SMACK EXPRESS

SMACK EXPRESS

HOW ORGANISED CRIME GOT HOOKED ON DRUGS

CLIVE SMALL & TOM GILLING

ALLEN&UNWIN

Every effort has been made to find the copyright holders of the photographs used in this book. Please contact the publisher should there be any issues of ownership of the photographs. The authors and publisher would be pleased to make the necessary corrections in any future edition.

First published in 2009

Copyright © Clive Small and Tom Gilling 2009

All rights reserved. No part of this book may be reproduced or transmitted in any form or by any means, electronic or mechanical, including photocopying, recording or by any information storage and retrieval system, without prior permission in writing from the publisher. The Australian *Copyright Act* 1968 (the Act) allows a maximum of one chapter or 10 per cent of this book, whichever is the greater, to be photocopied by any educational institution for its educational purposes provided that the educational institution (or body that administers it) has given a remuneration notice to Copyright Agency Limited (CAL) under the Act.

Allen & Unwin
83 Alexander Street
Crows Nest NSW 2065
Australia
Phone: (61 2) 8425 0100
Fax: (61 2) 9906 2218
Email: info@allenandunwin.com
Web: www.allenandunwin.com

National Library of Australia
Cataloguing-in-Publication entry:

Small, Clive.
    Smack express : how organised crime got hooked on drugs.

    ISBN 9781741756364 (pbk.)
    Bibliography
    Includes index.

    Drug traffic—Australia.
    Organized crime—Australia.
    Drug control—Australia.
    Drug abuse and crime—Australia.
    Crime—Australia—History.

    Other Authors/Contributors:
    Gilling, Tom.

364.1770994

Index by Trevor Matthews
Internal design by Lisa White
Set in 11.5/15.5 pt Sabon by Midland Typesetters, Australia
Printed and bound in Australia by Griffin Press

10 9 8 7 6 5

To all the honest cops past and present who
have fought the good fight against
organised crime

In memory of Sandra Harvey

Contents

Preface	ix
Acknowledgements	xi
About the Authors	xii
Cast of Characters	xv
1 Bob Trimbole: The 'ndrangheta and the Mr Asia gang	1
2 The Big Three of Organised Crime: Lennie McPherson, George Freeman and 'Stan the Man' Smith	33
3 Murray Riley: The gentleman gangster	41
4 'Snapper' Cornwell: A big fish in a big pond	54
5 Chris Flannery: Mr 'Rent-a-Kill'	65
6 The 1980s Sydney Gang War: 'We only kill each other...'	78
7 'Neddy' Smith: A life of crime and doing time	109
8 'Stan the Man' Smith and Lawrence McLean: Mates to the end	137
9 'Mikel' Hurley: From Balmain Boy to head honcho	162

10	The Coogee Mob: The head honcho's new gang	176
11	Cabramatta: Rise and fall of a heroin capital	204

Afterword	241
What Happened to . . .?	244
Bibliography	250
Index	256

Preface

In his 1979 book *The Godfather in Australia*, Bob Bottom surveyed organised crime's rise and coming of age. Drawing together the findings of a series of inquiries into aspects of organised crime, evidence previously hidden in the records of state and federal law-enforcement agencies, and crucial new information, Bottom demonstrated the growing power and reach of organised crime in Australia and detailed its attempts to form alliances with the American Mafia. A year later, Alfred McCoy's *Drug Traffic* focused on the scale of Australia's surging drug trade.

Bottom and McCoy exposed a situation that retired Justice Athol Moffitt, in his own book, *A Quarter to Midnight*, described as 'the Australian crisis'. In a damning swipe at governments and the police, Moffitt denounced the 'constant political wrangling and point-scoring on matters of organised crime and corruption, coupled with political apathy and fancy side-stepping in the face of an unrestrained escalation in organised crime'.

That escalation has continued. Organised crime has adapted its methods, but its focus on secrecy and self-protection is unchanged. So is the willingness to use violence, intimidation, and the corruption of state and federal politicians, police, and Customs, taxation and immigration agents. Criminals are becoming ever more adept at sheltering behind lawyers and hiding their profits and their investments—both legal and illegal—with the aid of accountants and business advisers. Occasionally investigators will break through one of these protective walls, but the edifice remains.

Despite the difficulties, our knowledge of organised crime has grown significantly in recent decades. Intelligence comes from 'rollovers', informants, telephone intercepts and covert listening devices, physical surveillance, the detailed tracking of financial transactions and court cases, the investigation of crime figures and their associates, and occasional media exposés.

Though imperfect and incomplete, all of this information is valuable. The picture it gives us may be obscure in parts, but it tells us much about the business of organised crime. And without studying where organised crime has come from, it is impossible to predict where it might go.

Acknowledgements

Our sincere thanks to those colourful characters on both sides of the law—many of whom must remain nameless—who helped directly or indirectly in the writing of this book. Thanks also to the journalists who over the decades have reported fearlessly on the growth and influence of organised crime.

Special gratitude to Bob Bottom, Steve Barrett, Keith Moor, Nick McKenzie, Stephen Gibbs, Kate McClymont, Neil Mercer, John Laycock, Bruce Provost, Peter Smith, the late Sandra Harvey and Marian Wilkinson for their support and advice.

About the Authors

During his thirty-eight-year career in the New South Wales Police Service, Clive Small spent much of his time on investigative work, and received several commendations. From 1977–80 he was an investigator with the Woodward Royal Commission into Drug Trafficking. For the next three years he was with the Commonwealth–state Joint Task Force investigating the Nugan Hand merchant bank and the activities of Murray Riley and his associates. In 1984 Small joined the policy team of newly appointed Police Commissioner John Avery, specialising in drug law enforcement and drug policy. In 1987–88 he was an investigator on Strike Force Omega, which reexamined the 1984 shooting of Detective Michael Drury. In 1989 he exposed the fiasco that was the investigation and attempted prosecution of former Police Superintendent Harry 'the Hat' Blackburn for alleged crimes of sexual assault, assault and robbery, and detaining for advantage. In the face of opposition from the police hierarchy and a smear campaign against him, Small insisted on Blackburn's innocence and recommended that all charges against him be dropped. A 1990 royal commission headed by Justice J.A. Lee supported Small's conclusions and exonerated Blackburn. In the early 1990s Small led the Backpacker Murders investigation, which resulted in the arrest of Ivan Milat for the abduction and murder of seven

ABOUT THE AUTHORS

backpackers in the Belanglo State Forest, south of Sydney, between 1989 and 1992. In 1996 Milat was convicted of all seven murders and sentenced to life in jail. During the mid-1990s Small led a secret investigation which uncovered widespread police corruption in the Fairfield–Cabramatta area. After the 1994–97 Wood Royal Commission into the New South Wales Police Service, Small was appointed to head the newly created Crime Agencies. In 2001 he was placed in charge of the Greater Hume Police Region, which covers western Sydney, to lead efforts to clean up Cabramatta, then Australia's heroin capital. Small spent his last two years in the Police on secondment to the Premier's Department as a Director of Community Solutions and Crime Prevention. He then joined the New South Wales Independent Commission Against Corruption as executive director of operations.

He left ICAC in March 2007. His police experience and contacts built up over several decades give him unrivalled insight into the workings of organised crime in Australia.

Tom Gilling is the author of *The Sooterkin* (1999) and *Miles McGinty* (2001), both of which were shortlisted for major awards and chosen as notable books of the year by the *New York Times*. They have been translated into several languages. His latest novel, *Dreamland,* appeared in June 2008. During his career as a journalist, Gilling worked for the *Sydney Morning Herald, The Australian, The Bulletin, The Guardian* (UK), *The Observer* (UK) and the *New York Times*, among other publications. He has co-written two non-fiction books: *Trial and Error* (1991, revised 1995), about the Israeli nuclear whistleblower Mordechai Vanunu, and *Bagman: The Final Confessions of Jack Herbert* (2005), about the events that led to the Fitzgerald Commission into police corruption in Queensland.

Cast of Characters

'**Aunty**', the name given by police to one of Australia's biggest cocaine importers, is a Colombian woman in her fifties who came to Australia with her family in the 1970s. She is the face of a Sydney-based syndicate that has been operating for two decades, importing and distributing around a tonne of cocaine every eighteen months.

Barry Richard Bull, born 25 July 1943. Bull was trafficking cannabis for a decade before becoming 'Snapper' Cornwell's partner. He spent long periods in jail during the late 1980s and '90s.

Leo 'the Fibber' Callaghan (aka Jack Warren and Patrick William Warren), was born in 1924. A professional shoplifter and member of Australia's infamous Kangaroo Gang during the 1960s, Callaghan fell in with Lennie McPherson and George Freeman and went on to become a major cannabis importer.

Daniel Michael Chubb, born 12 June 1942. Along with Michael Hurley, Chubb was one of the 'Balmain Boys' who, during the 1970s, stole from warehouses, bond stores and licensed clubs. A decade later Chubb was importing cannabis and heroin. Among his major distributors were Neddy Smith, Michael Sayers and Tony Eustace.

Richard Bruce 'Snapper' Cornwell, born 29 January 1946. Like Riley, Cornwell was a member of Michael Moylan's drug syndicate during the 1970s. When the Moylan syndicate collapsed, Cornwell and Riley set up their own operation. By the early 1980s Cornwell was importing cocaine and cannabis with Barry Bull. For a time, one of their biggest customers was Michael Hurley.

Kenneth Robert Derley, born 18 September 1949, was involved in drugs and property theft when he joined Murray Riley's drug operation in the mid 1970s. On Riley's orders he hired Neddy Smith as a heroin distributor and strong-arm man. After serving time for his role in Riley's 1978 cannabis importation, Derley stayed out of serious trouble until the late 1990s when he returned to the drug trade.

'Johnsonny' Bi Dinh, born in the mid 1950s, used his connections as a standover man and collector of money from illegal gaming machines to sell heroin for Barry McCann and George Savvas in Cabramatta. From the mid 1980s Johnsonny fed bulk heroin to Cabramatta's Vietnamese youth through pool halls and other hangouts. On 1 April 1987 he survived an attempted assassination—probably the result of a street war with rival illegal gaming operators. In October 1977 he was jailed for money laundering on behalf of an Asian controlled international drug syndicate.

Khanh Quang Do, born 23 May 1973. Do was the leader of a gang commonly referred to as the Bankstown Boys. Seen as intruders, they were in a state of constant conflict with the local Cabramatta gangs. In 2001, Do survived two assassination attempts by Hoang Ha La's gang.

CAST OF CHARACTERS

Thomas Christopher 'Tom' Domican, born 1 February 1943, hit the headlines in 1980 over allegations of vote rigging in the Enmore branch of the Australian Labor Party. During the 1980s, his interests were illegal gambling and protection. In Sydney's gang war he sided with Barry McCann against Lennie McPherson and George Freeman. Domican has been charged and acquitted of one murder, one attempted murder and five counts of conspiring to murder.

William 'Bill' El Azzi, born 25 December 1958, joined the police in 1981, using underworld boss Frank Hakim—the Lebanese Godfather—as a referee. He was a close associate of Tom Domican. El Azzi left the police and became an amphetamine cook for a major Sydney drug syndicate. In 2003 he was convicted of conspiring to manufacture amphetamines and sentenced to seven years' jail.

Anthony 'Pommy Tony' Eustace, born 26 November 1942 in England. Eustace arrived in Australia in 1964. By the early 1970s he was a close associate of the main players in Sydney's underworld. He was involved in illegal gambling, protection, drug importing and trafficking. A former boxer, he revelled in his reputation as a tough guy.

Malcolm Gordon Field, born 22 May 1941. After learning his trade with the Balmain Boys, Field was responsible for a spree of large-scale thefts. In 1973 he became an international thief and fraudster and was jailed in Paris and Stockholm. With Hurley, he imported cannabis and ecstasy using a network of companies and bank accounts in at least eleven countries.

Christopher Dale Flannery, born 15 March 1949. A relatively unsuccessful Melbourne criminal, Flannery moved to Sydney and became known as 'Rent-a-Kill'. He provided protection for George Freeman and formed a corrupt association with Detective Sergeant Roger Rogerson. His attempt to murder Detective Michael Drury in his Chatswood home left Drury severely wounded. Flannery killed several people during the Sydney gang war of the mid 1980s and wanted control of organised crime for himself.

George David Freeman, born 23 January 1934. After meeting in jail, Freeman and McPherson became lifelong friends and partners in crime. In the 1960s Freeman's SP bookmaking empire was protected by police and corrupt politicians.

Albert Jaime 'Flash Al' Grassby, born 12 July 1926, was elected the Labor MLA for the New South Wales electorate of Murrumbidgee in 1965. Four years later he won the federal seat of Riverina and became the Minister for Immigration. According to the underworld rollover Gianfranco Tizzone, Grassby was at the 'beck and call' of the Calabrian Mafia (whose existence he always denied) for forty years.

Shayne Desmond Frederick Hatfield, born in 1965, was a standover man and drug trafficker. He met Michael Hurley at Alcoholics Anonymous. By the late 1990s he was a major cocaine distributor for 'Aunty'. During 2004, Hatfield and 'Tom' sold 200 kilograms of cocaine. With Hurley and Les Mara, they imported 30 kilograms of cocaine before 'Tom' rolled over to the New South Wales Crime Commission.

CAST OF CHARACTERS

Graham John 'Abo' Henry, born 18 November 1951, was Neddy Smith's partner in drugs and armed robbery. After Smith was jailed for murder in 1988, Henry was given eight years for stabbing a police officer. In jail, he and Smith rolled to the Independent Commission Against Corruption.

Michael Nicholas 'Mikel' Hurley, born 5 November 1946. Another member of the Balmain Boys, Hurley committed large-scale thefts throughout the 1980s. He began importing cannabis, ecstasy and cocaine with another Balmain Boy, Malcolm Field. Hurley and another associate, Leslie Robert Mara, were arrested after a botched 2005 cocaine importation.

Duong Van Ia (known as Van Duong and Ah Sau or Brother Number Six), born 7 May 1955. Van Duong approached the heroin business the way he approached his gambling—with calculated risks aimed at huge wins. By the mid 1990s Van Duong was the sole supplier of heroin to the 5T gang. In one month alone Van Duong gambled $24 million at the Sydney Harbour Casino.

Hoang Ha La, born 3 March 1979. La's gang was a late arrival on the Cabramatta heroin scene. Its emergence prompted the final break-up of the already severely weakened 5T.

Warren Charles Lanfranchi, born 1958, met Neddy Smith in jail during the late 1970s. After his release Lanfranchi became a major heroin distributor for Smith. When Lanfranchi fell behind in his payments, Smith cut him off. Lanfranchi turned to drug rip-offs and armed robberies. As a potential rollover, he was a threat to both Smith and corrupt detective Roger Rogerson.

Van Ro Le (known as Madonna), born 13 January 1970. For a time Madonna was a leader of Cabramatta's 5T Vietnamese street gang, which was involved in murders, violence, protection rackets and drugs. More than any other gang, the 5T was responsible for the flourishing drug market on the streets of Cabramatta.

Barry Raymond McCann, born 28 July 1943. McCann was one of Murray Riley's partners in the infiltration of organised crime into licensed clubs in the 1960s. He trafficked heroin with the Mr Asia gang and later with his partner George Savvas. It was through the McCann–Savvas syndicate that large-scale heroin deliveries reached Cabramatta.

Bruce Michael 'the Godfather' McCauley, born 28 May 1937, was Danny Chubb's drug partner and financial advisor. After Chubb's murder in November 1984 McCauley continued to import and traffic in heroin, sometimes with Neddy Smith. In 1992 he was arrested in Sydney with 15 kilograms of heroin and sentenced to seventeen years' jail.

Lawrence Edward McLean, born 5 April 1931. McLean had a long criminal record in Melbourne before he moved to Sydney. By the mid 1970s he was growing and importing cannabis with Stan Smith. A decade later, McLean was masterminding importations from one of the world's biggest suppliers, Englishman Phillip Sparrowhawk, and forging links with another, Howard 'Mr Nice' Marks.

CAST OF CHARACTERS

Leonard Arthur McPherson, born 19 May 1921. In the late 1960s, along with George Freeman and Stan Smith, McPherson emerged as one of the big three of organised crime. Their main businesses were illegal gambling, SP bookmaking, protection and skimming money from licensed clubs.

Leslie Robert Mara, born 14 March 1953, played first grade rugby league from the mid 1970s to the early 1980s before turning to crime. Mara became a major player in the drug trade, importing cocaine with Michael Hurley and others. Their operation in 2005 came unstuck when an associate, 'Tom', rolled over and gave them up. Mara was arrested after eighteen months on the run.

Phuong Canh Ngo, born 9 July 1958, arrived in Australia as a refugee in 1981 and soon became involved in local politics. The Mekong Club was his power base in Cabramatta's Vietnamese community and he was closely associated with the violent 5T gang. Ngo and John Newman, the Labor member for Cabramatta, were bitter enemies. After Newman was assassinated in 1994 Ngo was charged with his murder.

Khanh Hoang Nguyen, born 8 May 1976. Khanh was a senior member of the 5T. In 1997–98 the gang splintered when Khanh Hoang Nguyen and David Nguyen (not related) broke away and formed their own gangs.

'David' Van Dung Nguyen, born 27 December 1977. Despite its small size, David's gang, as it was known, was particularly violent. They were the aggressors in a series of savage encounters with Khanh Nguyen's gang during 1999 and 2000.

The 'Rat' was a detective at Fairfield. There he led a small group of detectives known as the 'Rat Pack' which was involved in drugs and money rip-offs, the theft of money from illegal card games, perverting the course of justice and the fabrication of evidence.

Murray Stewart Riley, born 5 October 1925. Riley joined the New South Wales Police at nineteen and resigned in 1962. Riley had been in a corrupt relationship with McPherson since the 1950s. From the mid 1970s he was a major player in the cannabis and heroin trade, along with Snapper Cornwell and Neddy Smith.

Roger Caleb Rogerson, born 3 January 1941, joined the New South Wales Police and became one of its most decorated—but notorious—detectives. He formed corrupt relationships with various criminals, including Neddy Smith, and was accused (but acquitted) of having been involved in the attempted assassination of Detective Michael Drury in 1984. He was dismissed from the police in 1986 and was later jailed for perverting the course of justice.

George Savvas, born 1941, was a longtime political and criminal ally of Tom Domican. In 1984 Barry McCann and Savvas became partners. Over eighteen months they imported more than 100 kilograms of heroin and oversaw the first large-scale deliveries of heroin to Cabramatta. In 1987 McCann was shot dead. Two years later Savvas was jailed for twenty-five years for conspiring to import and to supply heroin. He was acquitted of murdering McCann.

Michael John 'Mick' Sayers, born 16 April 1946, moved to Sydney from Melbourne, where he was suspected of several

CAST OF CHARACTERS

murders. During the early 1980s he became a major player in illegal starting price bookmaking, race rigging and the drug trade. He was a close ally of Christopher Flannery.

Antonio 'Tony' Sergi, born 29 October 1935. Sergi ran the growing side of Trimbole's cannabis operation. The Woodward Royal Commission into Drug Trafficking identified Sergi as a senior member of the Calabrian Mafia.

Pasquale 'Pat' Sergi, born 1 January 1946, in Plati, Calabria, is a cousin of Antonio 'Tony' Sergi and married into the Trimbole family. According to the Woodward Royal Commission into Drug Trafficking, 'The distribution of the product [cannabis], and the channelling of finance back to the Griffith end of the operation, was carried out by persons in Sydney, including Pasquale Sergi', who were 'under the immediate control of [Aussie Bob] Trimbole'.

Arthur Stanley 'Neddy' Smith, born 27 November 1944. Smith was hired by Murray Riley in the mid 1970s as a heroin distributor and strong-arm man. Later he set up his own syndicate with William Sinclair and Warren Fellows. A close associate of Flannery, Smith sold heroin for Danny Chubb and was given the green light to commit crime by corrupt Detective Roger Rogerson.

Stanley 'Stan the Man' Smith, born 3 January 1937. One of the three original 'Mr Bigs' of organised crime, Smith later teamed up with Lawrie McLean to build a multi-million-dollar international cannabis operation. Smith was McLean's Sydney distributor until McLean was arrested in 1996.

Victor Thomas Spink, born 1942, moved from shoplifting and theft into the drug trade. He featured prominently on the so-called 'jockey tapes', along with Mick Sayers, another drug-running punter who was murdered in a gang war. In 1994 Spink and others were arrested over a 15-tonne cannabis importation. He was sentenced to nine years' jail, a light sentence that owed something to the unspecified 'assistance' he gave authorities.

Gianfranco Tizzone, born 1934. On Trimbole's orders Tizzone hired Melbourne criminal James Frederick Bazley to murder Donald Mackay and, two years later, drug couriers Douglas and Isabel Wilson.

'Tom' has been a drug trafficker since leaving school in the mid 1970s. By 2000, he was selling bulk cocaine for Shayne Hatfield. During 2004 he and Hatfield sold 200 kilograms of cocaine supplied by Aunty. They paid Aunty $24 million and made $6 million. With Hurley and Mara they imported another 30 kilograms of cocaine. In late 2004 'Tom' rolled to the New South Wales Crime Commission and gave up his colleagues.

Tri Minh Tran, born 10 December 1974, became leader of 5T gang in the early 1990s after Madonna was jailed. Under Tran the 5T dealt drugs, robbed illegal casinos and extorted money from local Asian businesses. Tran was a strong-arm man for Phuong Ngo but rejected his $10,000 offer to murder Labor MP John Newman. After his release from jail in 1995, Madonna challenged Tran for the leadership of 5T, but lost. Madonna formed his own gang.

CAST OF CHARACTERS

Bruno 'Aussie Bob' Trimbole, born 19 March 1931. Trimbole entered the cannabis trade in the late 1960s and soon joined forces with the 'ndrangheta, or Calabrian Mafia, centred on Griffith. When Donald Mackay threatened the mafia's operations, Trimbole had him killed. He went on to become a key member of the Mr Asia heroin syndicate.

Chapter 1

Bob Trimbole

The `ndrangheta and the Mr Asia gang

Griffith is a country town about 500 kilometres southwest of Sydney in the rich heart of the Murrumbidgee Irrigation Area, one of the largest wine, fruit and vegetable growing regions in Australia. In the 1970s it had about 12,500 residents, almost three-fifths of whom were Italian-born, the highest proportion in any town in New South Wales. Most were immigrants from Calabria, an impoverished region in Italy's deep south.

On 15 July 1977 a forty-four-year-old anti-drugs campaigner and local Liberal Party activist, Donald Mackay, left the Griffith Hotel after drinks with friends—and vanished. His disappearance was widely attributed to a 'mafia hit'. The 'mafia' tag referred to a group of local Calabrians whose homes were too opulent and whose cars were too flashy to have been paid for out of income from their farms and orchards. The money came, in fact, from growing and selling cannabis. It was rumoured that corrupt police and Labor politicians protected the Griffith mafia, whose drug activities were led by Robert 'Aussie Bob' Trimbole (also spelt Trimboli), the Australian-born son of Calabrian migrants. Tip-offs supplied by Mackay had recently been responsible for a series of police raids that resulted in the seizure of large cannabis crops and the arrest of several growers, all of Calabrian descent.

The public outcry over Mackay's disappearance forced the New South Wales Labor government to set up the Woodward Royal Commission into Drug Trafficking, which started its inquiries in Griffith within weeks and ran for the next three years.

The rumours were correct. The commission found that Trimbole was the 'practical leader' of a secret organisation known as the Onorata Società or Honoured Society, or, in the Calabrian dialect, 'ndrangheta (pronounced en-drang-*ay*-ta). It was the Calabrian version of the Sicilian Mafia. The 'ndrangheta is believed to have been born in the nineteenth century as a loose grouping of families who found kidnapping, robbery, bribery and extortion more lucrative than farming their rugged, rocky land. When Calabrians emigrated to the US and Australia, so did the 'ndrangheta.

Italian secret crime societies commonly referred to as mafia first took root along Australia's east coast, from the northern Queensland cane fields to Melbourne, in the late 1920s. The 'ndrangheta was one of these groups. It became prominent in the 1930s through a terror campaign that included at least ten murders and thirty bombings of Calabrians who had dared to resist or compete with its members.

By the early 1950s police were well aware of the 'ndrangheta, which had cells in cities and country towns across Victoria and New South Wales and thrived on protection and extortion rackets based around produce markets and labour exchanges. The threat of violence was usually sufficient to secure compliance. Murders were few. Violence, where it did occur, was rarely reported to authorities.

This changed in 1963–64, when a struggle for control of the growers' markets in Melbourne led to at least five murders and several attempted murders. But that mayhem was minor compared with what Trimbole unleashed when he introduced the 'ndrangheta in Australia to the drug trade.

Trimbole was born in 1931 and spent much of his early life on his parents' farm outside Griffith. At the age of twenty-one he broke with tradition and married an Anglo-Australian, Joan Quested. After a period on the farm they moved to a rented house in town. There Trimbole expanded a small motor-vehicle repair business into a petrol station with panel-beating and spray-painting facilities.

In 1968 Trimbole was declared bankrupt. About this time the petrol station burned down, along with all records of the business. Until now Trimbole's criminal activities had been limited to illegal gambling. Soon he began growing cannabis on a big scale. The profits enabled him to buy a series of businesses and he was regularly seen making extravagant bets at the races.

Trimbole knew of the 'ndrangheta from his family—his father is said to have been a low-level 'ndrangheta member in both Calabria and Griffith, and relatives in Calabria were active in it—but he was not a member. His nickname 'Aussie Bob' came from a preference for Australian ways. But now he turned to the Calabrian Mafia with a proposal: a national cannabis cultivation and distribution network that could yield millions of dollars a year and transform the 'ndrangheta in Australia.

Trimbole's family connections gave him quick and trusted access to the leaders of the Griffith cell, who found his offer too good to refuse. Making use of established extortion and protection networks and a ready supply of skilled agricultural labour, the drug business flourished.

For the 'ndrangheta it was a novel arrangement. Trimbole never became an initiated member: the relationship with him was chiefly a business partnership. For the purpose of the drug operations he became the society's 'practical' head but control of the 'ndrangheta itself remained with his partners.

By 1972 the crops were huge and so were the profits. Trimbole invested his share in seemingly legitimate businesses such as property, licensed premises, a wine cellar and a supermarket, and used sham loans to buy more farms. As the operation expanded, he handed over responsibility for the growing side to Antonio 'Tony' Sergi, born on 29 October 1935, of the House of Sergi Winery, now Warburn Wines. Woodward noted that 'It [the "Winery complex"] seems to have been financed with cash funds from unknown sources'. As an example, he observed Trimbole had 'loaned' Sergi more than $350,000 cash which was 'used in the Winery operations and construction' and that none of this 'loan' had been repaid. '[T]hese payments are not in fact "loans",' Woodward wrote, 'but constitute the introduction of organisational funds [i.e., cash from an organisation running the cannabis trade] into the Winery'. '[A] continual flow of organisational money poured into this business,' Woodward concluded.

Trimbole's focus now was the distribution networks, which he managed with his customary vigour. By the time of his discharge from bankruptcy in 1975, he had accumulated assets of more than $2 million and gambled away several million dollars more.

Between 1974 and 1978 police across Australia found twenty-two large-scale cannabis plantations. Most appeared to have produced multiple crops of the drug, and all were under the control of persons of Calabrian descent. Of forty-five people arrested, twenty-two were born in the Calabrian village of Plati, eighteen were born elsewhere in Calabria and two had Calabrian parents. The remaining three were from Sicily, Genoa and Nice. Many of the plantations had demonstrable connections with Griffith. The Woodward Royal Commission concluded that it could not be satisfied that any of the twenty-two plantations were 'unconnected' to Griffith and the 'ndrangheta.

It was an industry spread across at least four states and generating—in today's values—hundreds of millions of dollars a year in profits. Attempting to trace the source of the growers' funds, the commission uncovered never-repaid 'loans' between families; bank accounts whose owners could not explain where the money came from; cash from overseas, particularly from the sale of deceased estates in Plati; betting wins by occasional gamblers; and huge payments from the firm of Trimbole, Sergi and Sergi for 'farm produce' for whose cultivation no investments could be identified. Large sums of cash had also been found 'by chance' in the homes of deceased relatives.

As to the fate of Donald Mackay, the commission found that he had been murdered. His van had been found where he'd left it in the Griffith Hotel car park. Nearby were blood stains, Mackay's car keys and three spent .22-calibre shell casings. Trimbole and the other drug bosses had ironclad alibis: they'd been out of town that day, booked into hotels in Sydney and Surfers Paradise. Those who remained in Griffith had been in a restaurant in the company of local police officers. The commission concluded that these alibis were arranged because 'they knew what was going to happen'.

More details of the murder emerged after the commission ended. In March 1982 Gianfranco Tizzone, a Melbourne mafia identity, was arrested for cannabis trafficking. Not long afterwards, he 'rolled' and became a police informant. He said that since 1971 he had been the Melbourne distributor for Trimbole's multi-million-dollar cannabis network, selling more than $1.5 million worth of the drug each year. He also told police that in 1977 Trimbole had asked him to arrange for Donald Mackay to be killed because he was causing problems for the `ndrangheta's drug operations. Tizzone approached another well-known Melbourne criminal, George Joseph, who had excellent police connections: he was the patron of the Victoria Police gun club. Joseph put him in touch with James Frederick Bazley, a member of the Federated Ship Painters and Dockers Union, which was notorious for violence and intimidation. Bazley was a hitman who wore the scars of several shootouts and assassination attempts. He agreed to kill Mackay. It was not the last time Trimbole would use Tizzone to organise a hit.

Although Tizzone talked to police, it was not until 1 June

1983 that he made a formal statement. Part of this was released three years later by the special inquiry into the police investigation of Mackay's death. In the statement Tizzone claimed that by May 1977 'the threat by Mackay to our operations was considered so important that the problem was discussed at a meeting between Tony Sergi, Tony Barbaro [a brother-in-law of Sergi], Bob Trimbole and myself at the home of Tony Sergi in Griffith. During the meeting we discussed three alternatives designed to overcome the problem. One was to buy off Mackay at any price; another was to compromise him by getting him involved with a woman. The third alternative and the last resort was execution.'

Two days after making the statement, Tizzone retracted his claims against Sergi and Barbaro. He maintained this retraction during questioning by New South Wales police and during court proceedings.

One man closely involved in the Mackay murder investigation was Carl Mengler, an assistant commissioner of the Victoria Police. According to author Keith Moor, in his book *Crims in Grass Castles*, Mengler had 'no doubt that the first statement Tizzone made was the correct one'. He thought Tizzone 'decided to withdraw that statement to save his skin and protect his family'.

Neither Sergi nor Barbaro was charged in connection with Mackay's murder, although this allegation is contained in full in the 1986 Nagle Report of the Special Commission of Inquiry into the police investigation into the death of Donald MacKay.

A week after he disappeared, several thousand people attended a church service for Donald Mackay. Bob Bottom notes in his book *Shadow of Shame* that, while several

Liberal and National Party politicians attended, not one Labor politician did. When the then Premier, Neville Wran, finally went to Griffith, 'the local Labor Party MP, Lin Gordon, took him to see an Italian [Calabrian] political godfather, Pietro Calipari, but not [Mackay's wife] Barbara.' Many Griffith residents—and state police—saw Calipari as not just a political godfather but a mafia-style one.

Twelve years earlier, Calipari and others had been arrested and charged when police seized a number of firearms in a series of raids in Sydney and Griffith. The raids had followed Victoria Police investigations into the 1963–64 Melbourne market murders. A local Labor MP named Al Grassby gave character evidence for Calipari, as did a local detective, John Ellis. As a result, Calipari got off with a $40 fine. Ellis was one of several Griffith police who provided 'pre-arranged' alibis for Tony Sergi and others identified by the Woodward Royal Commission as 'ndrangheta members. He was later sentenced to a jail term.

Part of the profits of the Griffith drug trade was spent on buying the assistance of bookmakers and bankers (who could help launder drug profits), lawyers, police, public servants—and politicians. Prominent among these was Grassby. Tizzone claimed that the 'ndrangheta had started cultivating Grassby early in his career. They funded his election campaigns and delivered the Italian vote to Labor. 'The time and money they spent on Grassby was paid back in favours he did for them,' Tizzone said.

'Flash Al', as he was known (for his natty suits and colourful ties), had married into a local Calabrian family. In the mid 1960s he won the state seat of Murrumbidgee for

Labor. In 1969 he switched to federal parliament and won the seat of Riverina. Three years later he became Minister for Immigration. When Grassby lost his seat in the 1974 election, he blamed Donald Mackay and his claims about the local mafia and its Labor connections.

Ignoring Grassby's close ties to the powerbrokers of Griffith's drug trade, in 1975 the Whitlam Labor government appointed Grassby Commissioner for Community Relations, a position he held until 1982.

In the mid 1960s, as a member of the New South Wales Parliament, Grassby had strenuously denied the existence of the mafia in the Murrumbidgee area. He told the parliament that anyone who believed there was such an organisation 'had been watching too much late-night TV—probably Eliot Ness in *The Untouchables*'. He stuck to this position in the face of mountains of evidence in the hands of police that proved the 'ndrangheta had existed in Griffith since at least the early 1930s.

In February 1974, as Federal Minister for Immigration, Grassby visited Plati, in Calabria, as an honoured guest and was presented with a gold key to the town and honorary citizenship. In return, he used his ministerial authority to grant Australian visas to three Plati citizens who were known members or associates of the 'ndrangheta and who had previously been denied entry to Australia on grounds of bad character. One of them, Domenic Barbaro, had previously migrated to Australia but been deported after racking up a string of criminal convictions.

In the months after Mackay's murder, questions were asked in the New South Wales Parliament and the media about Grassby's role in granting the visas. Premier Neville Wran, who was also the Minister for Police, defended

Grassby's actions. Bob Bottom recounts in his book *The Godfather in Australia* how Wran 'blundered in' to the controversy, ridiculing suggestions that Barbaro was a hardened criminal and arguing that the visa decision had been made to enable him to 'see his dying mother for the last time before she met her Maker'. Unfortunately for Wran, it emerged a couple of days later that Barbaro had spent fewer than half his ten days in Australia with his 'dying mother' and that she was still alive and well three and a half years after the visit.

At the time Grassby authorised Barbaro's visit to Australia, he was a suspect in the kidnapping for ransom of an Italian industrialist's son. Not long after his return to Italy, Barbaro was arrested and charged over the kidnapping. A report of the Calabrian anti-Mafia police noted that the purpose of Barbaro's visit to Australia was to 'take money from kidnappings to that country [Australia] to . . . invest in Indian hemp plantations' and to launder the profits. Shortly after his arrest—and two years before Wran's defence of Grassby—an Italian court had declared Barbaro to be 'socially dangerous and associated with the mafia'.

Years earlier Grassby had sponsored 'ndrangheta figure Rocco Carbone's migration to Australia and settlement in South Australia. Carbone had been convicted in the late 1940s of exploding a hand grenade in a Calabrian police station, killing several police, according to a confidential police report.

In each case the sponsored 'ndrangheta member's family was closely related to the Griffith drug bosses.

Grassby also went to the assistance of Luigi Pochi, another Calabrian-born 'ndrangheta member identified by the Woodward Royal Commission. Pochi married a sister of

Tony Sergi and in 1975 went into business with Trimbole and Sergi in Vignali Wines in Canberra. The store was officially opened by Grassby eight months after Pochi and others had been arrested and charged over an $80 million cannabis crop at Colleambally. Pochi was subsequently convicted and served half of his two-year jail sentence. The Woodward Royal Commission found that Vignali Wines had been funded by the Griffith drug trade.

After Pochi's release from jail, the then Liberal government began proceedings to deport him. Several Labor MPs made representations on his behalf. So did Al Grassby, by then the Community Relations Commissioner. A long legal battle ended with the High Court upholding the deportation. However, in 1983 the government revoked the deportation order on the ground that it would place an unfair burden on the family of Pochi, who had lived in Australia since 1959.

Even as the government weighed up Pochi's deportation, he and others were under police investigation for cannabis growing. Roderick Campbell, Brian Toohey and William Pinwill, in their 1992 book *The Winchester Scandal*, note that despite the ongoing drug investigation's clear bearing on the deportation issue, 'no attempt appears to have been made to bring it to [John] Hodges's [the Immigration Minister's] attention.' This failure was never publicly explained.

More evidence of close relationships between 'ndrangheta members and Labor MPs emerged in late 1985, when Giuseppe Verduci, who had been committed for trial on cannabis charges, agreed to inform against the 'ndrangheta. His detailed police statement was passed on to the National Crime Authority. According to Andrew Keenan, in a 1987 *Sydney Morning Herald* article headlined 'Silence on Possible Mafia Arrests', Verduci, a longtime Labor Party fundraiser, claimed that in 1981 he had gone to the Canberra home of a Labor figure and warned him that the party should not be supporting Pochi's fight against deportation because he was still involved in the cannabis trade. According to Campbell, Toohey and Pinwill, Verduci produced cannabis from the boot of his car to support his claim. The Labor identity's response was 'to take a handful of the marijuana, explaining that his wife enjoyed it'.

Opposing Pochi's deportation, the South Australian Labor MP Mick Young told parliament, 'I am not sure that we are not taking this action [deportation] because we cannot get the real culprits [for the Mackay murder].' Ken Fry, the Labor member for Fraser, chimed in that the government had not considered 'the fundamental question', namely, 'whether he [Pochi] is likely to offend again . . . I do not see that there is any justification at all for believing that he would offend again . . . There is no evidence that he will offend again.' Fry went on to describe Pochi as 'a battler'. The idea that he was a Mr Big of organised crime 'is a product of the imagination of the police'. Outside parliament, Gareth Evans, the then Labor spokesman for legal affairs, added his voice to the chorus, saying there was nothing to suggest that Pochi had any continuing involvement with criminals or drugs. There is no suggestion that any of these was the 'Labor figure' to whom Verduci had spoken.

Apparently the Labor figure did not bother to tell his colleagues of his conversation with Verduci less than a year earlier. Instead, he allowed them to mislead parliament and the public.

A short time later, Pochi and others were arrested and charged over two more cannabis crops, this time at Bungendore, about 50 kilometres east of Canberra. Pochi was committed for trial over one of the crops, but the prosecution did not proceed and he was discharged.

At the time of this arrest, Pochi was associated with a company that had cleaning contracts for Australian Federal Police buildings, including AFP headquarters, as well as other government buildings in Canberra. This posed a potentially serious security risk.

After Donald Mackay's murder, with the Woodward Royal Commission throwing an unwelcome light on its activities, the 'ndrangheta again enlisted Grassby's help. His assignment echoed the line in the 1995 movie *The Usual Suspects* where Kevin Spacey's character, Roger 'Verbal' Kint, says, 'The greatest trick the devil ever pulled was convincing the world he didn't exist.' In Grassby's case, the devil was the 'ndrangheta. In 1979 Grassby began spreading rumours implicating Mackay's wife Barbara, their son Paul and their family solicitor in his murder. He tried without success to persuade politicians in the parliaments of New South Wales, Victoria and South Australia to read an unsigned document suggesting they were behind the killing. However, he got lucky when the *Sun-Herald* newspaper ran a story based on the document under the headline, 'Mackay Killing: Not the Mafia'. According to Bruce Provost, a former federal police agent and senior investigator with the then NCA, Trimbole paid Grassby $40,000 to circulate the document.

In 1986, despite being publicly named as an associate of violent mafia bosses and drug dealers, and being under investigation for maliciously spreading false information about the disappearance of Donald Mackay, and despite Bazley's conviction for conspiring to murder Mackay on Trimbole's orders, Grassby was hired by the Wran Labor government as an ethnic affairs adviser.

Barbara and Paul Mackay and their lawyer successfully sued Grassby for defamation. The civil case was followed by criminal charges against Grassby. In 1987 he was charged with conspiring with Trimbole and Giuseppe Sergi and his wife, Jennifer, to pervert the course of justice between 1979 and 1981 by circulating the false document. The charges were dismissed by a magistrate, then reinstated on appeal. In August 1991 Grassby was convicted of attempted criminal defamation. He appealed and a year later was acquitted and awarded costs.

In 2005 Bruce Provost claimed that Grassby had used his influence with the federal and New South Wales Labor governments to head off royal commission inquiries into his activities and that the NCA had bowed to political pressure to limit its own investigations. Once again the Labor Party was more anxious to hold onto the ethnic vote than it was to examine the party's links to organised crime.

In *The Winchester Scandal* Campbell, Toohey and Pinwill noted the peculiar make-up of the Belconnen, ACT, branch of the party, Grassby's 'home' branch. In 1988 twenty-one of the eighty-one financial members were ethnic Italians. No other branch had more than three. That year the Federal Police had begun investigating six members of the Barbaro family, five members of the Nirta family, six members of the Pelle family and four members of the Pochi family, all registered members of the Belconnen Branch—and all with the same address. At the time, Grassby's wife, Ellnor, was seeking preselection in that seat to stand as a Labor candidate.

Within weeks of Mackay's murder, Trimbole began distancing himself from Griffith and his colleagues in the cannabis trade. His new business was heroin. And his entrée was through a New Zealand-born gang that came to be known as the 'Mr Asia' syndicate.

Christopher Martin 'Marty' Johnstone started his crime career in his native Auckland in the early 1970s, when he teamed up with a Singaporean ship's crewman. The associate would bring in 'Thai'—sticks of compressed cannabis—and throw the packaged drugs overboard for Johnstone to pick up by speedboat.

Business prospered and Johnstone joined forces with a petty thief named Terrence Clark, who helped him set up a series of maritime-related companies as cover. Clark rapidly took the helm of Johnstone's organisation and switched its stock-in-trade to heroin. After a run-in with New Zealand police, Clark relocated to Sydney. As the syndicate continued to expand Johnstone moved to Singapore and became its 'Mr Asia' connection.

By mid 1977 Clark had couriers regularly bringing in heroin, which was distributed as far afield as Melbourne and Perth. On a conservative estimate, the syndicate imported 200 kilograms of heroin between late 1976 and 1979.

Bob Trimbole brought valuable assets to the syndicate: an efficient drug distribution operation, high-level criminal contacts, and a wide network of corrupt police and public officials.

By 1978 he was a key syndicate member, recruiting and supervising couriers, arranging false identities and passports, receiving tip-offs from corrupt police and narcotics officers, and helping arrested couriers evade prison. From time to time, just as he had done for the 'ndrangheta, Trimbole organised murders.

In June 1978 police investigating a huge cannabis importation by yacht (see Chapter 3) mistakenly thought Clark was part of that operation. Once arrested, he was extradited to New Zealand to face an outstanding heroin importation charge. The Australian police sweep also picked up two Mr Asia couriers. Douglas and Isabel Wilson, both heroin addicts, spent several days in custody—and talked, giving police a tape-recorded account of the syndicate and its business. 'I'm quite fucking frightened about it, you know,' Douglas Wilson said. 'I mean if he [Clark] thinks for one moment that I've given him up... if he can possibly organise it, he'll have me shot without compunction.'

He was right to be terrified. Within weeks, Brian Alexander, a law clerk in the firm that was representing the syndicate, told senior members the Wilsons had made a 'big statement' and that tapes existed of their interviews. The information, for which he was paid $10,000, was passed to Clark, who was still in jail in New Zealand. When Clark's heroin charge was dismissed, he returned to Australia determined to punish the Wilsons. He paid $250,000 for copies of the tapes—and decided the couple had to die.

Clark was quite capable of killing them himself. A year earlier he'd murdered another syndicate member, Harry 'Pommy' Lewis. A botched cannabis importation had seen Lewis arrested and facing a long jail sentence. Clark didn't trust him to keep his mouth shut. Brian Alexander arranged bail for Lewis, and within days he was dead. But while Clark plotted the Wilsons' demise, Lewis's handless body was found in bushland near Port Macquarie on the mid north coast of New South Wales. Clark knew he was a suspect. He would have to find someone else to kill the Wilsons.

He called on Trimbole. Just as he'd done two years earlier for the hit on Mackay, Trimbole sent Gianfranco Tizzone to give James Bazley the contract. On 13 April 1979 the Wilsons left Sydney for a syndicate meeting in Melbourne. Soon afterwards Clark left Australia for England, never to return. Within weeks the bodies of Douglas and Isabel Wilson were found in a shallow grave at Rye, near Melbourne.

A month later Trimbole visited Clark in England to discuss business. On his return he took control of the syndicate's Australian operations, but they were already doomed.

In August 1979 Clark's former mistress, Alison Dine, was arrested in Sydney and charged with possession of heroin. Granted $5000 bail, she fled to Britain—on a false passport supplied by Trimbole—before going to the United States.

Six weeks later Marty Johnstone's body was found in a flooded quarry in Lancashire, England. The order for his elimination had come from Clark. Johnstone had been stealing the syndicate's money, he had been ripped off in a heroin deal that cost the syndicate a quarter of a million dollars, and he had been attempting to establish his own importation network. Johnstone's killer was to be his close friend Andrew Maher.

Maher chopped off Johnstone's hands and smashed his face repeatedly in an attempt to destroy his teeth. There was a gaping hole in Johnstone's stomach. Bricks had been used to weigh down the body. Clark was charged with the murder and with conspiring to import and traffic heroin. Eleven other members of the syndicate faced similar charges. Clark was sentenced to a total of thirty-seven years' jail. He served only a fraction of his sentence and died in 1983.

During its short life the Mr Asia syndicate made so much money that Clark once boasted that he couldn't even spend the interest on his personal fortune of $50 million. The gang was responsible for at least a dozen murders. But most of its estimated ninety members and associates—including Trimbole—were never brought to justice.

The syndicate is known to have used more than 100 false passports and aliases to avoid detection. Clark alone used at least thirty while his former mistress, Alison Dine, had used at least seventeen.

Appearing at the 1980 Melbourne inquest into the deaths of Douglas and Isabel Wilson, Trimbole declined to answer questions on the grounds that his answers might incriminate him. In 1981, an illegal phone tap by the New South Wales Police Bureau of Criminal Intelligence recorded drug-dealing doctor Nick Paltos (see Chapter 6) advising Trimbole to leave the country. Two days later, using a false passport, Trimbole flew to the United States and then to Italy.

In October 1984 he was arrested in Ireland, where he had been living under the alias of Michael Pius Hanbury, a retired businessman. In February the following year, after a Dublin court refused Australia's request for his extradition, he fled to the Spanish resort area of Costa Blanca. From there he made several trips to other European countries, including Switzerland, for purposes unknown. In May 1987 Trimbole died of a heart attack in Spain at the age of fifty-five. His body was returned to Sydney and interred in the family plot at Eastern Creek. Fittingly, his funeral was marked by violence, when mourners attacked journalists and photographers.

In 1984 Gianfranco Tizzone was sentenced to eight years' jail for conspiring to murder Donald Mackay and the Wilsons. On his release in 1986 he was presented with a tax bill for almost $1 million. In 1987 Melbourne author and journalist Keith Moor found Tizzone living in Foligno, an ancient town in the Italian province of Perugia. In his book *Crims in Grass Castles*, Moor says that Tizzone told him, among other things, 'He [Trimbole] was protected in high places. The Family [the `ndrangheta] was, and still is, protected by corrupt politicians and crooked police officers.' The `ndrangheta cells in Australia, according to Tizzone, had strong links with those in America and Italy and the cells in Australia 'were required to send money regularly' to the organisation's headquarters in the Calabrian town of Plati. Tizzone died in Foligno in 1988 of natural causes.

George Joseph was sentenced to seven years' jail for his part in the murders of Mackay and the Wilsons. Released after less than two years, Joseph started a steak restaurant which counted several members of the Victoria Police, including some from internal affairs, among its regulars. After a few years he closed the restaurant—some say because he feared for his life—and later opened another small, but more discreet business in an inner south-eastern Melbourne suburb.

In 1986 James Bazley was convicted of the murders of Donald Mackay and the Wilsons. He served fifteen years' jail before being released in 2001, aged seventy-five. Within weeks of Bazley's release, Barbara Mackay died. Aged sixty-five, she had fought a long battle with the auto-immune disease, lupus.

In 1969 the Canberra-based Central Crime Intelligence Bureau of the then Commonwealth Police (later the Australian Federal Police) compiled a secret list of 341 suspected 'ndrangheta members who had migrated to Australia. Most arrived during the three decades from the mid 1930s and settled in New South Wales, Victoria and South Australia. A few settled in Western Australia and Queensland. Among the family names mentioned were Trimbole, Sergi, Barbaro, Condello and Demarte. The list was not given to the Woodward Royal Commission or to the police investigating the murder of Donald Mackay. To this day it has not been seen by the New South Wales Police.

Some members of the Mr Asia syndicate were still active in the early 1990s. Several carried their experience and connections into new criminal enterprises. New Zealander Darryl Leigh Sorby, a senior member of the syndicate, was convicted in 1984 of trafficking more than $10 million worth of heroin and served ten years of a twenty-three-year sentence. He went on to establish an ecstasy and cannabis-trafficking ring. In May 2006 he was convicted of importing ecstasy and money laundering and sentenced to twelve years' jail in New Zealand.

Mr Asia associates James 'Diamond Jim' Shepherd and Hans 'Bumbles' Czajkowski served time in the 1980s and both lived ostensibly quiet lives in Sydney. In 2000, however, they were arrested, along with Michael 'Popeye' David Hughes, a Mr Asia syndicate member who had escaped the earlier police net, over a $9 million, 50-kilogram ecstasy seizure, then the largest in Australian history. All three were jailed. While in prison Hughes committed suicide.

Sometime in the 1970s Reginald 'Mick' O'Brien met Bob Trimbole at the races. Not yet thirty, O'Brien was already a familiar figure at the track. He had spent more than a decade gambling, training horses and mixing with some of Sydney's more notorious racing identities. By the late 1970s O'Brien was using inside information and rigging races to ensure that Trimbole won. O'Brien and Trimbole became close friends, but O'Brien was more of a go-between and 'gopher' (a slang term meaning 'go for this; go for that') than an organiser. He was paid commissions on drug deals rather than given a cut of the profits.

After fleeing Australia Trimbole stayed in contact with O'Brien. Over the next five years O'Brien visited Trimbole six times in Italy, France, Switzerland and Spain, carrying with him—or getting others to carry—hundreds of thousands of dollars in cash which Trimbole would then convert into local currency. Once O'Brien was accompanied by Trimbole's son, Craig, and his wife, Josephine.

With Trimbole out of the country, O'Brien's income from the track and from drug commissions largely dried up. Desperate for money, he offered his services to a pair of career criminals, Victor Spink and Raymond Dumbrell. Never in the big league himself, O'Brien was persuaded to roll on his mates (see Chapters 8 and 9), including Craig

Trimbole, to the National Crime Commission. In 1992 he was murdered in a gangland hit.

In March 1989 Trimbole's son Craig and another man were arrested by the NCA and charged with supplying nine kilograms of cannabis in Sydney's western suburbs. Four years later Craig and his alleged accomplice were acquitted at trial. It was not Craig's first brush with the law. Years earlier he had been arrested on returning to Australia with the body of his father—there was no record of him leaving Australia. His passport simply showed him arriving in the Netherlands on 12 May 1987. Craig declined to assist authorities who told the court that the circumstances of his departure 'give rise to grave suspicions of illegality, or perhaps collusion with corrupt officials'. He was fined $5000. He had also breached a Tax Office order prohibiting him from leaving—he owed the Tax Office $726,000. The family resonances continued. In 1994 Rosaria 'Ross' Trimbole and Domenic Trimbole, nephews of Bob, were caught in a Victoria Police sting involving the sale of cocaine and cannabis and the importation of cannabis into Australia from Papua New Guinea. They and six others were jailed.

Though many of its members and methods lived on, the Mr Asia syndicate died with Clark. The 'ndrangheta proved more durable. The intense scrutiny that followed Mackay's murder badly disrupted its operations, but the distribution network remained largely intact. The 'ndrangheta retreated, regrouped, and emerged as a central node in an Australia-wide web of organised crime gangs with a focus on drugs and an undiminished willingness to use violence.

Some of Trimbole's old associates flourished. His mate Tony Sergi, whose dramatic increase in wealth during the 1970s was found by the Woodward Royal Commission to have come 'directly or indirectly from his involvement in the marijuana industry', was also named by the commission as being a senior member of the 'ndrangheta. He was one of several senior members the commission found to have contrived alibis on the night of Mackay's murder to ensure they could not be implicated.

In a November 1979 interview with ABC journalist Andrew Olle, Sergi was asked, 'You must have heard of the 'ndrangheta in your native Calabria,' to which he replied, 'I was too young, when I come from Calabria I was seventeen. But I heard of this when Mr Woodward asked me in the court, that's the first time I heard of it, and after it was in the paper, in the paper, and I heard it now, you're telling me now.' Within five years of the commission closing its doors, his family company began buying up farms for conversion to vineyards. In the late 1990s at least $40.5 million was invested in the family-owned winery, which by 2005 had an annual turnover of around $40 million.

Another who has continued to prosper is Pasquale 'Pat' Sergi, a cousin of Tony Sergi who married into the Trimbole family. The commission found that Pasquale Sergi and his brother, Antonio, had acted as 'dummies' for Tony Sergi in business transactions and that both Antonio and Pasquale 'acted in concert with Trimbole'. The commission found that the structure of the Calabrian marijuana organisation in Griffith 'could be divided between growing and distributing sections . . . The distribution of the product, and the channelling of finance back to the Griffith end of the operation, was carried out by persons in Sydney, including: . . . Pasquale Sergi, 1.1.46 [and] Antonio Sergi, 25.9.44 . . .' It added: 'This group was under the immediate control of Robert Trimbole.'

In the lead-up to the 1995 state election the Labor Party decided to nominate Pasquale Sergi for the Sydney seat of Fairfield—he was a long-time financial supporter of the party and for many years had been able to bring the Calabrian vote to Labor. However, according to a secret New South Wales police report, the plan 'may have been terminated when a "police probe" was conducted' and threatened exposure of Sergi's connections to Robert Trimbole and the 'ndrangheta's drug network and money-laundering operations. With Sergi's support, his close friend, Joseph 'Joe' Tripodi became the Labor nominee for the safe Labor seat and was elected. A year later Tripodi went into business with Sergi and others buying and selling government land and Department of Housing properties in Sydney's western suburbs for significant profit. Tripodi left the business four years later. He has been quoted as saying that he owned less than 2 per cent of the shares and had no management role. In August 2006 *Sydney Morning Herald* journalists Debra Jopson and Gerard Ryle reported Pasquale Sergi's connection with Robert Trimbole and the marijuana growers of Griffith and business association with Tripodi under the headline 'Pillar who put dark past behind him'. In 2007 Tripodi, now a minister, was advised by the New South Wales Independent Commission Against Corruption that 'the Commission did not find you or any other person engaged in corrupt conduct and it has decided to discontinue its investigation'.

Confronted by Ryle and Jopson during their investigation of Pasquale Sergi, Tripodi insisted, 'I was unaware that Mr Sergi had been named by the royal commission until last week. He has been a prominent member of the local community and we met through his charity work.'

Questions about Pat Sergi's association with Tripodi were brushed aside by the Labor Party. Tripodi's friend, the then Treasurer Michael Costa, chastised the *Herald* for even raising the issue. 'Coverage by Fairfax journalists is a "bloody disgrace",' he told *Herald* journalist Andrew Clennell. 'All those articles you've been writing about Joe and others . . . We're in politics, we meet all sorts of people, you can't hold people accountable for the fact their job leads them to talk to a whole range of people and then draw spurious connec-tions and make unfounded implications.' Perhaps not, but you can expect a Labor politician to be aware of a person's background when that person has been named by a Labor-instituted royal commission as having been involved in drug trafficking, money laundering and membership of an international crime society. That crime society has been implicated in numerous murders.

In 1995 an NCA report on its Cerberus project on Italo-Australian organised crime concluded that there was 'no Italian organised crime group that can be identified, in the Italian sense, as 'ndrangheta . . . in Australia'. Italo-Australian organised crime, it said, was 'simple criminal entrepreneurialism' and was in decline. There were only 'minimal links' between Italian 'organised crime figures in Australia and overseas-based Italian organised criminals'. Though there were 'ndrangheta-based 'cells' in New South

Wales, Victoria, South Australia and Western Australia 'their primary purpose appears to be socio-cultural rather than criminal, more akin to clans and fraternities'. The report notes, however, that 'associations between cell members probably provide one of the foundations for the formation of criminal syndicates'.

The NCA's conclusion—that there was no devil—was contradicted by at least forty murders, most of which remain unsolved, committed between 1977 and 1995 by 'mafia-like' organised crime groups. During the two years that followed the NCA assessment, state and federal law enforcement authorities arrested at least twenty-eight Griffith men—all related by blood or marriage to drug traffickers identified by Woodward—over their involvement in the cultivation and trafficking of cannabis valued at many millions of dollars in Queensland, Western Australia and Victoria. Several years earlier the former Australian Bureau of Criminal Intelligence updated the 1974–78 analysis of detected cannabis plantations conducted by the Woodward Royal Commission and referred to earlier in this chapter. In their book, *Mugshots 2*, Keith Moor and Geoff Wilkinson, who have seen the analysis, report the Bureau found that of 250 people arrested on more than 188 crops across Australia between 1974 and 1986, 60 per cent were connected 'to just 15 Calabrian Mafia families'. Fourteen of the 15 families 'were related by blood or marriage'. The fourteen included at least seven family names identified by the Woodward Commission as being involved in the drug trade. Testimony by Calabrian Mafia roll-overs, together with international telephone interceptions and evidence by the Italian Anti-Mafia Directorate, confirmed connections between the 'ndrangheta in Australia and its counterparts in Italy and the US, as well as proving the laundering of money between Australia and Calabria.

Just two years before the Cerberus project began its whitewash, the National Assessment Unit, Strategic Branch, of the Australian Federal Police concluded, in a report on Italian organised crime in Australia, that the 'ndrangheta was well established in Australia. The profound disagreement between the two reports has never been explained.

While the NCA worked on Operation Cerberus, two undercover Victoria Police, using the names Ben and Mark Gleeson, were themselves investigating the 'ndrangheta. In his book *Undercover*, 'Ben' (Damian Marrett) describes how they mingled with the young 'ndrangheta elite, including members of the Trimbole family. He recalls a conversation 'Mark' had with Bob Trimbole's nephew, Ross, about the mafia. 'All we are is family, Mark . . . We don't call it the mafia . . . "Mafia" is a very bad word. We are family. Family's very good. Family look after each other.'

As the conversation continued, Mark asked, 'So are the family just in Griffith?'

'No,' Ross replied, 'we have family everywhere, Mark. All over Australia, the world.'

Asked about Italy, Ross said, 'Of course we have contact with our family in Calabria.'

In what some might see as an ironic touch, the NCA report denying the Calabrian Mafia's existence was dedicated to 'Detective Sergeant Geoffrey Leigh Bowen of the Western Australia Police who was, on the 2nd March 1994, murdered whilst conducting investigations for the Cerberus Task Force'. A parcel bomb sent to the NCA office in Adelaide had exploded, killing Bowen and injuring several other staff. Two months afterwards, Ross Trimbole admitted to Mark and Ben that 'the family' had carried out the bombing. 'They hit one of our guys hard,' Ross said. 'We had to do it.' Ross Trimbole's admission of the Calabrian Mafia's involvement in the bombing wasn't even mentioned in the NCA bulletin.

In the Brisbane *Courier Mail* on 11 November 1995 Bob Bottom denounced the NCA's assessment as 'a blatant sop to ethnic sensitivities for what must rank as base political motives ... a convenient way to head off any further pressure for a national royal commission into mafia activity'.

In 2008 the South Australian government posted a $1 million reward for information leading to the conviction of the NCA bomber. The reward followed a seventeen-month review of the case which was unable to find any new evidence.

In her 2003 book *Mafia Brotherhoods: Organised Crime, Italian Style*, a former consultant to the Italian Anti-Mafia Directorate, Letizia Paoli, refers to the report of a 2000 Italian parliamentary inquiry into the Mafia and similar organisations and a 2001 Italian Ministry of Interior report, both of which identified Australia, among other countries, as having 'highly developed' `ndrangheta settlements. 'Though enjoying a high degree of operational independence,' Paoli writes, 'these units are considered by their own members and their Calabrian correspondents as belonging for all intents and purposes to the `ndrangheta.'

Neither the NCA nor the Australian Crime Commission, which replaced it in 2003, have seen fit to publicly revise the Cerberus findings.

Several times during the 1990s and early 2000s the police executive was warned of the threat posed to the state by organised crime—in particular, Italian organised crime. In its

2003–04 Annual Report, the New South Wales Crime Commission reported:

> Cannabis remains the most widely used illicit drug in Australia and accounts for more than half of the nation's illegal drug trade expenditure. The cannabis market continues to be controlled by established criminal networks, predominantly Italian organised crime groups as well as other ethnic criminal groups and outlaw motorcycle gangs . . .
>
> The Italian organised crime network supporting the activities of these various groups has received relatively little law enforcement attention over the past decade, yet continues to generate substantial wealth from its contribution to illegal cannabis cultivation and distribution.

In 2006 the long-time Italian Mafia prosecutor Dr Salvatore Curcio told Melbourne *Age* journalist Nick McKenzie that it was time Australian police woke up to the mafia menace in their midst. McKenzie cited a 2004 report by Italy's Interior Ministry that 'singled out Australia as one of the overseas countries in which the 'ndrangheta is most active and nominated the 'ndrangheta as the most "internationally dangerous" of Italy's Mafia groups'.

In 2008 the Italian Anti-Mafia Commission released its most recent assessment of the 'ndrangheta. It found that during the past three decades the society had become an international operation, evolving from its 'traditional rigid hierarchical and monolithic structure' into a more agile, flexible and effective form of mafia, 'like al-Qaeda with a similar tentacular structure'. Operating like a franchised 'fast-food chain', the report said, the 'ndrangheta 'offers the same, recognisable brand and identical criminal product all over the world'.

It has access to bases of support throughout Europe, North and South America and Australia. Several 'families' established in Australia—including the Sergi, Barbaro, Perre and Papalia clans—are named in the report.

In April Sydney's *Daily Telegraph* reported intelligence assessments by the Netherlands-based Synthetic Drugs Unit warning that 'ndrangheta, Dutch and Chinese criminals were planning to flood Australia with ecstasy. In May the Eurispes research group released a report that estimated the 'ndrangheta's turnover for 2007 at 44 billion euros (A$70 billion), of which about 27 billion euros came from drugs.

Around the same time US president George W. Bush announced sanctions under the US Foreign Narcotics Kingpin Designation Act in an attempt to cut off the 'ndrangheta's access to the US financial system. The sanctions prohibit US companies and individuals from engaging in trade or transactions with the 'ndrangheta organisation or its members.

On 8 August 2008 the Australian Federal Police, the Customs Service and other law enforcement authorities arrested more than twenty people across four states for importing ecstasy and cocaine. The arrests followed two enormous seizures. In June 2007, following a tip-off from overseas authorities, 4.4 tonnes of ecstasy (15 million tablets) was found in a shipping container in Port Melbourne. A year later, in June 2008, 150 kilograms of cocaine was seized from another container in Melbourne. In both cases the drugs had been loaded in Italy.

During the previous seven years Australian police and Customs had detected at least three major importations. One involved more than a tonne of ecstasy; the other two involved 500 and 434 kilograms of cocaine. In addition, they disrupted two planned cocaine importations of 300 and 500 kilograms. Each time the drugs had been or were to have been loaded in Italy. Yet these seizures had no significant impact on either the cocaine or ecstasy trade in Australia: there were enough successful importations to cover the losses.

Australian authorities continue to deny the existence of the 'ndrangheta in Australia.

During a 1986 ABC *Four Corners* program called 'The Family Business', Justice Woodward was asked by journalist Chris Masters, 'How serious was your investigation [royal commission] meant to be?' 'Well, by me, very serious,' he said, '[but] I'm afraid that it's like many commissions that are established by the government, it's never intended that they should find out too much because anything that's found out which casts a slur upon any part of the administration of the country or of the state is accepted without question by the government as a slur on them.'

'Let's get this clear,' Masters said. 'You're saying that your royal commission, formally, officially, from the government's point of view was meant to be a Clayton's royal commission. It was meant to pretend to look into it to satisfy the public.'

'I am afraid that's so,' Justice Woodward replied.

Despite the stench surrounding Grassby's involvement with the powerbrokers of Griffith's drug trade and those involved in the Calabrian Mafia, both in Australia and Italy, the Labor Party was not going to forget an old colleague who had served it well. In 2005 the ACT Labor government commissioned a life-sized statue of Grassby to honour his contribution to multiculturalism. The statue was unveiled in Canberra in May 2007. The insult to the Mackay family was obvious. Donald Mackay's son Paul told the ABC news, 'Grassby had a pattern of tending to gloss over events that occurred in Griffith and made a number of attempts to smear our family, and to defame us and to try to implicate us in Dad's death.' The National MP for Murrumbidgee, Adrian Piccoli, was more direct, saying of Grassby, 'He's named in just about every book written about organised crime.'

No member of a state Labor government or the then federal Labor opposition was prepared to criticise the decision to honour Grassby. A few Labor politicians offered muted support but most kept their silence.

In a culture focused on future elections, ongoing financial support, and the pragmatic repayment of past debts, politics carries more weight than principle.

Chapter 2

The Big Three of Organised Crime

Lennie McPherson, George Freeman and 'Stan the Man' Smith

While the `ndrangheta sowed the seeds of organised crime in the canefields of Queensland, Sydney and Melbourne had their own, home-grown crime organisations. During the 1920s Sydney's notorious razor gangs fought each other for control of prostitution, drugs, sly grog and illegal gambling, particularly starting-price bookmaking. Three gangs came to dominate the Sydney rackets. They were led by Tilley Devine, Kate Leigh and Phil 'the Jew' Jeffs, all of whom remained prominent figures in the city's underworld long after the power struggles had settled into a status quo of business as usual.

In the mid 1960s another gang war broke out as local crime bosses expanded their rackets and realigned their organisations. In four years there were at least nine assassinations and numerous attempted assassinations. The murders were, for the most part, carried out in public and involved the use of sub-machine guns, semi-automatic rifles and, in one instance, a car bomb.

In the years following the 1960s bloodshed, Leonard Arthur 'Lennie' McPherson, George Freeman and Stanley 'Stan the Man' Smith emerged as the Big Three of Sydney organised crime. They worked in loose partnership, but each had his own business interests and areas of responsibility.

McPherson was born in the dockside suburb of Balmain in 1921. When he was eleven, the Children's Court placed him on a good behaviour bond for stealing. By the late 1960s he had grown into a big, coarse-featured, physically intimidating man with forty-nine entries on his criminal record, including convictions for assault, firearms offences, fraud, housebreaking and theft. The charges he had beaten included murder, attempted murder, rape and interfering with a witness.

Freeman was born in 1934 in Annandale, a few miles from Balmain. He spent his childhood in and out of boys' homes before graduating to prison at eighteen. Identified in the 1955 Police Criminal Register as an 'active and persistent criminal', Freeman was less impressively described in a police profile as 'a not too successful criminal living in the western suburbs of Sydney and employed as a casual labourer at the State Abattoirs'.

From petty theft, safe-breaking and shoplifting, Freeman moved up to SP bookmaking. His small stature did not diminish his reputation for violence, and he served as an occasional bodyguard and provider of protection for well-heeled gamblers, illegal bookmakers and, later, casino operators. By the late 1950s he had racked up more than thirty convictions for firearms, theft and fraud offences, and resisting arrest. The crimes would continue, but Freeman was getting better at staying out of police view.

Freeman met McPherson during the early 1950s when both were serving time in Long Bay jail. From then on they were friends and partners in crime. During the early 1970s Melbourne's Toe Cutter gang, known for its members' habit of cutting off the toes of their rivals in the course of robbing them, tried to muscle in on Sydney's lucrative illegal casino and gambling trade. McPherson and Freeman met the challenge head on. Within a short time several of the Toe Cutters 'disappeared'; others fled back to Melbourne. By the end of 1972 the Toe Cutters were no longer a gang. The bones of one their most brutal leaders, Kevin Victor Gore, are said to rattle each time a jumbo jet lands at Sydney's Kingsford Smith Airport.

Sixteen years McPherson's junior and, like him, a Balmain boy on the make, Stan Smith avoided the police until he was seventeen. By his twenties, despite the age gap, he was a close friend of McPherson's, and the two were often seen drinking together in the pubs of Balmain. They were also colleagues, carving out reputations as hard men in the hard world of organised crime.

In 1963 Smith and several associates broke into the Paddington home of Robert 'Pretty Boy' Walker, a twenty-six-year-old gangster with a fondness for violence. Walker shot Smith several times and he spent several weeks in hospital recovering. Not long afterwards, as Walker strolled down the main road of Randwick—site of Sydney's top race-track—he collapsed in a hail of machine-gun fire from a passing car. There was no need for a doctor. Walker was dead, with six bullets in his chest.

Old-time cops and crooks say that in just over two decades, from the late 1950s, Smith was involved in around twenty-five shootings and murders. After that he had little need for violence: his 'advice' was enough to cow all but the toughest opponents.

By the mid 1970s Freeman's SP bookmaking and race-fixing operations were well established. At his office at Rockdale, half a dozen people gathered insider information and worked the telephones, placing and laying off bets and setting odds on races with around twenty 'agencies' scattered across Sydney. Each agency operated its own telephone betting networks.

McPherson supplied illegal amusement and gambling machines to clubs and bars and was heavily involved, with Smith, in the protection of Kings Cross nightclubs and small suburban gambling clubs. McPherson's gambling and prostitution interests extended to the Philippines and New Guinea. McPherson and Freeman infiltrated licensed clubs, taking control of them and skimming millions of dollars through scams ranging from the simple theft of cash to kickbacks on cleaning contracts and extortion disguised as payments for non-existent services.

The Big Three started looking for potential allies in the US underworld. Notable among these was Joseph Dan Testa, a forty-year-old described by the FBI as a 'member of the Organised Criminal Element in Chicago, Illinois . . . active in real estate development, cocktail lounges, financial institutions and other enterprises alleged . . . [to be] . . . front[s] or clearing house[s] for syndicate money'.

Testa first visited Australia in February 1965 as the guest of local illegal casino operator Ronnie Lee. Three years later, Freeman and Smith travelled to the US on false passports and, with introductions from Lee, met Testa, who squired them around during their six-week stay. On their return to Australia, Freeman and Smith were spotted travelling on false passports.

The next year Testa spent a month in Sydney, staying at Freeman's home. McPherson chartered an aircraft and took him on a shooting trip near Bourke. A year later McPherson visited Testa in Chicago. All expenses were paid by Testa, including the cost of a visit to Las Vegas, where McPherson claimed to have had some luck at the gambling tables. The next year, 1971, Testa again visited Australia as a guest of Freeman. Once more McPherson took him shooting. Testa also bought a racehorse and went into real estate investment and property development with Freeman, to whom Testa gave power of attorney.

Freeman and McPherson also had visits from Danny Stein, also known as Steinberg, who, according to the FBI, 'represented hidden interests in the Flamingo Sands and Caesars Palace Hotel' in Las Vegas and 'an illegal interstate gambling operation'. He was said to be an associate 'of the most notorious hoodlums to have visited Las Vegas, including Meyer Lansky'. Lansky, on whom the Hyman Roth character in *The Godfather* was based, has been described as 'the banker for the Mob' and the chairman of the 'national crime syndicate' in the US. He is supposed to have uttered the famous line, 'We [the Mob] are bigger than US Steel.'

Stein visited Sydney four times during 1972–73 and established a 'construction business' with Freeman. During 1973 Stein received payments from the then Associated Motor Club, which had been infiltrated by McPherson, Freeman and their crew, for 'work' as an 'entertainment manager'. Allegations of the mafia's involvement with the poker-machine manufacturer Bally and its infiltration into licensed clubs led the New South Wales government that year to establish the Moffitt Royal Commission into Allegations of Organised Crime in Clubs.

On 4 December Testa gave evidence before the Moffitt Commission, where another witness had described him as a 'psychopathic killer'—a charge he not surprisingly denied. Claiming to be a legitimate businessman, Testa insisted he did not know McPherson had a reputation as a criminal, and stood by his mate George Freeman.

The commission was unconvinced. It pointed to a series of meetings in Double Bay in July and August 1972 at which criminal alliances had been sealed and new opportunities discussed. Among those who attended the meetings were Freeman, McPherson, Frederick 'Paddles' Anderson, Karl Bonnette, Milan 'Iron Bar Miller' Petricevic, Leo 'the Fibber' Callaghan (known in later years as Jack 'the Fibber' Warren and Patrick William Warren) and a Labor MP named Albert Ross Sloss.

The commission exposed the existence of organised crime in licensed clubs, corrupt connections with police, and emerging alliances with recognised American Mafia members. Its report accurately identified individuals in this network who were already central to the growth of organised crime in Australia, as well as several who would emerge as major underworld figures in the years to come. But the government failed to act on the commission's findings. The underworld was left to police itself.

In September 1974, a month after the Moffitt Royal Commission released its report, John Stewart Regan, a particularly violent criminal, was gunned down in a Marrickville street. Regan had become a problem for the underworld, police and politicians alike because of his uncontrolled and public violence. But he overstepped the mark when a child he was supposed to have been minding disappeared, presumed murdered by Regan himself.

McPherson and Freeman had grown used to running their criminal operations without too much interference from the police. Regan's antics were making that increasingly difficult. To get rid of him, Freeman enlisted the help of Paddles Anderson, whose reputation as a standover man went back to the late 1930s. Anderson arranged a meeting between Regan and Freeman. At a hotel near the appointed venue, he took Regan's gun from him, assuring him that Freeman would be unarmed. When Regan arrived for the rendezvous, he was shot with bullets from three different handguns. Legend spread of Freeman stepping out from the shadows and juggling the three guns as he emptied them into Regan: it wasn't true but it added a pleasing lustre to Freeman's reputation as the fastest gun in the east.

Solving the problem was one thing, but what mattered to Freeman and McPherson was being seen to have solved it. Removing a nuisance like Regan stamped their authority on the criminal milieu while presenting both men as 'responsible' gangsters who could be trusted not to cause trouble for the police or politicians. A gullible press was happy to reinforce this view, and no one tried too hard to find Regan's murderers.

McPherson, Freeman and Smith shared power and profits and offered mutual support against rivals. To challenge one was to challenge all three—and few were prepared to take the risk. Reprisals were swift and without mercy. The triumvirate adjudicated on disputes and ensured that calm was maintained. In doing so they planted the seeds of organised crime in New South Wales: crime as a mafia-like business rather than an opportunistic, freelance activity, a business in which violence was a tool of internal control rather than public intimidation. As McPherson, Freeman and Smith bullied, stole and cheated their way to the top, they made sure police and politicians shared in the profits. McPherson and his allies also understood the need to manage political and police concerns and community fears.

As the gambling, extortion and protection rackets expanded, new opportunities—particularly to do with illegal drugs—emerged. So did new risks. The more the networks grew, the harder they were to manage. Recruits were often impatient to make their mark. Yet despite the difficulties, the criminal associations formed during these years would endure long after the triumvirate had lost its power.

Chapter 3

Murray Riley

The gentleman gangster

The McPherson–Freeman–Smith network nurtured several criminals who would go on to carve out notorious careers in their own right. Among the most influential was Murray Stewart Riley. One of the architects of organised crime in Australia, he started his career as a police officer.

Riley joined the police in 1943 at the age of nineteen. For a time he was one of the force's most promising young members. His prowess at rowing won him gold medals at the Commonwealth Games and the 1956 Melbourne Olympics, where his partner was Merv Wood, later a New South Wales police commissioner. He was taken under the wing of the corrupt detective Ray 'Shotgun' Kelly, who assigned him to protect Ray Smith, an associate of Lennie McPherson.

According to the Moffitt report, Riley became Smith's bodyguard after Smith's life had been threatened and his car bombed. He also 'formed some kind of business association' with Smith, and for a time lived in Smith's house. Riley also befriended McPherson.

His corrupt associations were discovered, and Riley was disciplined and put back in the uniformed ranks. In 1962 he resigned and went into organised crime full time.

Joining forces with McPherson and Freeman, Riley became involved in skimming money from licensed clubs. A key figure in the 1974 Moffitt Royal Commission into organised crime in clubs, Riley managed to disappear as soon as the commission began. Police could not find him, they said, though there were regular sightings of him in the city's better restaurants.

The commission found that Riley's activities in South Sydney Junior Leagues Club, the Associated Mariners Club and the Associated Motor Club had 'at least one important aspect in common with the US gangster pattern in the Las Vegas and London clubs,' namely that without being an office holder, he had begun taking over club affairs. 'In all three clubs he participated in and acted in organising the skimming, by illicit means and shams, of monies from the clubs.'

The Moffitt Commission blocked this source of revenue, but McPherson and Freeman found plenty of other opportunities to pursue.

Riley remained on McPherson's payroll, collecting protection money from illegal casinos, including the 33 Club, in Kings Cross, which became his gateway into the drug trade.

*

In late 1973 a group of cannabis- and LSD-using hippies from Australia, Canada and the US met while staying in Bali and decided to smuggle drugs into Australia. Two of the group travelled to Sydney with cannabis and opium hidden in their luggage. In January 1975 another four members of the Bali group flew into Sydney, each carrying about 10 kilograms of cannabis. When they were arrested, they contacted a Sydney solicitor whose number they had been given in Bali. The solicitor approached Michael Moylan, the owner of the 33 Club, and arranged for Moylan's wife, the club's co-owner, to lodge $28,000 bail. On their release they repaid the bail money and gave the Moylans $5000 for their trouble.

The Moylans had recently been forced to shut down the 33 Club. Michael had inherited the club from his late father, but lacked his father's business acumen and connections. He was also a compulsive gambler. The club went bust and the Moylans were left heavily in debt.

Drug trafficking seemed the perfect solution to their problems. The Moylans got a free seminar on importing from all six of the Bali smugglers and came to an arrangement whereby the six would flee the country and become the Thailand end of the syndicate. They would buy the cannabis, pack it in the false linings of suitcases and recruit couriers to bring it to Australia.

The Moylans's role was to meet the couriers in Sydney, take possession of the drugs and pay the couriers about $2000 each. If the couriers were arrested, the Moylans would hire a lawyer, arrange bail and, if necessary, provide false passports so they could flee the country. If the couriers preferred to stay and face the charges, the Moylans would support them financially. Michael Moylan invited Riley to join the syndicate because of Riley's reputation as a criminal 'heavy' and because of his local and American connections: the Moylans had plans to eventually smuggle heroin into the US.

With a few exceptions the syndicate's couriers were female. All were rehearsed in the story they should tell if arrested: in Thailand they had met and become infatuated with an American by the name of Michael Johnston. Before leaving for Australia, Johnston had given them the two suitcases as a farewell present. The bags had been packed by hotel staff while Johnston took them for a last drink. The staff also arranged for the suitcases to be delivered to the airport. The 'Johnston story', as it became known, enabled several couriers to beat charges in Australian courts. For a time there was even an international search for Michael Johnston.

After the Bali six had left for Thailand, the Moylan syndicate was beset by treachery. Graham Gerald 'Barney' Vesey, an American-born friend of Riley and a former employee of the Moylans at the 33 Club, organised an importation of his own, but the courier was arrested at Sydney airport. Despite the mutual distrust and threats, the Moylans and Riley realised that for the operation to work they needed Vesey's help. Instead of being thrown out of the syndicate, Vesey was made a full partner.

Gradually the Moylans and Riley recruited their own couriers and expanded the syndicate. One of its new members was Richard Bruce 'Snapper' Cornwell, a successful small-time cannabis importer who had been a regular gambler at the 33 Club. Cornwell had used several of the club employees, including his girlfriend, as couriers. His drug expertise and contacts made him a useful recruit.

Over four months, from May 1975, the syndicate brought in twenty-one shipments of cannabis, totalling more than 300 kilograms. At least three more shipments came into New Zealand, and another was landed in Perth, hidden in the luggage of a passenger on an ocean liner. These four importations totalled more than 50 kilograms. In September and November 1975 the syndicate brought in more than a tonne of cannabis hidden inside large cylindrical batteries. Vesey again double-crossed the Moylans and Riley, telling them that these last two shipments had been intercepted and keeping the proceeds for himself.

In late 1975, however, several couriers were arrested and started rolling over. The Michael Johnston story had been used too many times. Michael Moylan and his wife fled to England, where they were joined by Graham Twaddell, a principal of the syndicate from the outset.

In London the Moylans and Twaddell set up an operation using their established overseas contacts, but after only six months Michael Moylan and Twaddell were arrested trying to import cannabis into England. They were still serving their three-and-a-half-year jail terms when they, along with Moylan's wife, were extradited to Australia to face more drug importation charges. Moylan died in jail of a heart attack in 1980.

For the time being Riley, Vesey and Cornwell escaped punishment. While the Moylans had been drawing attention to themselves with their feverish cannabis trafficking, Riley had been exploring the feasibility of moving into heroin, which he would trans-ship through Australia into the US. He used his connections with American organised crime figures living in Sydney to gain entrée to the US underworld.

One contact was George Pierce 'Duke' Countis, a gambler and San Francisco restaurateur who came to Australia in 1967. He opened a restaurant in Double Bay and became a man about town. He was a frequent visitor to the 33 Club and other gambling dens, and soon became part of Riley's circle. He introduced Riley to Harry Wainwright, who had been an associate of, and lawyer for, mobsters on the US West Coast. Just as a US court was indicting him on tax evasion charges, Wainwright had become an Australian citizen. He and an American partner went into business growing marijuana in northern New South Wales. In 1976 he joined Riley's heroin syndicate.

Riley had then made several trips to the US, using his own and false passports. Sometimes he was accompanied by Countis, although they travelled separately. They later claimed the American visits were legitimate business trips to organise seafood exports to the US. But it was heroin, not prawns, that Riley was keen to ship. He also had a pipe dream of some day owning a Las Vegas casino.

In San Francisco Countis arranged Riley's introduction to James 'Jimmy the Weasel' Fratianno, Johnny George, Teamsters boss Rudy Tham and his brother Gus, and other Mafia heavies. Fratianno, who later became an FBI witness against several high-profile mobsters, admitted to taking part in more than twenty murders on behalf of the Mafia. Rudy Tham was an official of the notoriously corrupt Teamsters' Union who had Mafia and other organised-crime connections. These men would prove useful to Riley back in Australia.

During 1976 Riley's group—with him, Vesey and Cornwell at the helm—imported more than 50 kilograms of heroin into Australia in at least six shipments, using a variety of methods and routes. More than 18 kilograms were smuggled inside a cruiser transported to Australia as deck cargo. In early 1977 Vesey flew to the US and got involved in cocaine trafficking in California. Six months later he was arrested on an extradition warrant over his role in the Moylan syndicate, but skipped bail. While on the run, he joined Riley for another heroin importation. Vesey managed the Thailand end, buying and packaging the 'smack', while Riley distributed it in Sydney.

Riley now joined forces with an old partner in crime from the 1960s, William Sinclair, who dabbled in SP betting and heroin dealing. The Woodward Royal Commission described him as 'a man who did not follow any set profession, trade or business, but rather lived by his wits... His stock in trade was his extensive contacts on the fringe of business and politics.'

Sinclair's skills as a fixer and his ownership of the Wings travel agency made him an attractive ally for Riley. He had probably founded Wings Travel as a legitimate business, but it soon became a vehicle for organising trips by drug importers and organised crime figures. In two years the agency organised more than 200 itineraries for criminals and drug smugglers. Using Wings ensured they would be tipped off if law enforcement agencies made inquiries about their trips, and that no one would ask awkward questions if they made bookings under false names.

The Riley group's principal courier and overseas organiser was Warren Fellows, who had been introduced to the drug trade by an apprentice of his jockey father.

In his book *The Damage Done*, Fellows describes how, in rather amateurish fashion, he first smuggled hashish from India. He and Sinclair briefly teamed up with a Sydney publican in a small-scale heroin syndicate before throwing in their lot with Riley, who also brought in Arthur 'Neddy' Smith.

Smith was a standover man who worked for one of Riley's heroin dealers, Kenneth Robert Derley. Nearly two metres tall, and with a menacing presence and a background in armed robbery, Smith was just the kind of muscle Riley was looking for to protect his interests.

While he was putting his heroin network together, Riley was introduced to the American Michael Hand, a former Green Beret who had been decorated for bravery in Vietnam. Hand was one half of the recently established Nugan Hand Merchant Bank. The bank was only too eager to help Riley launder and transfer money around the world, and to accept any new customers he might introduce. Entranced by Riley's talk of millions from heroin trafficking and large cash deposits by the American Mafia, Hand set up a branch in Thailand's drug capital, Chiang Mai. Neil Evans, a Queenslander hired to work in the Nugan Hand Bank's Chiang Mai office when it opened in late 1976, later told police, 'I was never under any illusion at any time that I was to go over there for any other purpose but to seek out drug money.' He claimed to have secured $3 million from six Thai-based drug traffickers in the nine months the office was open.

Riley and Countis also approached Hand for a $23 million loan to buy a block of land in Las Vegas for a casino. The construction money would be raised once they owned the land. Riley and Countis arranged for Stephen Hill, a manager of the Nugan Hand Bank, to go to Las Vegas and meet their partner, the US mobster Johnny George. Hill told Hand the plan was not feasible. A furious Riley immediately severed all relations with the bank.

But by then it had its own network of contacts in the

Southeast Asian drug underworld. Over the next three years the bank laundered and transferred millions of dollars between Sydney, Hong Kong, Bangkok and Singapore for as many as twenty heroin traffickers, including members of the international Chinese heroin syndicate Pak Leung and the soon-to-be-notorious Mr Asia syndicate. The bank collapsed in 1980 amid rumours that it was a front for the CIA.

The failed casino bid convinced Riley he would have to get the money on his own. One big drug importation was all he needed. Now he set about finding the cash to fund it.

In late December 1976 a parcel of travellers cheques to the value of US$274,700 was consigned by registered mail from the Corryong, Victoria, branch of the Bank of New South Wales to the headquarters of American Express in Sydney. Somewhere inside the Redfern Mail Exchange, the parcel was stolen. Three months later Riley paid the thieves $50,000 cash for the cheques, confident they would yield a handsome profit.

Riley recruited a number of women who had worked in illegal casinos (some of whom had also carried drugs for him) and provided them with false passports. Over the next few months cheques to the value of about US$100,000 were cashed in Sydney, Hong Kong, San Francisco, Auckland, Miami, Rio de Janeiro and Zurich. Several of Riley's proxies were caught. Riley himself would eventually be arrested, but that was years away.

Throughout 1977 the heroin importations continued, with Neddy Smith as the principal distributor. It was a loosely run organisation. People like Smith and Sinclair were on the inside of every deal, while the Sydney publican,

Fellows and some members of Riley's 1976 group were included in only some of the shipments. In his memoir *Neddy*, Smith claims that he and Riley did several million dollars' worth of business during 1977 and that he had ten distributors working for him, largely in Sydney's eastern suburbs.

That year Riley began loosening his ties both with Smith—who became senior partner in a heroin syndicate that included Sinclair and Fellows—and with Snapper Cornwell. By now he had the cash to set his one-off importation in motion.

Through contacts in the Chinese Triads, he approached Thai drug suppliers with an order for five tonnes of cannabis. He was told that such a huge quantity would need to be grown and wouldn't be ready for delivery until the end of 1977. A price of $48,000 a tonne plus $50,000 for 'protection' was agreed on: $200,000 was to be paid up front; the balance shortly after delivery. The deposit would come from heroin sales.

While the grass grew, Riley hunted for a boat to ferry it to Australia. Unknown to him, another Sydney-based syndicate, led by one Wayne Thelander, was preparing to import two tonnes of cannabis into Australia. In early 1978, as Riley and Thelander tried to find vessels for their contraband cargoes, by chance they both hired the same man, a New Zealander named Graham Lyall Cann who had a yacht called the *Choyro Maru*.

Cann, a member of the Mr Asia heroin syndicate, told neither Riley nor Thelander of his arrangement with the other, hoping to be paid twice for the same trip. As he prepared to collect the consignments, he told each syndicate that a second consignment existed, but did not identify the owner.

In late March 1978 Cann sailed to Hua Hin, on the western side of the Gulf of Thailand, and loaded Thelander's two tonnes. He then sailed to Pattaya, where he met Riley and two Thais, one a senior military officer. A couple of days later, the *Choyro Maru* went to a nearby military harbour and took on Riley's cargo. It was only four and a half tonnes: half a tonne of the cannabis had been destroyed by fire while awaiting collection.

As it made its way to Australia, the *Choyro Maru* developed engine trouble. Cann arranged for the cannabis to be dropped off at Polkington Reef, between Papua New Guinea and the Solomon Islands, from where it would have to be retrieved by boat or seaplane.

Chaos followed as each syndicate struggled to organise for its own cargo to be picked up. Cann arranged a meeting in Sydney between Riley and Thelander, and both parties finally agreed to cooperate. A yacht, the *Anoa*, was bought in Cairns. It sailed to Polkington Reef, loaded five tonnes of the shipment, and headed for New South Wales.

Near Coffs Harbour, the crew was spooked by a low-flying aircraft. The following night they docked at a small inlet south of the town and unloaded nearly three tonnes of cannabis. Their fears were well founded. The *Anoa* had been under surveillance by the federal Narcotics Bureau ever since it left Cairns.

Over the next six weeks police arrested most members of both syndicates and recovered the cannabis unloaded from the yacht. Later, they located another two tonnes of cannabis still at Polkington Reef. The final two tonnes were never found.

Riley and several others immediately pleaded guilty. Three months later Riley was sentenced to ten years' jail (the maximum penalty at that time). He was later given a similar sentence for his role in the American Express travellers' cheques fraud. Wayne Thelander also got a ten-year sentence.

Released on parole in May 1984, Riley teamed up again with Neddy Smith, now a big player in the heroin trade. Over the next few years they pulled off a few more importations, attempted importations and drug rip-offs. At times they were joined by their old partner William Sinclair, following his nine-year stint in a Thai jail for his role in one of Smith's heroin deals (see Chapter 7).

When Smith resumed his old career of armed robbery, Riley began casting around for new opportunities. In 1990 he changed his name by deed poll to Murray Lee Stewart, obtained a passport in that name and travelled to Britain, where he went about setting up what was to be his biggest scam. He opened a bank account on the Isle of Man, telling the manager that British Aerospace would be depositing a large sum which was to be used as part of a secret government operation to assist with the release of hostages in the Middle East. If they succeeded, Riley and his two British associates stood to make nearly $100 million. He lived the life of Riley in the five-star London Hilton and Mayfair hotels and ran up hotel bills of almost $200,000 before he was arrested.

In July 1991 Riley, aged sixty-five, was sentenced to five years' jail. During the next few months his security classification was dropped from the second highest category to the lowest and he was transferred to a prison farm without walls or fences. A few weeks later he simply walked out. His escape was not reported for seven weeks.

By then Riley was in Hong Kong with his longtime

Australian girlfriend, Carol Dean, who had flown there to meet him. When Dean returned to Australia, Riley followed. At the time of writing, the two are still together.

A retired detective who knows Riley from days gone by claims that in 2002 he was at a country racecourse in northern New South Wales with a currently serving detective when he noticed a dapper old man with neatly trimmed grey hair in the company of a well-dressed, middle-aged woman. They appeared to be enjoying the races. He stared at the old man, who stared back. They nodded, smiled and went their separate ways. The young detective said, 'Who was that?'

'Murray Riley.'

'Never heard of him.'

Riley played in the big criminal leagues, but he lacked the ruthless streak and the capacity for violence that made McPherson, Freeman and Stan Smith so notorious.

Now in his eighties, his skin mottled from the removal of skin cancers, Riley has remained beyond the reach of the law since his return to Australia. He is said to have been involved in a few poker machine scams and frauds with colleagues from the 1970s, but it has been strictly small-time crime for a man who knows that if he ever returns to jail he will almost certainly die there.

Chapter 4

'Snapper' Cornwell

A big fish in a big pond

While several drug networks from the early 1970s survived in changing forms into the 1980s and even 1990s, few were as enduring or played as significant a role as the one built by Richard Bruce 'Snapper' Cornwell.

Tall and lean, a smooth talker and flashy dresser, Cornwell was a well-known gambler at the race tracks and in the gambling dens that dotted Sydney in the late 1960s and early '70s. He had several convictions for violence, but it was not until 1974, after being arrested in Townsville in possession of a small quantity of cannabis, that he was first convicted of a drug offence. Along with Riley, Cornwell became a distributor for Michael Moylan's drug syndicate. He also brought in his own shipments using the Moylan couriers and his then girlfriend.

'SNAPPER' CORNWELL

When the Moylan syndicate collapsed in late 1975, Cornwell joined up with Riley for drug importations—later Neddy Smith would also join the syndicate. Having visited India and Thailand and established his own Asian drug contacts, Cornwell moved to Thailand in mid 1977. Not long after, a series of shocks upset the status quo in the Australian drug trade. The *Anoa* debacle had smashed Riley's syndicate, and the arrests of Neddy Smith and his associates in Thailand (see Chapters 3 and 7) and Sydney had temporarily crippled his network. The Woodward Royal Commission had severely disrupted several other major drug networks. Now, with the commission winding down, the opportunities were too good to miss. Cornwell returned to Australia.

Using his contacts in Sydney's underworld and his well-established drug distribution networks, he began building his own power base. He enlisted as his partner Barry Bull, who had done time in Darwin for importing cannabis on a ship he and his associates sailed to and from Bali. After moving to Sydney, he continued dealing drugs and was arrested three times for theft, forgery, and the possession and supply of cannabis. Each time he got off with a fine.

Bull moved to Noosa Heads, where he helped Cornwell orchestrate huge importations of cannabis, heroin and cocaine—at least a dozen shipments in a few years, according to Queensland police. Ships were used to bring the drugs to agreed locations off the Queensland and New South Wales coasts. Local boats would collect the drugs and bring them to shore. Cornwell and Bull expanded their distribution network until it reached from Noosa all the way to Melbourne. They were soon making so much money they had to employ accountants and corrupt businessmen to launder it and hide their assets.

In August 1982 two principals in their network, Terrence Basham and his partner Susan Smith, were found shot in the head on their horse stud near Murwillumbah on the far north coast of New South Wales. Their two-year-old daughter, Sara, was snuggling up to her parents' bloodied corpses. Photographs in the house showed Sara playing with bars of silver and sitting on her mother's knee playing with bundles of $50 notes. Another photograph showed a suitcase full of money. It was said that they had failed to pay Bull and Cornwell for several large drug transactions.

Eight days after the murders, Cornwell left Australia for a vacation that lasted a year. While he was away, Victoria's Costigan Royal Commission on the Painters and Dockers Union examined his finances. It focused on a series of transactions in the weeks before Basham and Smith were murdered. Its report observed: 'The possibility that some of this cash was assigned to a murder contract is irresistible.' Tax authorities also took a close interest in Bull's finances aand stripped him of millions of dollars in assets.

With Bull short of money and demand for cannabis unabated, he and Cornwell could not resist the temptation. After Cornwell returned from overseas they began to plan their next importation. By May 1985 they'd purchased two tonnes of the drug in Thailand and had it sailed to a location off New Guinea. There, Bull's yacht took the cannabis on board and brought it to Australia.

The shipment made them millions, but Cornwell and Bull wanted more. Their next importation was planned for the summer of 1985–86. By this time, however, the National Crime Authority had them under almost constant surveillance. Perhaps they were tipped off by corrupt agents or police; perhaps they noticed something amiss. But in mid

September they abandoned their 'safe house' in Sydney's Edgecliff and flew to Singapore and then Britain using false passports. Planning for the importation continued.

The NCA asked New Scotland Yard to help locate the runaways. In November Cornwell's then wife, Carmen, flew to London and was immediately put under surveillance. At the time, New Scotland Yard was also on the hunt for Robert Trimbole, who had left Ireland after beating an extradition bid and was believed to be on the loose in London.

Carmen Cornwell was seen meeting with two men, one of whom the police thought was Trimbole. The police pounced and arrested the three. 'Trimbole' was actually Jack Levy, the de facto husband of Carmen's mother. It took him several weeks to convince Scotland Yard of his identity. The second man was Cornwell, who had a false passport and refused to identify himself—until he'd spent a few nights in the police cells. But the NCA had wanted Cornwell watched, not arrested. Hurriedly, extradition papers were put together.

Almost a year later in mid 1986, as the legal wrangling over Cornwell's extradition dragged on, Bull was arrested in Austria. On his way from court to jail he forced open the door of a moving police van and leapt onto a motorcycle ridden by his longtime partner, Sylvia Lux, who had fled Australia with him.

The escape gained international attention and was a major embarrassment to local police, who pulled out all stops to arrest Bull and Lux. Lux eventually got off with a three-year suspended sentence for helping Bull escape. Bull was deported to Australia, where Cornwell had finally arrived—flown home under heavy guard in the Prime Minister's own RAAF Boeing 707.

In 1987 Bull and Cornwell, along with others, pleaded guilty to importing the two tonnes of cannabis and conspiring to import a second shipment. They were sentenced to twenty-three years and eighteen years respectively. Bull's sentencing was delayed by the presiding judge for three weeks so he could marry Lux. Stephen Angelini, a Californian associate of the two men, told the court Cornwell 'reminded me of some guy who had watched too many gangster movies'.

Cornwell's assets were estimated to be worth around $23 million. They included properties and mining investments in Australia, a variety of investments in Hong Kong and the UK, and twenty-four bank accounts in different aliases and company names in Australia, Switzerland, Jersey, the UK, Liechtenstein and Hong Kong. The courts eventually confiscated $6.9 million of assets, but there was plenty left. Only about $300,000 was confiscated from Bull, whom the Tax Office had seen to a few years earlier. The NCA's 1987 report said Cornwell had headed one of Australia's biggest drug syndicates since the late 1970s and had also been involved in 'corruption, taxation and foreign exchange offences, and murder'. While he was in London awaiting extradition to Australia Cornwell wrote to an associate: 'I don't give a fuck what they do, or how they treat me, as long as we save, or keep safe all that I have worked for, and secure our futures.'

By 1992 both Cornwell and Bull were being allowed out of jail on daily work release, though it's doubtful either did much work. In February 1993 Cornwell was seen and photographed in a festive mood at Sydney's Gay and Lesbian Mardi Gras. A political outcry led to cancellation of his work release. But less than a year later Cornwell was free after serving just over seven years of his sentence.

Bull's work release was also stopped, but only briefly. It was cancelled for good in late 1993 when people noticed him in the pub enjoying a beer. He died at home on Queensland's Sunshine Coast in 2004, with Sylvia Lux at his side.

Cornwell had been out of jail for only six months when a former associate named Neil Hoffman started talking to him about 'business' opportunities. Hoffman said he could get hold of large quantities of locally grown cannabis and weapons ranging from handguns to missiles. He also had an 'in' with the head of a Japanese Yakuza crime family that had interests in Australia.

Hoffman's information came from a person who can only be named as Fred. Picked up by law enforcement agents, Fred quickly confided that his stories were a scam, but to the police that didn't matter. They were after Hoffman, and Fred, their new paid informant, could set him up for them. When they learned Hoffman could lead them to Cornwell, they could hardly believe their luck. They had Snapper on the hook. All they had to do was play the line and reel him in.

Fred offered Hoffman and Cornwell access to more than two and a half tonnes of cannabis said to have been grown near Casino, in northern New South Wales. In mid 1995 Snapper accepted the deal and demanded delivery of a twenty-pound sample. Fred offered 100 pounds, and arranged to meet Cornwell in the car park of the Racecourse Hotel at Randwick. As Cornwell went to check the sample, heavily armed police pounced. Cornwell and Hoffman spent the next three years in jail fighting charges of conspiracy to supply cannabis. They were convicted but acquitted on appeal.

Cornwell's defence was, at that time, unique. He argued that long experience as a professional drug trafficker had told him from the outset that the proposed deal was a sting. Fred was a 'bullshit artist', Cornwell told the court. At $1000 a pound the price he had asked was 'bullshit', less than a third of what it should have been. Ten years earlier, Cornwell said, he had been getting $3500 a pound. Besides, he went on, no one in Australia could have a two-and-a-half-tonne forest-grown crop ready to harvest in July: it was the wrong season. And no one would grow that much cannabis without an established network to distribute it. The jury believed Cornwell. On his acquittal, he declared, 'I believe in miracles.'

Fred, meanwhile, dissatisfied with the wages of a police informer, approached Hoffman after the two men's arrest and offered to change his evidence for $250,000. He spent six months in jail for attempted extortion.

During the early 1990s law enforcement agencies began using the term 'East Coast Milieu' to refer to a loose group of organised crime figures centred on Sydney. Criminals though they were, the Milieu members had certain standards. They gave each other preference when organising new ventures. They dealt in cannabis and later cocaine and ecstasy, but heroin was banned. Traitors, or 'dogs', were not tolerated. Prominent in the Milieu at that time were the so-called Coogee Mob (see Chapter 10) and Cornwell, who always gave the Mob first dibs on selling his drugs.

But the alliance between Cornwell and the Mob, always uneasy, was soon to fall apart.

*

When Cornwell got out of jail in 1998 he decided to focus on cocaine. His partner in the venture was Juan Guillermo Diez-Orozco, a native of Colombia who had become an Australian citizen. During the 1980s he had been a mid-level cocaine importer, and Cornwell had distributed the drug for him.

In July 1996 several of Diez-Orozco's associates were arrested. He slipped off to Colombia, where he worked on expanding his cocaine networks and acted as a go-between for his Sydney connections. In 2000 he returned to Australia and started planning a 120-kilogram importation with Cornwell. Diez-Orozco left for Medellin, Colombia, to meet his contact, Adolpho Zapata, described as a 'mover and shaker in the Medellin cocaine trade'. Zapata was in jail at the time, but that was not a problem. He met Diez-Orozco in his 'office', the prison coffee shop, and they worked out the details. A yacht would be used, manned by a crew of professional cocaine smugglers who usually sailed their cargo to the US. To cut costs, the boat would transport two cargoes: after the Australian drop-off, it would rendezvous with a mother ship and take on another load of cocaine for delivery to the UK.

In Sydney, Cornwell put together the Australian end of the importation. To head it, he recruited John Lawrence, a long-time colleague of Cornwell's in the drug trade. Lawrence's crew included Dominic Brokenshire, who had served time for his role in Murray Riley's *Anoa* importation. Police soon had several of the conspirators under surveillance. They recorded Cornwell complaining on the phone to Lawrence, 'I've got all the buyers, all bar the Coogee fucking Mob.' The reason he didn't have the Mob was that they had their own cocaine supply, which was too big for him to compete with. Cornwell told Lawrence they could expect to make about $110,000 a kilogram.

But the Coogee Mob's cocaine imports had caused a glut. Cornwell was having trouble selling the cocaine he already had. Payment was overdue, and Diez-Orozco's Colombian connections had no patience with delays or excuses. Diez-Orozco, who went by the alias 'Mr Carlos', told Cornwell: 'I am dealing with very, very, very heavy people there . . . [they are] putting pressure on me.'

By April 2001, however, the consignment was ready to be shipped to Australia, and Zapata was out of jail. He would set sail on the delivery vessel with two other associates as crew and supervise the handover of the cocaine and the collection of payment. They would take the cargo to a position 120 nautical miles off Port Macquarie, from where Colombians working with the Cornwell–Lawrence team would pick up the drugs. One of the conspirators, Wouter Van Bommell, later told authorities, 'Mr Zapata told me Mr Carlos would have a fast boat in Australia and what I have to do is take the drugs from the sailing boat and bring it back to the shore and then I finish my job.' Van Bommell said he had met up with 'Carlos' and 'Josie' (John Lawrence) at the Sydney Opera House and other venues to confirm the plan. The rendezvous was to occur some time after 19 June 2001.

Around that date, Zapata received a call on the yacht telling him the planned seaborne exchange of the cocaine was off. The call is said to have come from someone in authority in Colombia, who urged Zapata to dump the drugs into the sea for retrieval. At the same time, Australian police briefly detained several members of the Australian and Colombian gang. A new drop-off point was quickly chosen:

Kelso Bank, about 350 nautical miles off the Queensland coast. The cocaine, packed in weighted waterproof bags, was thrown overboard in about twenty metres of water for collection.

A few weeks later the NCA swooped, charging almost a dozen people, including Cornwell, Lawrence and Diez-Orozco, with conspiring to import the 120 kilograms of cocaine. When the authorities went to Kelso Bank, the cocaine was missing, but the anchors and chains used to weigh it down were found on the sea floor. What happened to it is unknown, but police believe Zapata retrieved the drugs with the help of Victorian contacts and sold them on his own.

As the arrests were being made, Zapata was detected trying to board a plane for South America. He was held for a short time, then released. He returned to Colombia and was not pursued over the Cornwell importation by either Australian or Colombian authorities.

In July 2003, after a four-month trial, Diez-Orozco and Lawrence were each sentenced to twenty-four years' jail. Dominic Brokenshire, Lawrence's longtime drug partner, was found not guilty. Looking for another miracle, Cornwell gave evidence at the trial on condition that what he said couldn't be used against him in other proceedings. Cornwell told the jury he had previously sold cocaine supplied to him by Diez-Orozco, but had not been part of the conspiracy to import the drug. His role was to have begun only after the drugs were landed in Australia, and there was no evidence that they had been landed. His argument apparently swayed the jury, which was unable to reach a verdict in his case.

A year later Cornwell and four others over whom the jury had been deadlocked stood their second trial. Cornwell and one of the South Americans were convicted. Cornwell, then fifty-eight years old, argued for a light sentence, saying his previous time in jail had left him with depression, possibly unresolved post-traumatic stress disorder, anxiety and panic disorder. He was also a suicide risk, expert witnesses said. He was given the same twenty-four-year sentence as Diez-Orozco and Lawrence had received.

Still seeking a miracle, Cornwell appealed. In 2006 his conviction was overturned and a new trial ordered. Meanwhile, he would remain in jail. But his success was short-lived as the Crown succeeded in a further appeal to the High Court. Cornwell must now take his case back to the Court of Appeal to try and overturn the conviction again on different grounds.

Chapter 5

Chris Flannery

Mr 'Rent-a-Kill'

Christopher Dale Flannery began his life of crime at the age of fourteen. He spent the next few years housebreaking, stealing cars and escaping from the detention centres and prisons where he was periodically locked up.

A 1964 youth parole board report describes Flannery, then fifteen, as 'rather spoiled' and 'not orientated towards rehabilitation'. Another report describes him as 'a nervous, sensitive lad' and records his mother and grandmother—who raised him after his father walked out on the family—as saying Christopher was 'a good hearted lad . . . [a] very likeable boy . . . who loves his mother'. Nevertheless, he 'does not like direction; [is] quick tempered; he stays out at night without permission; he truants from school . . . he does not like being controlled, he cannot settle down in one place'. He also stole money from his mother and grandmother. Flannery's sentences were often extended because of his constant clashes with the authorities, and jail records include such comments as 'will not accept authority', '[behaviour] unsatisfactory, shows no signs of improvement', 'assaults fellow inmates', and 'a definite parole risk'.

In 1968, at the age of nineteen, he was jailed for seven years for two rapes. Also jailed over one of the rapes was Laurence Prendergast, who had been Flannery's partner in crime for some years and would remain so for the rest of his life.

During an interlude in a low-security prison farm, warders identified Flannery and six others as 'hard-core strong-arm' inmates. The then governor of the farm wrote, 'I ask that as many as possible of these mentioned prisoners be returned to Pentridge to disorganise the present stand-over set-up that exists.' Released after four years, Flannery resumed his relationship with Kathleen Jones, the daughter of a prominent member of the Painters and Dockers Union. They had had a brief romance as teenagers, after which Kath had married and had a child. The marriage over, she had begun visiting Flannery in jail. Kath's father gave the newly free Flannery a job in his decorating business, and the couple soon had a baby son.

Within four months of his parole, Flannery was back before the courts charged—with Prendergast—with the attempted armed robbery of a bank and other offences. Granted bail, Flannery absconded to Perth with Kath and the two children.

For a short time Flannery appeared to settle down. He got a job as a menswear salesman and was even promoted.

CHRIS FLANNERY

Then, with two old jail pals, he tried to rob his employer, the David Jones department store. A security guard was shot. Now wanted for armed robbery in two states, Flannery fled to Sydney with Kath. Three weeks later he and one of his accomplices were arrested as they retrieved a gun and other items used in the Perth robbery attempt.

The arresting police included detective Roger Rogerson. Rogerson later said the arrest had been a 'very violent struggle, which ended up on the railway lines. It was a fight to the death, almost.' It also marked the beginning of an association that would lead to corruption, murder, gang warfare, and Flannery's own death.

Flannery's reputation for violence scared off commercial airlines and he had to be flown to Perth in a straitjacket aboard a RAAF Hercules. Flannery beat the charges, but his problems weren't over. He was extradited to Melbourne and sentenced to three to five years' jail for the bank robbery and other charges.

During his first year inside, Flannery pleaded almost non-stop for transfer to an open prison farm, claiming he wanted to get away from 'criminal elements' and prove himself 'a changed person'. He got the transfer, but the prison farm governor was unconvinced that he'd reformed. Describing to the parole board how Flannery 'would go into a wild rage' if crossed, he wrote presciently, 'I feel Flannery is suffering some persecutory delusion and this could be his undoing in life.' Despite the governor's reservations Flannery served just three years.

In mid 1978 he and Kath got married. For a short time he kept out of trouble by working as a doorman at clubs around

Melbourne, but crime and violence were never far away. He soon hooked up with Alan Williams, an old crime mate he'd met again in Pentridge jail. According to Williams, Flannery judged himself a bit of a failure: 'He would get done for everything he did.... He was an absolute jinx.... everything he touched turned to dust. He just couldn't take a trick in the crime department.' Looking for a new way to prove himself, Flannery started thinking about murder. Williams remembers him saying: 'The only way I think I can earn a quid [and get away with it] is killing people, and I think that's what I'll try next.'

Melbourne was the perfect venue. The city's underworld was in the throes of the so-called waterfront war, in which factions of the Painters and Dockers Union fought over territory and drug profits—and piled up at least forty corpses. On one side was a gang led by Brian and Les Kane; on the other, a rival gang led by Raymond 'Chuck' Bennett, also known as Ray Chuck. Flannery's mate Laurie Prendergast was on Bennett's side; Flannery joined the Kanes.

In 1978 the body of Raymond Francis 'the Lizard' Locksley, a notorious Melbourne criminal and close associate of Flannery, was found on a dirt track in bushland near Menai, southwest of Sydney. He had been murdered the night before, shot four times by a .38-calibre handgun. Flannery was the prime suspect. According to police, Locksley had been involved in the gang war in Melbourne and had gone to Sydney with Flannery, whom he trusted but who had accepted a contract to kill him. Flannery returned to Melbourne, where his car was cleaned and given new tyres to ensure it could not be linked to the tracks at the murder scene.

The Flannerys were regular visitors to Sydney. Seven months later, on New Year's Eve, they attended a party at the home of Kath's sister and her husband in suburban Earlwood. During the night Kath accused a young woman of flirting with her brother-in-law and after threatening her, grabbed her from behind and threw her down a flight of stairs. As another guest went to see what was going on, Flannery punched him and bashed him with a chair, breaking his jaw.

In August 1979, as the investigations of the Locksley murder and the New Year's Eve assault ground on, Melbourne detectives searched Flannery's Aspendale home and found a pistol. Chris and Kath were arrested. In court, Flannery claimed that two weeks before his arrest he had been at a St Kilda nightclub part-owned by his wife—and where he acted as bouncer—when a fight broke out. According to Flannery, he'd had to step in and confiscate a pistol. He took the weapon home and forgot about it. A man claiming to be the owner of the pistol corroborated the story, and Flannery beat the charge.

Meanwhile the gang war had escalated. In October 1978 three men armed with .22-calibre machine-guns fitted with silencers had waylaid Les Kane and bundled him into a car. He was never seen again. Prendergast, Bennett and a third man were charged with his murder but acquitted.

A year later Bennett himself was shot dead while walking between courts at the Melbourne Magistrates Court complex. At the time he was on remand for a $69,000 payroll robbery. Mark 'Chopper' Read, a well-known Melbourne criminal, would later tell police Flannery was widely believed responsible for the killing. Flannery had found his vocation —and his nickname: Rent-a-Kill.

In February 1980 a Melbourne lawyer named Roger Wilson disappeared. Wilson had been involved in a number of dubious financial deals with Mark Alfred Clarkson. Clarkson believed Wilson owed him money. Police allege that when Clarkson went bankrupt, he hired Flannery to murder Wilson. Flannery in turn hired his old friend Kevin 'Weary' Williams. Within days of Wilson's disappearance, Flannery and Williams had left Melbourne. Williams, accompanied by his girlfriend, nineteen-year-old Deborah Boundy, drove to Surfers Paradise, where they met Flannery. One month later, Flannery and Kath left Australia separately for the US and Canada. After three weeks they returned to Australia together.

In July 1980 Williams, Boundy and two other Melbourne criminals were arrested at Nyngan, in northern New South Wales, on relatively minor charges. One of the men said he was Christopher Flannery. Local police immediately notified Sydney Detective Sergeant Bill Duff, who was investigating the 1978 Locksley murder. He went to Nyngan, only to find that it was not Flannery who had been arrested, but Williams.

Boundy told Duff that both Flannery and Williams had told her they'd carried out the Wilson murder and that she had seen them preparing for it. They had dressed in suits to look like detectives and made up a police sign to get their target to pull over. They said they had stopped Wilson while he was driving along the Princes Highway near Pakenham, Victoria, handcuffed him, dragged him into the bush and shot him. Boundy said Williams had told her Flannery shot Wilson in the head but had not killed him. When Wilson tried to escape, Flannery chased after him and put 'six or seven more bullets into him, and the body was buried'. A hire car used by Flannery and Williams had travelled almost 1000 kilometres in two days. Boundy also told police Kath had helped Flannery clean the vehicle used in the murder. Speaking to Melbourne police, Boundy said Flannery had telephoned Williams in Surfers Paradise to say he wanted her dead because she knew too much. The next day Williams had lied to Flannery that he had killed her. Terrified that Flannery would find out the truth, Williams and Boundy spent several months driving around New South Wales, committing petty crimes to support themselves.

A few weeks later Melbourne detectives charged Flannery, Kath (who had recently been convicted of the New Year's Eve assault), Williams and Clarkson with Wilson's murder. All but Flannery obtained bail. Despite the threats to her life and the violent record of those she was to give evidence against, Boundy was not placed in protective custody. On Boxing Day 1980 she disappeared. She had been abducted and murdered. Soon afterwards, Flannery was granted bail. The case was now fatally undermined and all four accused of Wilson's murder were acquitted.

Years later Ian Victor McLean, a cousin of Kath, told police that shortly after Wilson was killed he got a call from Flannery asking him to come over and clean his car. He said the car had been full of dirt and a 'white powder stuff like lime'. Some months later, McLean said, Flannery told him that to prevent the police finding Wilson's body, he had dug it up, put it in the boot of his car, and taken it to another location. McLean's former lover told police that Flannery had seemed to be ill just after Wilson's disappearance, but she'd been told he was suffering from the after-affects of moving the decomposing corpse.

By now Melbourne had become a dangerous place for Flannery. He had fallen out with Brian Kane and was offside with the remnants of both main gangs in the waterfront war.

And his legal problems were far from over. In October 1981 Detective Duff extradited him to Sydney over the still unsolved 1979 murder of Raymond Locksley. Despite his criminal record, his repeated escapes, and his breaches of parole and bail conditions, Flannery was soon free on bail. And through the corrupt Duff, he was reintroduced to the man who would become his guide to Sydney's underworld: Detective Roger Rogerson.

Rogerson was hand-in-glove with several Sydney criminals, including Neddy Smith. When rumours spread that Flannery was going to kill Smith, it was Rogerson who brokered peace between them. In his book *Neddy*, Smith says the whole thing was a misunderstanding—two violent men mouthing off at each other. In years to come Flannery would become a close associate of Smith—an enforcer who could be relied on in a crisis. Flannery introduced his old Pentridge mate Alan Williams to Smith when Williams's Melbourne heroin sources dried up, and Smith became Williams's supplier.

Rogerson arranged for Flannery to meet Lennie McPherson and his Lebanese protégé Louis Bayeh, taking him to lunch with them at a city restaurant. Bayeh later told the Wood Royal Commission that Flannery spent most of the time talking to 'the Big Man'. McPherson asked his colleague George Freeman to arrange a job for Flannery and pay him a retainer. For a short time Flannery worked as a bouncer at an illegal casino operated by Bruce Hardin, a longtime friend and ally of Freeman and McPherson. Flannery soon moved up the food chain to become Freeman's minder, enforcer and debt collector, and to provide security for gambling dens that paid Freeman and McPherson for protection. At the same time, he started doing odd jobs for Neddy Smith and others.

CHRIS FLANNERY

Flannery liked to put about a different story of how he broke into the Sydney crime scene. In his version he came to Sydney determined to drive McPherson mad. He boasted to Alan Williams how he used to ring McPherson and then 'bump into him on purpose, different places, spit on him, call him a dog, then goaded him and I do believe that McPherson rang Freeman and said, Get hold of that Flannery and take him under your wing. Will you calm him down; give him a quid to keep him happy.' The story that Williams told to police after he rolled was nonsense, but it demonstrated how eager Flannery had been to show he could go toe to toe with the hard men of Sydney.

It wasn't long before Flannery found himself in trouble with Barry Raymond McCann, the well-connected Sydney criminal who had been one of Murray Riley's associates in the 1960s and who owned an inner-city hotel, the Lansdowne. He had been involved in the distribution of heroin for Robert Trimbole and the Mr Asia syndicate and now had his own operation. Flannery and Kath were drinking at the Lansdowne with some of Flannery's new underworld friends when they got into a fierce argument. McCann's wife, Janice, told them to quieten down as they were annoying other patrons. Flannery lashed out and hit her, bruising her jaw. A hotel resident produced a shotgun and threatened Flannery, who immediately left with his wife.

McCann was in the Philippines at the time, but Flannery was well aware of his reputation. 'He was sending apologies and flowers, which were not accepted,' McCann later told police. 'After a while I agreed to meet him . . . He apologised again and said he didn't mean it. I told him to keep away from the pub and my wife. That was the first time I met him.' While McCann claimed that he and Flannery had resolved their differences, their lingering animosity would become one of the triggers for a gangland war.

In June 1982 Flannery was committed for trial for the Locksley murder. Two months later, Snapper Cornwell's associates Terrence Basham and Susan Smith were murdered on their horse stud near Murwillumbah, New South Wales (see Chapter 4). George Tsingolis, a violent drug dealer with close links to organised crime in both Sydney and Melbourne, told police that Flannery had admitted killing the couple. Alan Williams also claimed Flannery had admitted both murders to him.

At the Locksley murder trial, the jury failed to reach a verdict. It would be two years before Flannery faced a retrial.

Back in Melbourne, the Painters and Dockers feud raged on. In November 1982 Les Kane's brother Brian was shot at the Quarry Hotel, Brunswick. Later that month Leslie 'Johnny' Cole, a painter and docker with a history of violence, was assassinated in Sydney. Cole was a close ally of the Kanes and a friend of Lewis Moran, the father of Melbourne crime figure Mark Anthony Moran, who twenty years later would be one of the casualties of that city's next gangland war. The chief suspect for the murder of Johnny Cole was Michael Sayers, one of Flannery's old friends from Pentridge. Like many of Melbourne's worst criminals, Sayers had moved to Sydney, where he became involved in gambling, SP bookmaking and drug dealing.

In May 1983 Flannery pleaded guilty to the five-year-old charge of assault at the New Year's Eve party. Detective Bill Duff gave evidence on his behalf. Sentenced to a year's jail, Flannery immediately lodged an appeal and was granted bail. According to Duff's police diary, he and Flannery went straight to the Armed Robbery Squad offices, picked up Roger Rogerson and went for a celebratory lunch.

A few weeks later Flannery met Melbourne criminal Peter James Cross. The pair joined forces in a range of activities including the importation of cocaine from Bolivia. According to Alan Williams, Flannery was using cocaine himself. Tsingolis told police that before Flannery went to kill anyone he would sit down, 'put headphones on and turn the stereo up with loud classical music. While listening to the music he would snort cocaine.'

Cocaine dealing would never be more than a lucrative sideline to Flannery's main business as a hitman, which continued to keep him busy between court appearances. While he waited for the outcome of his appeal, Alan Williams got involved in a heroin deal with (unbeknown to him) an undercover detective, Constable Michael Drury. Drury had arranged to meet Williams and make the buy in North Melbourne. But Williams had been able to obtain only three-quarters of the half-kilogram of heroin he had promised to deliver. As the police swooped, he escaped. It took four months before he was arrested in Melbourne. In December 1982 the charge against him was dismissed. His troubles were over, or so he thought. Another four months later Williams found out that he was going to be tried after all over the drug bust. Michael Drury would be a principal witness. Williams was desperate. What would it cost to beat the charge? Could Drury be bribed?

Williams turned to his friend Flannery. Flannery had helped him out by putting him in touch with Neddy Smith, who was now supplying him with a kilogram of heroin a week for the Melbourne market. It is entirely possible that the heroin Drury was to buy from Williams had been supplied by Smith. But the favour Williams needed this time was a lot bigger.

According to Williams, Flannery approached Rogerson to bribe Drury, but Drury said no. Williams flew to Sydney in February 1984 to meet Rogerson in person. He made another visit in May, telling Flannery to keep the pressure on Rogerson to talk Drury round. When it became clear that Drury could not be bribed, the discussion turned to murder. Over dinner with Flannery and Rogerson, Williams agreed to pay $100,000 for the hit.

On 6 June Flannery shot Drury through the window of his home as Drury stood in the kitchen; his children were in another room. Flannery's old Melbourne partner in crime Laurie Prendergast sat in a getaway car around the corner listening to a scanner tuned to the police radio frequency. McPherson later told trusted colleagues that in the weeks before the shooting, Flannery had asked him for a gun. McPherson referred him to an unnamed supplier who sold him two handguns, one for Prendergast. The day after Drury was shot, Flannery returned one gun, telling McPherson, 'I shot a bloke last night. He's alive, but I think he will die.' Drury survived. Two years later, McPherson told the story to a police officer.

Rogerson claimed that he and Flannery had been drinking at a club some distance away at the time Drury was shot. Kath Flannery claimed she had phoned her husband at the club to ask if he would be home for tea. Rogerson and Flannery had in fact been at the club that night, but was it at the time of the shooting or half to three-quarters of an hour *after* it? The precise time could not be verified. Williams told police that after he and Flannery left their dinner meeting with Rogerson, he asked Flannery, 'Do you trust Rogerson that much?' to which Flannery replied, 'Yeah, I do, but just on the off chance something happens, it won't be done unless he's with me.' The Arncliffe alibi was consistent with Flannery's plan.

Two weeks later, Flannery's long-delayed second trial for the murder of Locksley began. He was in luck. Two important witnesses, the government medical officer and a senior detective, had died—both from natural causes. After two days Flannery was acquitted. A fortnight later he and Kath flew to England and Ireland for a month's holiday.

Free of all criminal charges for the first time in years, Flannery set his sights on taking over organised crime in Sydney. By December the city's gangland had erupted into open war (see Chapter 6). Four months later Flannery was fined $1500 for the New Year's Eve assault. He would have been better off with his original twelve-month jail sentence: within weeks he was to become one of the casualties of the gang war.

Chapter 6

The 1980s Sydney Gang War

'We only kill each other . . .'

The Sydney gang war of the mid 1980s was in reality a series of wars within a war. It was a time of unrivalled prosperity for Sydney's crime elite. The profits from drug importations and trafficking swamped them with cash, which flowed over into gambling. Huge bets were made. Fortunes were won and lost. But greed and jealousy brought conflict, upheaval, and new opportunities for those able to take advantage of them.

The war began with unpaid debts, which led to murder, paybacks and more murders. It finally ended in 1987 with the assassination of Barry McCann.

*

The unpaid debts belonged to Michael Sayers, who befriended Chris Flannery in Melbourne while doing time for armed robbery. Moving to Sydney, Sayers became involved first in SP bookmaking with his father, Robert, then race fixing and heroin dealing. Inevitably, he once again found himself rubbing shoulders with Flannery.

Sayers was also a heavy gambler, whose huge debts put him on the wrong side of George Freeman and his associates—a dangerous place to be. Sayers's efforts to avoid paying up only made matters worse. In May 1984 he agreed to settle an overdue debt of $120,000 with Albert Tabone, an SP bookmaker. As Sayers approached Tabone with a briefcase, he was grabbed by two men in suits, pushed into a car and driven off. Half an hour later he returned to the meeting place, where Tabone was still waiting. He showed him the empty briefcase and said the two men who had grabbed him were Federal Police officers. (One was actually Chris Flannery.) They had found a kilo of heroin in his briefcase and, in return for not charging him, had stolen it and the $120,000 in cash that was meant for Tabone. Sayers pleaded for more time to repay the debt, and Tabone reluctantly gave it to him.

Freeman was neither as gullible nor as forgiving as Tabone. When Sayers held out on him, he asked his trusted debt collector Flannery to kill him. Business, for Flannery, was always business. He agreed to murder his mate, and discussed the hit with his wife and, according to her, with 'Pommy Tony' Eustace who was well credentialled in Sydney's underworld with the usual SP bookie, drug dealing resume. Eustace was a former boxer who revelled in the reputation of being a tough guy. He advised against the hit, saying Sayers was a 'good bloke' and that police had told him that Sayers was about to be arrested for drug offences. A few days later he was charged with, among other things, having unlicensed pistols and supplying heroin, cocaine and cannabis. Four months in jail waiting for bail saved him, for the moment, from death.

But Sayers had an even bigger problem with his heroin supplier, Danny Chubb, to whom he owed around $400,000. There too, however, fate was about to intervene in Sayers's favour.

Chubb was a career criminal yet never spent a day in jail. He was one of the first 'Balmain Boys' to move from large-scale thefts from the docklands to drug dealing. By the late 1970s Chubb was importing container loads of 'Lebanese gold' hash through associates of Fayez 'Frank' Hakim, the so-called Lebanese godfather and the Lebanese connection for Freeman and Lennie McPherson. Using his waterfront contacts, Chubb would have his containers smuggled off the wharves.

Chubb rapidly expanded his interests to heroin. Using as many as half a dozen couriers at a time, he would bring it into the country in shipments of up to 50 kilograms. Soon his drug networks stretched throughout Australia and Southeast Asia. In addition to Sayers, his distributors included Neddy Smith and a Who's Who of Sydney and Melbourne organised crime.

Chubb would have his cannabis containers placed in such a way that they could be watched from a distance. In March 1982 Customs seized a container with over 2 tonnes of hashish mixed in among Middle Eastern foodstuffs. It was Australia's largest detected hash shipment, but no one was ever charged. Chubb had been sitting on the balcony of a Balmain house watching Customs and the Federal Police agents watching the container. He had written off the entire shipment rather than risk getting caught.

Less than a year later Chubb was preparing for an even bigger importation: more than 7 tonnes through Darwin. It was to be his biggest mistake.

The ship and crew that would bring in the hash were provided by Chubb's Greek contacts. To liaise with them he chose Nicholas 'Nick' Paltos, a Greek-Australian who was doctor to some the most notorious criminals in Sydney. A heavy gambler, Paltos was also deep in debt. He jumped at Chubb's offer and brought Graham 'Croc' Palmer, a former illegal casino operator, and Ross Karp, a solicitor, into the syndicate as well.

Two months later Paltos travelled to Greece to negotiate the hire of a freighter and stayed in contact with the Greek-based coordinator of the shipment after his return. North of Australia, the freighter ran out of fuel. A fishing trawler was dispatched to meet it, and after transferring the cargo, the Greek crew scuttled the freighter. In late February 1984 the shipment was landed north of Darwin, loaded onto semi-trailers and driven to Sydney, where it was stored at a number of locations. The crew of the sunken freighter were smuggled to Bali before flying to Greece.

It looked like a successful operation, but it had cost a lot more than Chubb planned. The hash was of poor quality, and Chubb had difficulty selling it. Many of his buyers felt cheated.

But if Chubb's cannabis business was in trouble, his heroin dealings were thriving. He was now importing about 100 kilograms a year with the help of Singapore-based Ho Chin Hoon, also known as Vincent Ho, who worked for

Chinese triads and sourced the heroin from Malaysia. The couriers were from Singapore, and false passports came from Indonesia. Operations were compartmentalised to minimise the risk of detection and limit the damage to the syndicate in the event of an arrest. Couriers were taken to a hotel in Singapore, where about 2 kilograms would be strapped to each man's body. As many as four couriers would travel on a single flight. A supervisor, not carrying heroin, would know all the couriers, but the couriers would not know each other or the supervisor. If one or two couriers were caught, the operation would still go ahead. After passing through Customs, the couriers would be approached by the supervisor and directed to a hotel in Sydney where the heroin would be taken from them. The supervisor would ring Hoon in a Singapore café and confirm the success of the operation, whereupon he would fly to Sydney, pick up the heroin and contact Chubb or his partner, Bruce McCauley, known as 'the Godfather' to his Asian heroin suppliers and as 'the Smuggler' to his Sydney-based colleagues. Chubb would make the collection and have the heroin tested. Once he was satisfied, McCauley would hand over the money.

Chubb owned several homes and blocks of land and at least a dozen prize greyhounds. He was a partner in a seafood business and was regarded as a mammoth punter—most bookmakers had placed limits on his betting. McCauley had been changing more than $100,000 a week in $5, $10 and $20 notes for $50 and $100 notes for Chubb, and was himself a multi-millionaire.

During 1984 more than $7 million cash had been changed into large denominations, and most of it had been smuggled to the Philippines. In all, over four years, $15 million of Chubb's cash was sent to the Philippines.

Its whereabouts remain a mystery. It is rumoured that the money was taken by the Godfather and an eastern suburbs lawyer Chubb entrusted with the task of hiding it.

For all Chubb's success, greed and rivalry were starting to undermine his organisation. Neddy Smith, in particular, was unhappy with the way Chubb was running his heroin operation. Smith didn't like being, or being seen to be, one of 'Danny's boys'. He wanted to be the boss and talked with Murray Riley, crooked detectives Bill Duff and Roger Rogerson and others about setting up his own heroin importation operation through Papua New Guinea.

Chris Flannery also wanted to be the boss. That meant getting rid not only of Chubb but of his own employer, Freeman. That was not going to be easy. Flannery would have to bide his time. Meanwhile Flannery was still preparing for the hit on Sayers.

He was also a target himself. Barry McCann still held a grudge over the assault of his wife by the Flannerys at the Lansdowne Hotel. He also believed Flannery and Sayers had been involved in the theft of $300,000 worth of drugs from the boot of his car near the Lansdowne Hotel. Flannery was becoming a nuisance. McCann enlisted the help of his ally Tom Domican, a standover man. But after weeks of failed efforts to set Flannery up, the hit was finally called off: Flannery was safe—for the time being.

Chubb, however, was a marked man. As well as resenting his power, Neddy Smith owed Chubb money. Lennie McPherson was to tell police it was 'a huge amount'. For four years Smith had been one of Chubb's biggest distributors, moving about three kilograms of heroin every ten days in Sydney and Melbourne with his partner in crime, Graham 'Abo' Henry. In his book, *Abo: A Treacherous Life*, Henry claims he and Smith knew Chubb was to be murdered.

On 8 November 1984 a heroin shipment worth $2 million dollars was waiting for Chubb just around the corner from his mother's place in Millers Point, at the southern end of the Harbour Bridge. Chew Suang Heng, a courier who had made eight trips to Australia, would later tell police: 'We check into the Cliveden Hotel and Vincent [Ho] came about three days later . . . we then book into Bridge Street apartment [near Millers Point]. We stay there together and the drug was there in the suitcase. Vincent then tried to contact Godfather [McCauley] but was unsuccessful for the first few days.'

That morning, Chubb received a phone call at his mother's house and went to the nearby Captain Cook Hotel. He met Neddy Smith and Abo Henry and confirmed the shipment's arrival by phone. He left the hotel, bought a packet of fish and chips, and went back to his mother's. As he got out of his car he was hit by a shotgun blast in the throat and four bullets in the chest. His unopened fish and chips fell to the pavement. The Godfather was in the house at the time. Hearing the shots, he fled.

McCauley resurfaced a few days later. According to courier Chew, 'On twelfth we contact Godfather and arrange to meet at Menzies Hotel Coffee House on thirteenth. The Godfather arrive and told Vincent [Ho] there is trouble in Sydney and to leave Australia immediately and he would not collect his consignment. Vincent took the suitcase to Sydney

Apartments York Street and left it there in the name of Chow Indonesia. We flew to Singapore.'

Nine months later, investigating police arrested Ho in Sydney in possession of more than 4 kilograms of heroin. A further 3.5 kilograms was in a suitcase recovered from the Chateau Townhouse in Melbourne. Three others, Chun Choi Chan, Man Yuan Chuk and John Tran, were also arrested. Chan and Chuk were both Hong Kong residents who had arrived in Australia only a few days earlier. Chuk had visited Australia seven times in the previous year; Chan was on his second visit in four weeks. Tran had lived in Sydney for about fourteen years.

McCauley's fingerprints were on items in the heroin suitcase, but it was to be another seven years before he was charged. In February 1992 he was arrested in Drummoyne, in Sydney's inner west, in possession of about 15 kilograms of heroin, and later sentenced to seventeen years' jail. Eight million dollars, covering the years he was in the drug business with Chubb, were seized by the tax office.

Immediately after Chubb's murder, there was an uneasy calm in the underworld. But it was the lull before the storm. The two main criminal alliances were hardening their positions. On one side, aligned to McPherson through Freeman, were Flannery, Neddy Smith, Abo Henry, Tony Eustace, Sayers, and Louis Bayeh and his gang.

The other side was led by Tom Domican, whose main interest was protection rackets, and Barry McCann, who not only wanted Flannery dead but increasingly saw Chubb's heroin operation as an impediment to his own ambition of a network to rival the Mr Asia syndicate. McCann's network included Kevin Theobold, Joseph Meissner, Roy Thurgar, Victor Camilleri and George Savvas.

The Domican team made the first move by expanding its interest in illegal gambling clubs and amusement machines. Domican had formed a business relationship with a corrupt policeman, Bill El Azzi, who was close—perhaps related—to Frank Hakim. Domican and El Azzi asked Hakim if they could put some of their amusement machines in an ethnic club at Enmore. Hakim managed the protection of ethnic-based illegal gambling clubs and amusement machines on behalf of McPherson and Freeman. He knew they had a stake in the Enmore club. Nevertheless, he gave the nod to Domican and El Azzi.

It appears that Hakim 'forgot' about McPherson's existing arrangement with the club and also 'forgot' to tell him Domican and El Azzi were putting machines in there. When McPherson found out, he was not impressed. He contacted Louis Bayeh and together they rounded up about twenty musclemen, who went to the club and threw Domican's machines into the street. McPherson and Domican threatened, over the phone, to blow each other's 'fucking head off'. Later that night McPherson met Domican's partner McCann, at Kings Cross to determine whether the conflict could be resolved peacefully. It couldn't. The gang war was about to explode.

Flannery initially closed ranks with the McPherson side. Warning shots were fired at Domican's home. Domican suspected Flannery and used police contacts to find him. Flannery and Kath were outside their house in Arncliffe when a green Jaguar pulled up and unleashed more than thirty shots from an automatic weapon. Flannery was hit in an ear and hand, but declined to help police with their investigations.

At first Flannery thought the attack was a spillover from the Melbourne gang wars and assumed that Raymond 'Muscles' Kane, whose brothers, Brian and Les, had both been murdered in the conflict, was responsible. The ongoing feud between Flannery and the Kane brothers had been a major reason for the Flannerys moving to Sydney. But when he learned Domican was behind the shooting, he set his mind on revenge.

To Flannery, the gang war was starting to look like the opportunity he had been waiting for. It was his chance—if he played it right—to establish himself as a boss of bosses. According to several of his colleagues, both Flannery and his wife wanted him to be the next George Freeman. Flannery's 'Rent-a-Kill' reputation had grown considerably during the previous six months. He was widely known to have been responsible for the attempted murder of Detective Michael Drury, yet he not only seemed to have got away with the shooting but had been given an alibi by a serving detective. The way Flannery saw it, one gang was going to lose this war and the other would be seriously weakened. He had a big say in who was going to die. It was time to lay the foundation for his own empire.

Flannery and Neddy Smith paid Sayers a call and told him Flannery was setting up a protection racket backed by Smith. Sayers told them to 'get fucked'; he wasn't paying. He had a will drawn up and started placing pillows in his bed under the blankets as a decoy for would-be killers. Sayers rightly believed that he was likely to be murdered. But it would not be Flannery who murdered him.

Sayers was not a popular man. Chubb and George Freeman weren't the only others who had wanted him dead. Sayers was widely believed to have been responsible for the 1982 murder of painter and docker Johnny Cole, who was allied to McPherson and Freeman. He also had huge gambling debts, and now Chubb's death had cut him off from the heroin that had previously been his source of cash.

Despite his debts, Sayers wasn't exactly broke. He owned five properties in Sydney, as well as racehorses and luxury cars, and had several hundred thousand dollars in various banks. None of it would save him.

One night in February 1985 Sayers and his partner arrived at their home in the beachside suburb of Bronte. Sayers was in the driveway when two masked men in dark clothing shot him several times. Bleeding copiously, he tried to flee down the street. He got fifty metres before he collapsed. One of the shooters walked up to him, pointed a gun at his head and fired.

Just three years after Sayers was murdered, his father Robert, a former SP bookie, was shot in the back at point blank range as he walked along a suburban street. He had been due to give evidence at the inquest into his son's murder. Sayers Snr spent two days in hospital under police guard before signing himself out and leaving New South Wales in fear of his life.

Even though Freeman had wanted Michael Sayers dead, he and McPherson now saw themselves as having lost an ally. In the days after the shooting, Neddy Smith visited his friend Detective Rogerson at home and told him that Domican and McCann had 'delusions of grandeur. They believe that the time is ripe for them to take over everything from McPherson and Freeman. Their idea is to get rid of Flannery, whom they fear, and then it will not take much effort to eliminate Freeman and then McPherson last.'

For the next fortnight McPherson, in fear of his life, stopped going out at night. He kept a loaded shotgun and rifle in his lounge room and started recording the registration numbers of cars parked near his Gladesville home. During the night of 28 February an orange Ford Falcon was seen making several slow runs past McPherson's house. The two men inside seemed to be trying to peer through the windows.

A few weeks earlier, the same vehicle had been spotted outside the Flannerys' home. Kath identified Domican as the driver. The vehicle was registered in a false name but its owners were Victor Camilleri and Kevin Theobold, two members of the Domican gang who trained every day in Domican's home gym. Camilleri was a known thug and thief, while Theobold was a small-time crook. Domican's ally Barry McCann had employed Thurgar at his Wollongong casino and Camilleri at one of his Sydney casinos during the 1970s.

Three days after it was seen crawling past McPherson's home, the orange Falcon cruised through Kingsgrove with Theobold driving and Camilleri in the passenger seat. Looking over his shoulder, Camilleri noticed a Valiant containing three men draw alongside. One of the men was Flannery. He and the other passenger fired a hail of bullets into the Falcon. Camilleri was wounded in the neck, shoulder and stomach. He and Theobold abandoned the car and ran into a house, where they called the police.

The Valiant was found a few hours later, abandoned not far from the Flannery home. The rear window had been shot out and several bullet holes were found. Clearly, Camilleri and Theobold had fired back. The Valiant had been bought a few days earlier by two men in their twenties for cash, in the name of Thomas Domican. One of the buyers is believed to have been Flannery. The use of Domican's name and an address where he had previously lived was a clear sign that he was the intended target of the shooting. The shooting of Camilleri had been a mistake.

The attempts on Domican's life continued. In early April, Domican showed up at Kingsgrove police station to be interviewed by detectives. They were interested in several matters, including his knowledge of the gang war, but he didn't trust them and believed they were actively helping the other side. At almost 9 p.m. he left the station and was looking for a taxi when two helmeted men on a motorcycle chased and shot at him. Domican hid behind a wall and the shooters sped off.

Domican believed the police had set him up. Who else would have known that he'd be at the station? The NCA later claimed that Domican had identified the pillion passenger and shooter as Chris Flannery. Kath confirmed this, saying Chris had told her that he and Domican had been involved in a shootout one night near the Kingsgrove police station, but no one was hurt. Years later Louis Bayeh was to tell a similar story to the Wood Royal Commission, saying that Domican had named Flannery as the shooter and that Flannery had admitted it. The driver of the motorcycle was rumoured to have been Flannery's Melbourne mate Laurie Prendergast, his back-up in the attempted murder of Detective Drury ten months earlier. As one local underworld figure said of the rumour, 'One thing's for sure, no Sydney crim would have been mad enough to get involved.'

At about 7 p.m. on 23 April 'Pommy Tony' Eustace was shot six times from behind with a .45 pistol as he waited beside his Mercedes not far from Sydney airport and the Flannery home. At the time he was on bail on charges of conspiring to import cannabis valued at more than $8 million. He had been waiting to meet Flannery and was carrying an envelope stuffed with cash. The money disappeared after the shooting. Witnesses saw the gunman run to a nearby car and flee the scene.

Eustace was still alive when help arrived. Asked if he knew who had shot him, Eustace said that he didn't. He didn't even know how many shooters were involved but he thought he had been shot four or five times. Later, in hospital, detectives asked Eustace about the shooting. His only response was 'Fuck off.' He died an hour later, a tough guy to the end.

A few days later the vehicle used by the shooter—another Valiant—was found abandoned in the airport car park. It had been bought ten days earlier from a car yard by a man using a false name.

Seven hours before the shooting, Eustace and Flannery had had a long meeting at Surry Hills. Eustace drove his Mercedes to the meeting, while Flannery drove the Valiant. That afternoon Flannery had gone to the airport and hired a car before setting off in the Valiant again in search of Eustace. After shooting him and dumping the Valiant, Flannery and his accomplice made their getaway in the hire car.

Why would Flannery kill a friend and confidant? Eustace was a threat to Flannery's imperial ambitions. Moreover, Flannery knew that he had let slip to a detective friend Flannery's boast about shooting Detective Drury. Paranoid from cocaine, the increasingly erratic Flannery decided

Eustace had to go. Two days after the murder Flannery and Kath went to Noosa Heads for a holiday. While he relaxed, his own fate was being sealed in Sydney.

At first McPherson was determined to eliminate Domican and his gang. But the Freeman–McPherson alliance had now been on the losing end of several shootouts. Flannery, who had once been considered an asset, was a liability. His uncontrollable behaviour was a threat to the survival of both gangs.

During March and April 1985 a series of meetings was held between McPherson, Domican, McCann, Smith, Bayeh and others, including Rogerson and Duff, at Bayeh's home and in coffee shops and other places around Sydney. They ranged over many topics of common interest, including a truce.

Around this time McPherson received an anonymous letter, which he identified as having been written by a serving police officer. It claimed that Constable Bill El Azzi was threatening to have McPherson 'loaded up' with drugs and arrested. McPherson knew El Azzi—he was a close associate of Frank Hakim and had been Domican's partner in the pokies incident. Running into El Azzi at Domican's house one day, McPherson shouted, 'If you try and load me with drugs, I'll blow your fucking head off.' El Azzi shouted back, 'If you do anything to hurt Tom, I'll fix you. I would do anything for Tom, even die for him.'

The threats over, McPherson and Domican got down to the serious business of trying to resolve the gang war. The Domican and McCann gang held the upper hand, and the price they demanded for a truce was Flannery. McPherson argued for an alternative solution, saying, 'You just can't go shooting people left, right and centre.' But Domican and McCann would not be dissuaded. McCann told McPherson, 'He's got to be killed one way or another. Either you and George get him or I'll get him.' In the end, McPherson gave in: 'Me and George will take care of it, leave it up to us.'

As Roger Rogerson later told Channel 9's *Sunday* program in 2004, 'Flannery was a complete pest. The guys up here in Sydney tried to settle him down. They tried to look after him as best they could, but he was, I believe, out of control. Maybe it was the Melbourne instinct coming out of him. He didn't want to do as he was told, he was out of control, and having overstepped that line, well, I suppose they said he had to go.'

Flannery's long-time mate, Alan Williams, saw the murder of his mate as inevitable: 'You're not gonna start up a new regime with Chris Flannery heading the helm. It would have been nightmare on Elm Street.'

Two days after returning from his holiday at Noosa Heads, Flannery went to Freeman's home for a meeting with Freeman and McPherson. According to Louis Bayeh, McPherson told him that Flannery asked for a machine gun, saying the rifle McPherson had given him to murder Domican wasn't suitable. Freeman agreed to supply the gun. On 9 May Flannery left his unit in the city for Freeman's home, where he was to collect the machine gun. He was never seen alive again.

The opposing gangs now declared the war over, but Kath Flannery was not so easily pacified. Her husband was missing and someone was to blame. Kath believed, correctly, that it was Freeman.

Two months after Flannery's disappearance, Freeman drove to Nick Paltos's surgery. While getting his youngest child out of the rear car seat he realised he was being watched by two men wearing caps and gloves who were sitting in a Holden sedan parked nearby. He jumped into his car and fled. The Holden followed. Freeman managed to lose his pursuers and reported the incident—and the registration number of the car—to police. Later the same day Freeman and his family flew out of Australia on an overseas holiday. Years later some people involved admitted that the incident had been an intended hit on Freeman.

Three weeks after the attempted assassination, Kath called the police after noticing something unusual under her car, which was parked in the driveway of her home. It was a bomb. According to army bomb experts, it had been built by a person 'with expertise in the area of electronics' and was capable of being detonated by remote control from a distance of 300 metres. Kath's 'war' with Freeman would continue for years.

Years later, Kath Flannery's mother, Dorothy Jones, recalled her son-in-law telling her how George Freeman had warned him, 'the one that gets you will be the friend you think you've got but haven't'. That friend was Freeman, a man who always put business first.

In what many police and criminals consider too much of a coincidence, Flannery's Melbourne mate, Laurie Prendergast, met the same fate as Flannery. On 23 August he disappeared from his Warrandyte home near Melbourne. In an inquest in 1990, the Victoria State Coroner, Maurice Gurvich, said of Prendergast's disappearance: 'In many ways the story that unfolded here resembled the plot of a gangster movie ... there was evidence of deception, alias[es], disguises, fraud, strange property and financial transactions, large sums of money in a paper bag, a missing gun and other evidence . . . And there were allegations of cover-up and conspiracy. All this together with the intervention of a clairvoyant make the ingredients of a good B-grade screenplay.'

The Coroner stated that there were a number of explanations for Prendergast's disappearance and made an open finding. Neither Flannery's body nor Prendergast's has ever been found. Prendergast had enemies in Sydney and Melbourne, but none of the parties in the Sydney gangland murders could guarantee peace while Prendergast was still alive. It was not enough to get rid of one crazed killer, Flannery, and have his sidekick still on the loose.

While Sydney's gang war officially ended with the murder of Chris Flannery, Barry McCann's smack network seethed with internecine rivalry. The network had grown considerably since the demise of McCann's associate Bob Trimbole and the collapse of the Mr Asia syndicate. In the three years from 1982, it imported about 60 kilograms of heroin.

In 1984 McCann took on a new partner, George Savvas, a fellow ally of Tom Domican. Savvas and Domican were aspiring politicians: they appeared as No. 1 and 2 on the same independent ticket in the 1984 Marrickville Council elections. Domican had previously been accused of vote-rigging in the Enmore Branch of the Labor Party. Unfazed, Savvas said of his long-time partner: 'I've found Tom to be a hard working, scrupulously honest man who knows a hell of a lot about local government. I am proud to be on the same ticket as him.'

In 1980 the left-wing Labor MP Peter Baldwin had been badly bashed. He said his attackers were Joe Meissner—who had served jail time for the theft of submachine guns and was secretary of the ALP's Enmore branch—and Domican, who Baldwin said had threatened him a month before.

Within a month of the assault, Domican, Meissner and others were charged with conspiracy and forging the books of the Enmore branch with intent to defraud. Dismissing the case two years later, magistrate Bruce Brown noted: 'It seems that some force or forces were working improperly to undermine the strength of the prosecution.' Domican later told a British TV reporter that he had visited witnesses and they had had 'a lapse of memory'. Officials high up in the Labor Party were involved, he claimed.

Savvas was elected to Marrickville council; Domican was not. Savvas openly described himself as 'the king of Marrickville' and suggested he had protection because of his connections with police. When he hooked up with McCann's operation, the effect was immediate. Through a corrupt airline employee, Savvas had access to the international luggage-handling and Customs bond areas. That meant McCann no longer had to rely on couriers to bring in heroin. Now, up to 20 kilograms at a time would be packed into a briefcase in Singapore and placed on an Olympic or British Airlines flight to Sydney as unaccompanied luggage. The Singapore connection, Ong Jong Tai, also known as 'Chinese David' and described at one stage in an NCA report to be one of the world's biggest heroin suppliers, would then contact McCann with the message, 'That horse is racing today.' He would give McCann the flight number and its arrival time. Savvas would alert his airport connections, who would replace the heroin-filled briefcase with an identical bag, bypassing Customs in the process.

In eighteen months more than 100 kilograms were imported in at least five consignments. The drug was distributed around Kings Cross, where prostitutes were good customers, and—through a thirty-year-old Vietnamese named 'Johnsonny' Bi Dinh—to Cabramatta, in Sydney's west.

Johnsonny ran a pool hall and coffee shop in Marrickville, which he leased from Savvas, and a similar club in Cabramatta. The two men were in business with Leslie 'Les' Jones, who the 1974 Moffitt Royal Commission said had 'been to the [United] States with the mafia'. Jones, along with McPherson, Freeman, Murray Riley and McCann, had been vying for control of video poker machines and skimming money from clubs.

One night in January 1983 two masked intruders, posing as policemen and armed with sawn-off shotguns, approached Jones's home in outer-western Sydney. Spotting them from a window, Jones grabbed an M1 carbine and waited. As they burst through the front door, a dozen shots were exchanged before the gunmen fled. Jones packed up his family and moved to Surfers Paradise.

Cornelius 'Con the Cobra' O'Connor, a standover man with a long record for violence and theft, was charged over the murder attempt, but before he could face trial he was murdered himself—shot through the head and neck. His body was then locked in the boot of a car, driven to a dirt track on the edge of the city and set ablaze. No one was ever charged with the murder.

In the late 1980s the Queensland Criminal Justice Commission identified Jones as one of the Mr Bigs of Australia's illegal gaming industry. It found that he had been a partner in various business deals with Savvas and named Johnsonny as having been Jones's top standover man and 'principal collector' of proceeds from gambling machines in the Cabramatta area.

Like the Mr Asia syndicate, the McCann–Savvas operation was beset by greed, drug and cash rip-offs, intimidation, violence and murder. At the time he joined the McCann gang, Savvas was under remand on fraud charges. A business partner, Dr Peter Papapetros, said Savvas had cheated him out of $160,000. Papapetros soon got a visit at home from two armed and hooded men. McPherson, Domican and others also threatened him, and there were menacing 'offers' to buy his hotel. In November 1985 a Marrickville alderman, Jack Passaris, suggested on TV that Savvas should resign from the local council. His comments were also printed in a local newspaper. Passaris soon received an anonymous phone call warning him: 'We know how to deal with people like you who have a big mouth.' Within hours his car yard was firebombed.

About six weeks later a witness in the Savvas fraud case, Joseph Magros, was found dead, shot three times in the back of the head. He had phoned a friend on the evening of the murder and said he was going out to meet Johnsonny. Magros had already been visited by McPherson and two of his henchmen and warned against giving evidence in the case. A month later, Papapetros's medical practice was firebombed.

Papapetros said Joe Meissner had been one of the men pressing him to sell his hotel and drop the charges against Savvas. Meissner would later tell a court that in August 1985 Domican had invited him to lunch with Papapetros, McPherson and Magros. Papapetros had claimed Savvas owed him $160,000 and said he was 'prepared to pay me [Meissner] $60,000 to take care of George Savvas'. The money was to be divided between Meissner, Domican and McPherson. Meissner had a tape which he said was of a conversation he'd had with Papapetros. On it, a man Meissner claimed was the doctor said, 'Just put the sword into the c—, mate.' Savvas was found not guilty. Papapetros left the country.

Conscious of his declining status in Sydney's underworld, Neddy Smith became increasingly envious of those on the rise: McCann's operation was one that was rising faster than the others. Always a big drinker, Smith was now drinking more heavily than ever before. In March 1986 he was involved in a fight with some of McCann's gang at the Lansdowne Hotel and assaulted McCann's son. A fortnight later McCann tried to murder Smith as he left the Quarryman's Hotel in Pyrmont. Fortunately for Smith the shooter missed, though Smith's drinking mate caught pellets from three or four shotgun blasts. He survived, but it was enough to make Smith back off, at least for a few months.

On 21 April an attempt was made to kill Detective Jim Wooden of the Criminal Investigation Branch as he was leaving a greyhound meeting at Sydney's Harold Park. The shotgun blast missed him, hitting his car. No one was ever arrested over the shooting, but it is believed to have been connected with his investigations into the gang war. Wooden left the police and moved to the Philippines.

A year later Johnsonny was shot in the stomach as he walked along the street with his wife one night. He refused to talk to the police, and no one was ever charged. The Queensland Criminal Justice Commission found that the shooting was the result of a street war between rival illegal gaming operators and noted that some of those involved 'are also suspected of involvement in narcotics'.

In August 1987, four months after Johnsonny was attacked, Barry Croft, a major heroin distributor for McCann, was driving in the inner-city suburb of Chippendale, not far from

McCann's Lansdowne Hotel, when a car pulled up alongside him. He was shot in the head and died instantly. In the end it was Neddy Smith who was charged with his murder.

About the time Croft was killed, a large heroin importation belonging to McCann 'disappeared'. McCann accused Savvas of stealing it and demanded $2.2 million compensation to enable him to pay his Chinese suppliers. Savvas denied having anything to do with the theft, but McCann told associates, 'That fucking Savvas has gone the knock on it. I am going to kill him... Savvas pays or Savvas gets killed.' Told of McCann's threat, Savvas responded, 'If Barry is coming to get me, don't think that I am just going to be standing there and cop it. I will get him first.'

Three days after Christmas, McCann's body was found in a park. He had been shot twenty-five times with two .22-calibre weapons. After he was dead eight shots had been fired into the crown of his head. The hit was not just business, it was personal.

A year later Savvas was charged with a number of offences relating to McCann's murder and the importation and trafficking of heroin. He was eventually sentenced to twenty-five years' jail on the drugs charges and fined $200,000. The court heard that Domican had been a central figure in McCann's original heroin importing scheme and that before Savvas's arrest the gang had brought in heroin with a street value of more than $160 million. Nancy Dufek, a former prostitute and Savvas's lover, denied claims that heroin worth $200,000 had been hidden in a kitchen tidy in her flat. She later fled to Chile, successfully fought extradition, and is believed still to be living the high life in South America. Although Savvas had admitted to police that he'd been involved in the McCann shooting—he claimed it was a knee-capping gone wrong despite the fact that not a single bullet had hit McCann in the legs—he was acquitted of the murder charges.

Imprisonment was little impediment for Savvas, who soon began plotting with fellow inmates to set up a heroin and cocaine importation operation which he would run from the jail. Roy Thurgar, an old mate, would arrange for the drugs to be imported with the help of a contact in Customs. Thurgar's murder in 1991 interrupted the planning only briefly. But the plot was being monitored by the federal and state police. Eighteen months later, Savvas, four other inmates, including two women, and a couple on the outside were charged with conspiring to import 40 kilograms of cocaine from South America. Savvas, the other male inmates and the pair outside jail were also charged with conspiring to import 20 kilograms of heroin from Thailand. Related operations in Brazil resulted in the seizure of 14 kilograms of heroin and 750 kilograms of hash. In 1994 Savvas got another twenty-five-year jail sentence.

Savvas was not the last person to be charged with the murder of McCann. A decade later, Neddy Smith couldn't help bragging to a cellmate about his role in a series of murders, including several committed during the gang war. The cellmate was an informant and he taped the confessions. Among the people Smith bragged on tape about killing was Barry McCann. Smith was charged with that murder, but the charge was eventually dropped after Smith was given his second natural-life sentence for another murder in 1983.

Smith's feud with McCann had lasted for years. Killing him had seemed like a way to get back on top of the heroin trade—as Savvas's new partner. Throughout 1986 and 1987, quite unknown to McCann, Smith had been distributing heroin for the Savvas–McCann operation. There were strong rumours that McCann's missing heroin importation was a rip-off Smith pulled with the support of Savvas. In any event, getting rid of McCann became a top priority. With his rival out of the way he and Savvas could take over the operation, and Neddy would be back where he felt he belonged. Savvas's arrest, however, scuttled the plan.

Smith lied and exaggerated as well as boasting, a tendency he frequently reminded courts about when defending himself against crimes he had been taped admitting to. In the case of Danny Chubb, Smith claimed that he had personally committed the murder. He hadn't. However, one of his close friends and a fellow member of the Chubb drug network, John Lawrence Stout, was investigated by the police. He had no alibi. At the time, Stout was under remand for a string of safe robberies in New South Wales and Victoria. Two months after Chubb's assassination police seized a large amount of hash and a stash of firearms from an apartment block in Cronulla. It was Smith and Stout's safe house. The hash was found to be identical with Chubb's Darwin importation a year and a half earlier. Ammunition found in the flat included Focchi shotgun cartridges, a brand that was very rare in New South Wales at the time but was used in the murder of Chubb. Despite this, police lacked enough evidence to charge Stout.

Also in 1985 a police bug picked up Dr Nick Paltos talking to solicitor Ross Karp about Chubb's murder. At the time they knew they were under investigation by the Australian Federal Police over Chubb's seven-tonne hash importation:

Paltos: Oh, it was my shot that Danny's dead, you know.
Karp: Yeah, that's right.
Paltos: Yeah, really Ross, he would have brought us all undone.
Karp: Oh, look at the way he used to talk on the phone.
Paltos: Yeah.
Karp: We'd visit him, they'd be looking at his joint, watching the cars coming and going. You'd come undone from things that aren't really, you know, anything vital.

Paltos was bragging, but unlike Neddy Smith, his boasts lacked even a germ of truth.

In 1986 Domican was charged with the shooting of Flannery in the driveway of his home. The following year he was charged with Flannery's murder. That charge was later dismissed, but Domican was sentenced to fourteen years for the attempted murder.

Domican spent six years in jail before the conviction was quashed on appeal. During that time he was charged with conspiring with Roy Thurgar to murder the Corrective Services chief, Ron Woodham. Both men were acquitted. In 1988 Domican and Thurgar, along with Victor Camilleri, Kevin Theobold and corrupt cop Bill El Azzi, were charged with conspiring to murder Michael Sayers. The charges against Thurgar and El Azzi were dismissed; Domican, Camilleri and Theobold were acquitted at trial.

Domican, McCann, Thurgar and Alan Stapley were charged with conspiring to murder Kath Flannery—the charge related to the gelignite bomb that had been found under her car—and with conspiring to murder Chris Flannery. The charges were dismissed. Domican was convicted of conspiring to murder a man named Franciscus

Vandenberg while in jail, a matter completely unrelated to the gang war. His conviction was overturned on appeal.

Since his release from jail, Domican has been a prominent figure in several state and federal investigations, including a number into the building industry. In June 2002 he was fined $5000 for threatening an NCA officer three years earlier. He is still involved in the building and construction industry and is well connected to major crime figures in Victoria and Western Australia, where he now lives.

Garry Nye, a criminal whose record includes armed robbery and assault, and a car dealer named John Harlum, were charged with Thurgar's murder in 1991 but later acquitted when it was established that the two alleged killers had never even met. The trial judge, Justice James Wood, who would later head a royal commission into police corruption, described the police case as 'a complete load of rubbish'. In December 2003, a decade after Nye's acquittal, the Supreme Court found he had been maliciously prosecuted and awarded him $1.35 million in damages.

In a December 1997 raid on the Waverley home of a well-known criminal, Eric Leonard Murray, police seized a shotgun later identified as the one that killed Thurgar. The shotgun had also been used in the June 1992 gangland hit on fifty-six-year-old Desmond Anthony Lewis, a former boxer and standover man involved in illegal bookmaking. The shotgun, with a home-made pistol grip, belonged to long-time underworld figure Robert Douglas 'Bertie' Kidd. Kidd had used it in a string of home invasions and an attempted bank robbery for which in 2004, at the age of seventy-one, he was convicted and sentenced to twelve years' jail. Kidd was a close associate of the murdered Mick Sayers. Murray, who is two years older than Kidd, had often acted as Kidd's driver and lookout. He was convicted of related crimes and jailed for three years.

George Savvas thought eight years in prison was enough. Eighteen more was out of the question. In July 1996 he walked out of Goulburn jail wearing a blond wig, a light-coloured jacket and dark glasses. To the embarrassment of authorities, he avoided recapture for eight months. During that time he was the state's most wanted man.

In March 1997 Savvas took two women to dinner at Sydney's most expensive Japanese restaurant. A man calling himself the Black Fox rang the police, who swooped. The $300 bill was left for the women to pay. They told police they had met 'Andy' a month earlier at an Italian restaurant. He'd told them he was a property developer. Speculation spread as to the identity of the Black Fox: was he a criminal rival, the jilted lover of one of Savvas's girlfriends, or just a community-minded citizen? While Australian police and Interpol had been hunting for Savvas as far away as Europe and South America, he had been doing a bit of quiet cocaine trafficking in Sydney. He had also taken to using the drug—a gram was found in his pocket when he was arrested.

Savvas was no sooner back in jail than he started planning his next escape. He formed a close relationship with fellow Maitland jail inmate Ivan Milat, who had been convicted of murdering seven backpackers and was never to be released. Both men were desperate and their escape plan was a crazed fantasy. They intended to scale an eight-metre prison wall topped with razor wire and under constant electronic surveillance, then somehow get through gates flanked by guard towers to reach accomplices who would be waiting outside to drive them to freedom. The New South Wales Crime Commission, jail authorities and police all learned of the plan, and foiled the escape before it got started. That night Savvas hanged himself in his cell. Milat is still in jail.

McPherson's and Freeman's grip on the underworld was severely weakened as a result of the gang war. In 1990, at the age of fifty-seven, Freeman died in his own bed from an asthma attack. He was buried at Waverley Cemetery in Sydney's smart eastern suburbs. Five years earlier Freeman, McPherson and a fair slice of Sydney's underworld had attended the burial service of their old mate Paddles Anderson at the same cemetery.

McPherson continued to run protection rackets in Kings Cross and elsewhere across Sydney until December 1994, when he was convicted and jailed for organising the violent assault on Darron Burt. Burt had worked for a McPherson company that imported bourbon whiskey. When Burt left the company he took with him a multi-million dollar importing contract. In true mafia fashion, McPherson hired a number of his henchmen, including Branko Balic, to teach Burt a lesson in business ethics. In a taped telephone conversation, played at the trial, McPherson was heard to tell Balic, 'The boys just done a job for me, a fucking good job . . . they got this fucking bloke and broke his fucking arm and bashed his head.'

But putting McPherson away was never going to be easy. Following the example of the American Mafia godfather Vincent 'the Chin' Gigante, who feigned mental illness for almost twenty years to escape conviction, McPherson had himself admitted to a Sydney psychiatric clinic, ostensibly with severe depression. He fed stories to the media about his fear of going to jail and suggested that a jail term would be a death sentence. The notorious hard man who hadn't shied from bashing and even killing his rivals could now be heard mumbling about suicide.

Given a sentence that many thought was light, the judge explained he had taken into account 'the special circumstances and his [McPherson's] health'. Brought from his cell to appear before the Wood Royal Commission into the New South Wales Police Service in 1995, McPherson turned on another memorable performance. 'I've done nothing wrong,' he declared, 'and I'm put in a position where I've got to answer questions so you can judge whether I'm saying something wrong. It's like the Spanish inquisition. You shot me in the water and if I come up I'm guilty even if I say I'm innocent.' He professed to remember little. He claimed never to have paid police but speculated that some had because it was just 'common sense'. Questioned about allegations of widespread bribery and corruption in the New South Wales Police, McPherson maintained that, 'I never met any crooked cops. Only met the bludgers who wanted to put me away.' Explaining how he'd managed to stay out of jail for nearly thirty years, McPherson said that he had been verballed by police when he was last jailed and that after his release,

> I said, 'Never again' and that's been my attitude all the way through. I've said on the phone a thousand times, 'Don't do anything you can go to jail for.' The police can verify that. They've listened to my phone for 35 years. I've said

to people, 'Don't do anything that can put you in jail', and none of my friends have been to jail in 35 years.

On 28 August 1996, at the age of seventy-five, McPherson died in jail.

Chapter 7

'Neddy' Smith

A life of crime and doing time

Before Murray Riley gave him his start in the heroin trade, Neddy Smith had had a long and violent, but not particularly successful, criminal career. He was arrested more than twenty times and spent long periods in boys' homes, juvenile detention centres and jails, including six years for robbery and twelve for the pack rape of a young mother. Released from jail in early 1975, Smith found the going tough. He immediately returned to crime, but wasn't making the kind of money he wanted. As soon as Bobby Chapman, one of his partners in the rape, got out of jail Smith teamed up with him in a spree of armed robberies.

In October 1976 the pair, along with Chapman's wife, Gail, tried to steal the Fielders Bakery payroll. As two bakery employees drove away from the bank with the $16,000 payroll, a hooded Chapman approached their car, pistol drawn. The driver accelerated, but the car stalled. Chapman fired through the window and the driver was hit with shattered glass. Chapman fled without the payroll. Smith drove him to where Gail Chapman was waiting in another car, and they abandoned the getaway car.

Hearing they were suspects, Smith approached a police informer and gave up his mate of fifteen years as the shooter. Smith would later claim that the only people he ever gave up were corrupt police. In fact, the betrayal of Chapman marked the start of Smith's long career as a police stooge. His motive was always the same: to ensure his own survival. Sometimes he informed to help police get a result while still protecting his own interests; sometimes he did it to get rid of competition; sometimes he obliged the police by getting rid of troublesome offenders. From time to time police paid Smith for his information. When Detective Roger Rogerson revealed this in 1986, Bob Bradbury, a former chief of the Criminal Investigation Branch who had controlled the informant reward fund, told the media: 'If he said he [paid rewards], I probably would believe him.'

When police arrested the Chapmans, however, Gail gave up Smith as the driver of the getaway car, and he had to be arrested. Smith remained in custody for a few weeks before being freed on bail. While Chapman was on bail, he committed another armed robbery. Bail was refused for eight months until Rogerson spoke up in his defence, telling a bail hearing that he had helped police on various occasions, giving 'valuable assistance in relation to the clearing up of a number of very serious crimes'. Chapman later pleaded guilty to armed robberies and was sentenced to thirteen and a half years' jail. When he was tried a year later on the attempted-murder charge, Rogerson intervened again, claiming to have information that it was not Chapman but another person who had fired at the payroll car and repeating the 'valuable assistance' claim. Other police had no knowledge of Rogerson's claims and were astonished by his decision to speak up for Chapman. The trial was aborted. Chapman later pleaded guilty to lesser charges of shooting with intent to commit grievous bodily harm and escaped additional jail time. Gail Chapman also pleaded guilty and, also with Rogerson's assistance, was released on a bond.

Chapman would later tell the Independent Commission Against Corruption he had never provided Rogerson with information or done any 'business' with Rogerson. He suggested that Rogerson's intervention at his trial had been at the behest of Smith, who had cause to fear Chapman—and had something to offer Rogerson.

Smith later insisted he was no 'dog': he said he paid police to get bail after his 1976 arrest and paid them again to let him beat the charges. But as Chapman was to tell ICAC: 'I know Smith had no money. No one knew that better than me . . . Smith had four bob, so if Smith paid money it must have been time payment, $50 a week, because he never had any money to give to anyone.'

Smith put his freedom to good use: by the time of Chapman's second trial, with Murray Riley as his mentor he was on his way to becoming a major heroin trafficker. Smith now had plenty of cash and was 'connected'. He wanted to placate Chapman and turned to Rogerson to help him do it. Despite Rogerson's efforts in court on his behalf, Chapman never spoke to Smith again.

Released after five years, Chapman wasted no time getting back into crime. Abandoning robbery, he dived into drugs, importing and dealing heroin, cocaine and cannabis. He amassed more than $1 million in assets, including a penthouse at Noosa Heads, several luxury cars and a stake in a $200,000 racehorse. Despite being charged with a string of importation and trafficking offences, he always managed to get bail. On Good Friday 1995 he was murdered near his outer-suburban home, bashed and then shot in the chest as he lay in the gutter.

Smith was introduced to Murray Riley in 1977. After serving as Riley's muscle during drug deals, he established his own distribution network and the good times began. Now that he was no longer causing headaches for Rogerson's Armed Hold-up Squad, Smith could also afford a more stable relationship with his bent-cop mates.

Smith's heroin syndicate included Bill Sinclair, an associate of Murray Riley's who now ran the Texan Bar in Bangkok, and Warren Fellows, whom Smith had met through Sinclair and who now worked for him as a courier. In October 1978 Fellows, travelling on a false passport, flew to Bangkok to make another smack run. With him was footballer Paul Hayward, the brother of Smith's de facto wife, Debra. Australian police had them under surveillance. They had a drink with Sinclair, but Smith had ordered him dropped from the deal. Sinclair tried to pump them for information and his agitation convinced watching police that he was part of the plot. On 11 October Thai police pounced and found 8.5 kilograms of heroin in Hayward's hotel room. Threatened with execution, the two men implicated Sinclair, though Fellows later insisted 'the Old Man' was innocent.

'NEDDY' SMITH

The morning after the Bangkok arrests, police searched Smith's inner-Sydney home and found $90,000 in cash and letters containing tips on importing drugs in containers and getting a container past Customs. Smith was arrested. Over the next few days, other properties were searched. Smith's step-brother, Edwin, was found with almost 2 kilograms of high-grade heroin from an earlier importation. A further $300,000 was found in various homes and banks.

Although Smith was the syndicate's central figure, police had little evidence against him and certainly not enough to secure a conviction. While he was in jail on remand, his parole on the 1968 rape conviction was revoked, keeping him inside. But the lack of evidence against him on the heroin charge was still a problem for police. The solution came in the form of Edwin Smith. Facing a heavy jail sentence, Edwin initially resisted police efforts to get him to talk. But as the seriousness of his situation sank in, he rolled and exposed Neddy's heroin network to the Woodward Royal Commission. Admitting that he'd lied in his five interviews with police shortly after the Thai heroin busts, he told of previous heroin importations and described the network of traffickers around the Smith–Sinclair–Fellows group. Tested by lawyers representing some of the drug traffickers he named, Edwin stuck to his story. Much of his evidence was corroborated. He agreed to give evidence in criminal proceedings against Neddy and was sentenced to ten years' jail for his role in the heroin ring.

In jail Neddy renewed his partnership with Murray Riley. For a time they virtually ran the jail. In return for keeping the peace, they were allowed privileges, including, as Smith boasted in *Neddy*, a larger cell, private toilet, TV set, radio and fan, as well as increased access to the jail library.

Smith's time in jail was littered with court appearances. Most of the 1976 charges arising from the botched Fielders Bakery robbery had been dismissed two years earlier, but he still had to face trial on the charge of possessing an un-licensed pistol. Smith had previously claimed police planted the gun, but now he said it belonged to the father of his de facto wife and that she had hidden it in the house without telling him. Just as he was to do a week later in the trial of Bobby Chapman and later in the trial of Gail Chapman, Rogerson appeared and without warning gave evidence for Smith. Rogerson was well and truly on Smith's payroll by this time, but his evidence couldn't prevent Smith from being sentenced to six months' jail. Three months later, however, the conviction was overturned on appeal. According to Smith, Rogerson's evidence cost him $10,000—though the pistol charges meant nothing to Smith either way. He was already serving time for rape and he still had to face the Sinclair–Fellows heroin charges.

A magistrate dismissed the charge of supplying heroin when police were not ready to proceed with the case, but a few months later they laid a new charge of conspiring with Sinclair, Fellows, Hayward, Edwin Smith and others to supply heroin. It was still hanging over his head when he was released from jail in October 1980.

By now, however, Smith had learned the value of the bribe and of having police onside. They were two assets he was determined to keep and consolidate. He lost no time seeking out Rogerson. Their former loose association became a partnership that would continue until the late 1980s. He also started rebuilding his heroin network.

While Smith was in jail, Danny Chubb had graduated from being a successful thief to a large-scale importer of hash and heroin. Now Smith became one of Chubb's top distributors, and the cash flowed. A few months later Warren Lanfranchi, a young thief Smith had met in jail, was released. Lanfranchi needed money and Smith was eager to help. With his support Lanfranchi was soon a major smack dealer in the eastern suburbs, raking in $10,000 a week. He also acquired a lover who would become a big drain on his business. Sallie-Anne Huckstepp, a blonde, ponytailed prostitute, had expensive tastes and a heroin habit that cut into Lanfranchi's profits.

Lanfranchi started falling behind in his payments to Smith. By April 1981 he owed Smith more than a quarter of a million dollars; much of that was owed in turn to Danny Chubb. Smith cut him off: no more heroin until the debt was paid.

They were desperate. Huckstepp needed money to buy heroin and both wanted to maintain their extravagant lifestyle. Smith—himself under pressure from Chubb—was also making ever more threatening demands for his money. Lanfranchi tried to make ends meet, committing at least five armed robberies or attempted armed robberies and several drug rip-offs, some ending in violence. During a botched raid on a bank, he attempted to shoot a police constable, Ray Walker, who just happened to be in the area. About a week later Walker identified Lanfranchi as the shooter.

Lanfranchi had been Smith's protégé. Now he was a problem. Lanfranchi's armed robberies and the attempted murder also made him a headache for Rogerson, who was under pressure to make some arrests. Even more of a problem was the fact that Lanfranchi knew about Smith's drug operation and about Rogerson's corrupt links with it.

If Lanfranchi were arrested and jailed for a long period, Smith and Rogerson could be in big trouble. Lanfranchi might cut a deal, rolling over and telling what he knew to reduce his sentence. The danger signs flashed even brighter when the Armed Hold-up Squad arrested Lanfranchi's accomplice and he named Lanfranchi as his partner in the armed robberies.

Meanwhile Smith's trial on the 1978 conspiracy to supply heroin charge began. It was now almost three years since his step-brother Edwin had testified to the royal commission. By now Edwin was a reluctant witness. Fearing for his life, he had changed his evidence. Then the heroin discovered in his possession three years earlier, which had formed a significant part of the evidence against Neddy, was found to have been tampered with. It had gone from being 85 to 90 per cent pure to being mostly glucose powder. The loss of Edwin's evidence and the unexplained dilution of the heroin wrecked the Crown case, and Smith was acquitted.

Smith later claimed to have paid $30,000 to police, via Rogerson, for the heroin to be diluted. Someone profited handsomely, both from the bribe and from the sale of the substituted heroin. Edwin Smith was released from jail soon after Neddy's acquittal, having served about four years of a ten-year sentence. Neddy has never forgiven him for turning 'dog'.

When he was sure the prosecution case in his own trial was fatally weakened, Smith turned his attention to getting Lanfranchi out of trouble, and had several discussions with him about how best to go about it. To Lanfranchi the solution was simple. Smith was bribing Rogerson, so why couldn't he? For Smith and Rogerson, though, a bribe, no matter how big, was not an option. In any case, Lanfranchi owed Smith too much already. The solution was going to have to be more drastic.

The next day, as Smith's trial progressed, Smith met Rogerson outside the District Court at Darlinghurst. Rogerson later claimed that Smith was concerned about the police: he wanted to avoid a situation in which a police officer might be shot attempting to arrest Lanfranchi. Police found that idea laughable. During the weekend break in his trial, Smith met Lanfranchi for a drink, then dropped him off in inner-city Chippendale, where he was to meet Rogerson to discuss a bribe. To show he was unarmed, Lanfranchi had been told not to wear a coat. He met up with Rogerson and they walked together into nearby Dangar Place, where eighteen police officers were on hand to help with his arrest. A few minutes later Rogerson shot Lanfranchi dead. According to Rogerson, Lanfranchi had gone for a gun when he realised he was about to be arrested. During the previous week police had had several opportunities to arrest Lanfranchi without violence, but they had not taken them.

A few days after the shooting Smith's trial ended. He was free, there were no outstanding charges against him, and Lanfranchi was out of the way. To Smith, his treachery was simply a matter of self-preservation. It also sent a strong message to other criminals: Neddy was a powerful person who was not to be messed with.

To avoid the media and police spotlights, Smith and his family moved to Kiama, south of Sydney, where he was harder for police to watch but close enough to Sydney to continue with his heroin business.

Rogerson didn't have to worry about leaving town. He still had plenty of support within the police. Tony Lauer, a Police Association spokesman who later led the failed crackdown on corruption in the New South Wales Police and became police commissioner, came out strongly in support of Rogerson and denounced as 'anarchist elements' those who criticised him over the shooting.

The inquest into Lanfranchi's death was held over three weeks during November 1981. The Coroner held that as a matter of law there was no evidence upon which he could find that an indictable offence had been committed. But the jury declined to find that Rogerson had shot Lanfranchi in the course of self-defence. The extent of the relationship between Rogerson and Smith was not known at the time of the inquest, but quite a few police who gave their loyalty to Rogerson then would before long feel betrayed.

There was, however, one factor that both Rogerson and Smith had underestimated. It was the attention the media would give to Sallie-Anne Huckstepp.

Huckstepp began courting the media as allies in her crusade for the truth about Lanfranchi's death. And they responded with gusto. She was a great story: the heroin whore and gangster's moll fighting for justice for her slain lover against a corrupt police force. But while she was right when she declared Neddy Smith and Rogerson had a corrupt relationship, some of her claims were highly doubtful. For instance, she insisted that Lanfranchi had $10,000 stuffed down the front of his pants when he met Rogerson near Dangar Place and that Rogerson stole the money. But she also claimed she and Lanfranchi were broke. Lanfranchi's father said that his son had told him just six days before the shooting that he was in trouble with Rogerson and would have to borrow money to get Rogerson off his back. He did

Left: Robert Trimbole. Right: Pat Sergi. (Both photos courtesy of News Limited)

Tony Sergi outside his house in 1977. He told journalists, 'We're in the liquor business, not the marijuana business'. (Courtesy of News Limited)

Donald Mackay shortly before his murder.

The Donald Mackay murder scene. (Courtesy of News Limited)

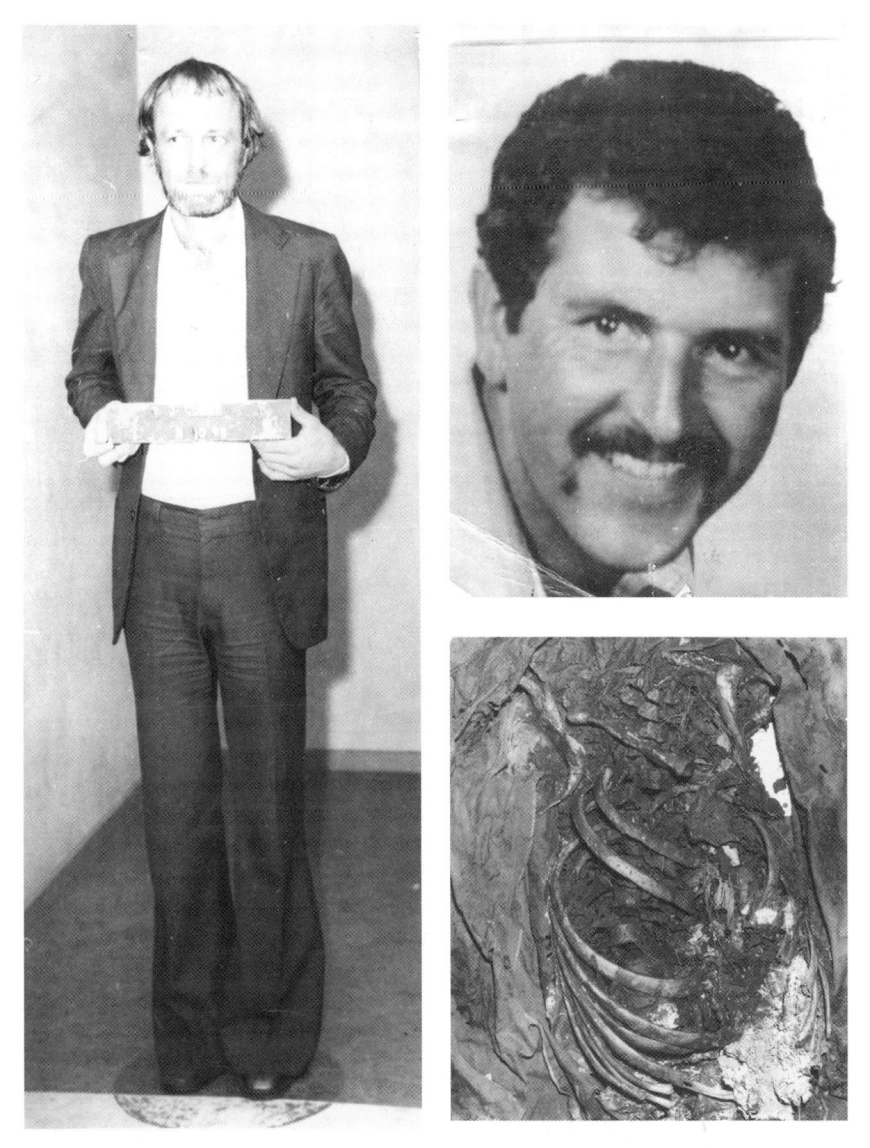

Left: Terrence John Clark. Top right: Pommy Lewis. Bottom right: Pommy Lewis's remains found at the crime scene. (Courtesy of the New South Wales Police)

Left: Douglas Wilson. Right: Isabel Wilson. (Both photos courtesy of the New South Wales Police)

Lennie McPherson (left) with Joe Testa (right) on a kangaroo shooting trip.

George Freeman (right) in Sydney with Danny Stein.

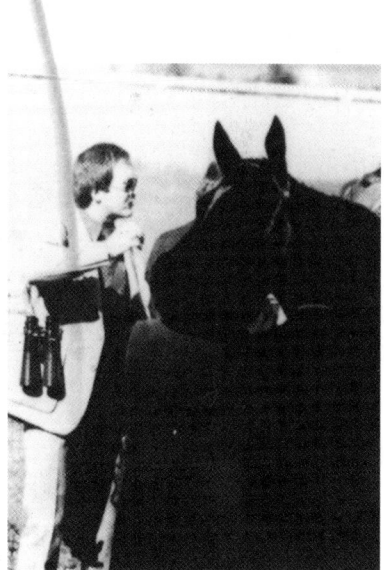

Left: Murray Riley (left) with US Mafia figure Sam Amarena.
Right: Snapper Cornwell at the races.

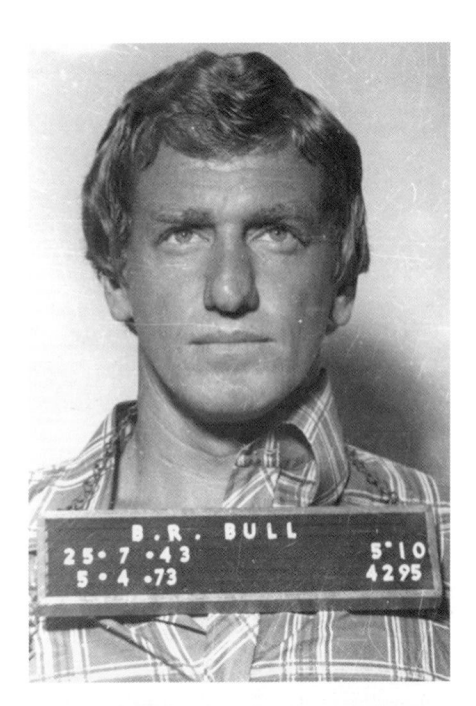

Barry Bull. (Courtesy of the New South Wales Police)

Terrence Basham and his partner Susan Smith. (Courtesy of the New South Wales Police)

Left: Christopher Flannery arriving at court in 1982. (Courtesy of News Limited) Right: Alan Williams.

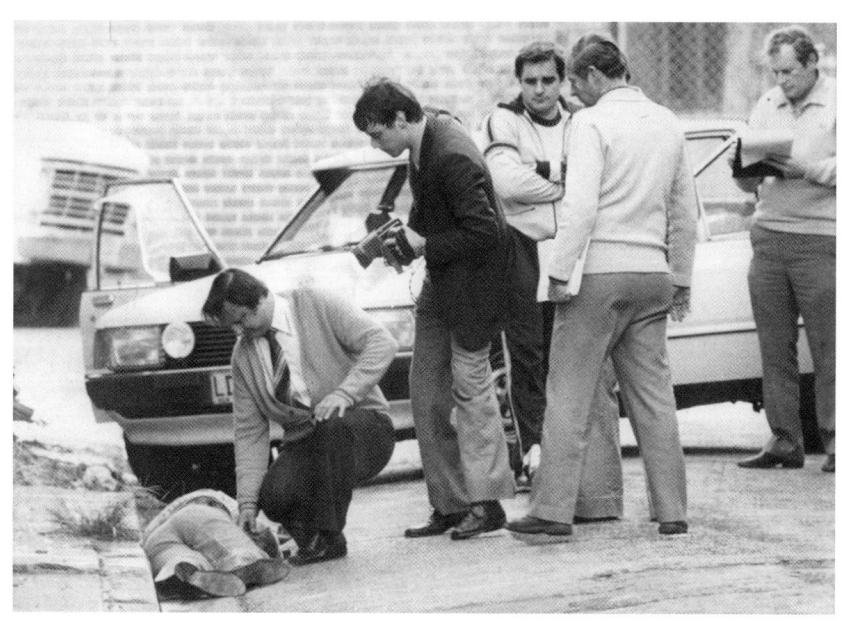

Roger Rogerson (centre with folder) at the scene of Warren Lanfranchi's shooting. (Courtesy of News Limited)

Left: Heroin from Danny Chubb's last importation. (Courtesy of the New South Wales Police) Top right: Bruce 'The Godfather' McCauley at Abe Saffron's funeral. (Courtesy of News Limited) Bottom right: Danny Chubb. (Courtesy of the New South Wales Police)

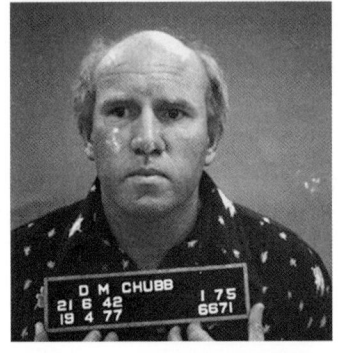

Police at the scene of Danny Chubb's murder. (Courtesy of News Limited)

Left: Neddy Smith being driven away in a police van. (Courtesy of News Limited) Right: John Stout. (Courtesy of the New South Wales Police)

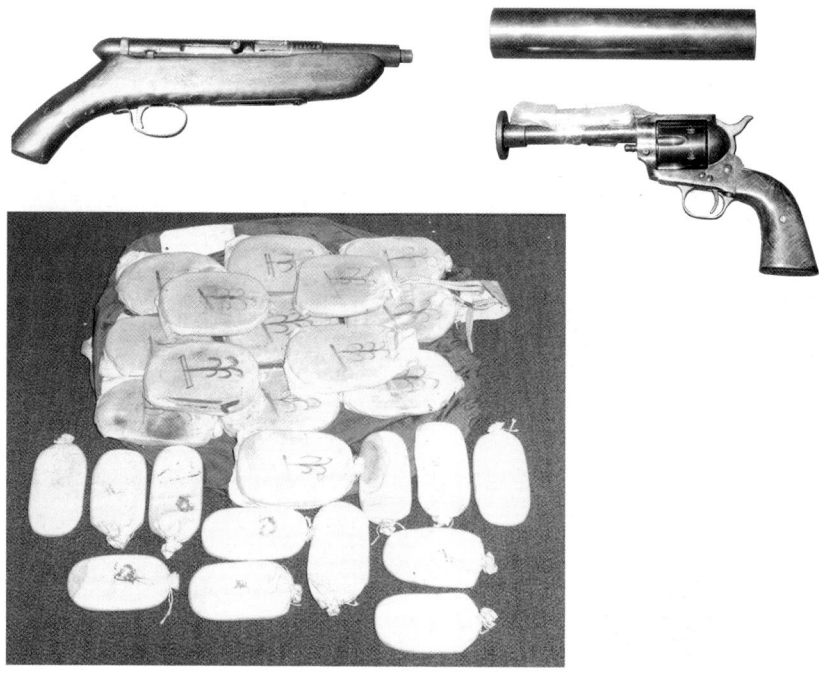

Some of the drugs and weapons found at Neddy Smith and John Stout's safe house. (Courtesy of the New South Wales Police)

Mick Sayers enjoying time with his greyhound before his murder. (Courtesy of News Limited)

Barry McCann

Police at the scene of Barry McCann's murder. (Courtesy of News Limited)

Left: Convicted drug dealer and prison escapee George Savvas with girlfriend Nancy Dufek during a visit by her to the maximum security Parklea Prison. Right: The cell in which George Savvas hanged himself.

A police surveillance photograph of Stan Smith meeting Laurie McLean.

Left: Michael Hurley's passport photograph. Right: The yacht *Charles Sydney* believed to have been used by Michael Hurley and Malcolm Field for the importation of drugs in the early 1990s.

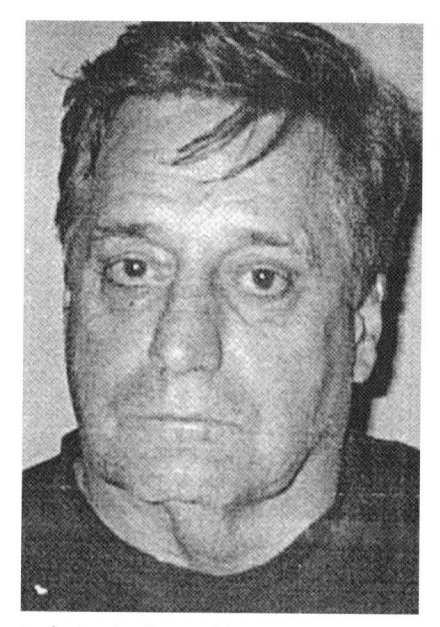

Left: Malcolm Field. Right: Les Mara handcuffed after his arrest by Federal Police at Callala Bay, 200 kilometres south of Sydney. (Courtesy of News Limited)

Shayne Hatfield wearing a balaclava with the piles of $100 bills.

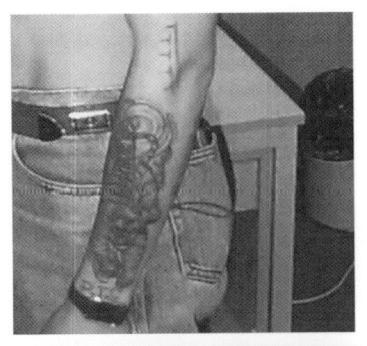

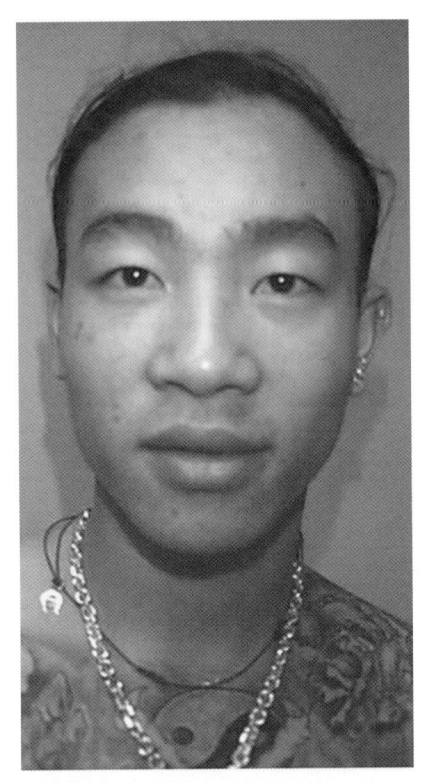

Top Left: The gang tattoo of 5T. Bottom Left: David Nguyen Van Dung. Right: La Hoang Ha. (Courtesy of the New South Wales Police)

The original members of 5T, circa 1990.

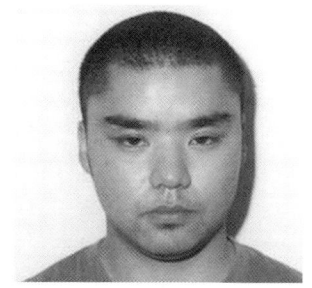

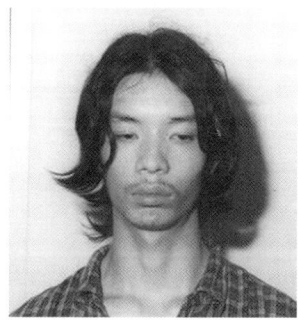

Convicted of the 2004 pool hall killing were Khanh Hoang Nguyen (left), Minh Thy Huynh (top right) and Duong Hai Nguyen (bottom right). (Right hand photos courtesy of the New South Wales Police)

Security camera footage of Duong Hai Nguyen entering the pool hall and leaving with Khanh Hoang Nguyen (right). (Courtesy of the New South Wales Police)

The world's biggest ecstasy bust. In 2007 over 15 million tablets were imported by the Calabrian mafia. (Courtesy of the Australian Customs Service)

The complete ecstasy haul laid out in a Customs Service warehouse. (Courtesy of the Australian Customs Service)

not borrow the money, he didn't have access to heroin, and he did not commit any known robbery during those few days. Huckstepp's claim that Lanfranchi simply had the money on the morning he was to meet Rogerson is implausible. Just after the shooting, Sallie-Anne told friends that she had been pregnant to Lanfranchi and had a miscarriage after the shooting. It was a lie, but it won her public sympathy. By the time of John Dale's 2004 book *Huckstepp: A Dangerous Life*, Sallie-Anne's story had blurred into myth. Her time in a Kalgoorlie brothel had become a place where she found 'stability in a whorehouse' and happiness. 'I was happy there,' she was quoted as saying. Yet she'd once told police that she and her then husband were forced to leave Kalgoorlie because 'the police continually demanded free sex and money, and any money I had left was taken by the brothel's madam'.

While she continued to crusade for Lanfranchi, Huckstepp soon acquired another lover, David Kelleher. A heroin dealer and violent criminal, he had been a distributor for Smith and took over the business when Smith was arrested in 1978. The relationship was interrupted by short jail sentences for both Huckstepp and Kelleher, but in September 1985 Kelleher was charged with conspiring to import 11 kilograms of heroin and eventually sentenced to life in jail. Huckstepp was once again on her own, addicted and broke.

While Kelleher was in jail, Huckstepp began a romance with a federal policeman, Peter Smith. On visits to Kelleher, she told him she was using Smith to get information that Kelleher might use in his defence. At about eleven o'clock one night in February 1986, Huckstepp got a phone call at home and, according to her flatmate, went out in a hurry to meet someone called Wozza—believed to be Warren Richards, a heroin dealer. The next morning she was found dead in a pond in nearby Centennial Park. She had been struck in the face, strangled, then dragged into the pond and drowned. A coronial inquest heard various theories about the identity of her murderer. Among those named were Richards, Kelleher (who supposedly had her killed out of jealousy), Rogerson and Neddy Smith (who later claimed he had committed the murder because Huckstepp was 'bugging Roger' with accusations of corruption). Smith's wife corroborated his claim that he had been at home that night.

Despite their hatred of each other, Huckstepp and Smith had several things in common. They were deeply involved in the heroin trade. Neither had any honour; they ripped off friend and foe alike. They both knew a lot about corruption in the New South Wales Police and legal fraternity. They were both liars and exaggerators and they were both willing to sell out others to ensure their own survival. In many ways it was these last characteristics that would bring about their respective downfalls.

After the Lanfranchi shooting Smith was given the green light to commit crime as long as Rogerson and a few of his cronies were kept in the loop and looked after, and Smith continued to give up crooks who were causing problems. With Danny Chubb as his supplier, Smith had access to as much heroin as he could sell and more money than ever before. According to Smith, he was selling about 3 kilograms every ten days, two in Sydney and one in Melbourne. One of his Melbourne customers was Alan Williams, the man who would later hire Chris Flannery to kill Detective Michael Drury. Smith also got to know Flannery, who was introduced to him by Rogerson and became a distributor and part-time enforcer for Smith's operation.

Smith was paying Chubb about $100,000 a pound and cutting the heroin before selling the same quantity for about $250,000. Smith was to brag: 'I used to spend $10,000 a week on clothes. I used to buy a new car every three months. And the young ladies did quite well; I bought twelve women new cars. I kept them in apartments. I spent $75,000 on jewellery just for myself.' He also claimed to have spent $6000 on one night in a brothel.

By May 1984 Flannery was openly telling fellow criminals that Neddy was No. 1 in the heroin scene and was going to wipe out the opposition. Smith himself was only slightly more modest. He was expressing his dissatisfaction with Danny Chubb's control of the smack trade and discussed with a number of crime figures the feasibility of bypassing Chubb and importing heroin through Papua New Guinea. Among them were Smith's old mentor Murray Riley, now out of jail after a comfortable few years as a 'model prisoner', Rogerson and Detective Bill Duff.

Their attention focused on Pel Air, a small airline with which Duff was associated. (The airline still exists today, although it has been taken over by new owners and new management who have no connection with the former operation.) Riley would use his drug contacts from the 1970s to hook up with the Thai suppliers. Pel Air would fly the heroin to Sydney, and Smith would be responsible for its distribution from there. Duff had been involved with Pel Air's predecessor, Wings Australia, since about 1980. For a few years the company operated as a charter airline and cargo carrier, but in late 1984 it collapsed. Pel Air was formed, taking over Wings Australia's planes and contracts. One of its pilots was Peter Johnstone, who had been previously charged with bird smuggling and conspiracy to murder. According to police, Johnstone described himself as a member of an international organisation with corrupt political connections that was 'capable of disposing of anyone they wanted removed'.

Two months after Danny Chubb was murdered in 1984, Pel Air did a dry run to Thailand. There Johnstone made contact with one of Riley's Sydney heroin-dealing associates from the 1970s, Kevin Leith, who introduced Johnstone to Szeto Yin Wah, described at the time as one of Thailand's biggest heroin exporters.

Meanwhile Duff approached an old colleague, Detective John McNamara, who had just taken up a position in the Criminal Intelligence Unit. He asked McNamara to let him know if Pel Air or any of its staff were under surveillance, telling him there would be a 'big drink' in it. McNamara told his superiors and then the Australian Federal Police, who tapped the phones of Duff and others. Two months later they asked police in Port Moresby to keep under surveillance a Pel Air plane suspected of carrying drugs.

On the day the plane was due to leave Papua New Guinea the then Prime Minister Michael Somare had lunch with the plane's passengers: two principals of Pel Air and a prominent Melbourne businessman. A couple of hours later, police moved in and searched the plane. Learning of the search, Somare intervened; local police claimed the search was aborted. Drug-sniffer dogs had reacted positively when inside the plane, but the luggage was not searched (there is no suggestion that Somare knew this when he intervened).

Later, Somare claimed that Australian authorities had never told him of their suspicions about Pel Air and its personnel. Had he known, he said, he would not have met them. The Papua New Guinea government ordered an official inquiry into the matter. It found that Somare had done nothing wrong, but his relationship with Pel Air and those associated with it played a significant role in his ousting in 1985. To this day, it is the only occasion in Australia's history when local criminals can claim to have directly dealt with the leader of a foreign country, albeit without his knowledge. (Somare later resurrected his political career and was elected prime minister for the third time in 2002. He was knighted in 2005.)

After the Port Moresby raid, Duff spoke with McNamara several times. The group was still determined to import heroin through Papua New Guinea. Duff claimed that $15,000 had been paid to a federal police officer to warn him if any member of the airline were put under surveillance. He offered McNamara $5000 for the same information. In late March–early April 1985 Duff laid out the plan to McNamara:

> The first flight is going to be on Tuesday week but he [the pilot] is only going to bring down one kilo and if there is any problem he is just going to throw it over the side. It will be just a training exercise to see if everything is sweet. The next one after that will be eight and the third will be forty . . . After that that they can jam this job [as a detective in the NSW Police] up their arses and I can sit back and retire.

The first two runs were to provide cash to fund 'the big one'.

Within weeks Duff, Riley, Smith, Rogerson and their partners knew they were under investigation. A month later Duff was charged by the police with misconduct and put before the Police Tribunal. His conversations with McNamara formed the core of the evidence against him. Lawyers for Duff attacked McNamara's evidence but it was never alleged that he had fabricated any of the conversations. Duff did not give evidence or call any witnesses in his defence. The tribunal found against him and he was sacked from the police in March 1986.

The investigation of Pel Air was a major disruption to Smith's plans to dominate the heroin trade, and it cost him a lot of money. There was more bad news to come. Without telling their Pel Air partners, Riley and Smith had invested in a second heroin importation network, but it too came unstuck. In April 1985 five men, including a former police officer, were nabbed when they attempted to collect a parcel from the North Sydney post office containing almost 400 grams of heroin. One of the five had earlier travelled to Bangkok, bought the heroin and mailed it to the North Sydney *poste restante*. But despite their underlings' arrests, Smith and Riley were still free—for now.

Financially, however, they were in dire straits. After Chubb's murder his partner, Bruce 'the Godfather' McCauley had continued to import heroin. Sometimes Smith bought his supplies from McCauley, but it was risky. It was known that McCauley was the target of several Federal Police investigations. Smith was still at loggerheads with Barry McCann, who was now a large-scale importer of heroin and supplier to several of Smith's old distributors. Rogerson, meanwhile, was preoccupied with his forthcoming trial for attempting to bribe Detective Michael Drury to change his evidence in the case against Flannery's colleague, the Melbourne drug trafficker Alan Williams. Smith had little option but to return to what he knew: armed robberies, drug rip-offs and the occasional murder.

Over the next two years Smith committed at least seven armed hold-ups, netting more than half a million dollars. Once he'd paid off his partners, however, what remained was not enough to pay for Smith's lavish lifestyle of expensive lunches and drinking binges.

Disgraced cop Duff and his wife ran the Iron Duke Hotel in Alexandria. Smith claimed to have bought the hotel when the previous owner went broke and given it to Duff, but he never backed this up. Duff insisted that he and his wife had bought the hotel without Smith's help, but rumours of Smith's involvement persisted. In April 1986, about 100 metres from the hotel, a car mounted the footpath and ran Smith down before trying to reverse over him. Smith's left leg and six ribs were broken. Duff was one of the first on the scene. The day before, Rogerson had said on TV that Smith was a police informer. Smith linked this disclosure, which he denounced as a lie, to the attempt to run him down.

A day after the attempt on his life, Smith was interviewed on TV. He claimed that he had recognised the driver of the vehicle that ran him over, though the driver was wearing a wig and a false moustache. This person, he said, worked closely with certain police, whose names Smith knew. Terrence Ball, a former professional boxer turned drug dealer, was charged by police with wounding Smith and attempting to murder him. Ball was a member of Barry

McCann's gang, which at the time was involved in its own gang war as it sought to expand its heroin business.

Ball told police that two years earlier, when he was working for Barry McCann at the Lansdowne Hotel, he had been shot in the head after an argument between Smith and McCann. Ball claimed that since then he had been receiving death threats from Smith. Detective Sergeant Gordon Beaumont gave evidence that, when asked, Ball admitted to running over Smith. 'I did. But you would have done the same thing. He had it coming.' Smith, however, told the court that he and Ball had been lifelong friends and that Ball was definitely not the man who had run over him. The case was thrown out.

The botched hit-and-run was the second attempt on Smith's life that week. A few days earlier he and another criminal associate were leaving the Quarryman's Hotel at Pyrmont when a shotgun fired several blasts in his direction. Smith wasn't hit, but his associate was, and was rushed to hospital.

By early 1986 Smith and Rogerson appeared to be in open conflict. Failed crime ventures, the gang war and the scrutiny they were receiving from the media and police had badly strained the relationship. Or so they wanted people to think. The public show was, in part, an attempt to take some of the heat off Rogerson, who was under investigation on several fronts. In fact, the relationship, though sometimes uneasy, would continue for several more years. Rogerson's longtime friend and partner, Bill Duff, was closer to Smith than ever before.

In June 1986, three months after Duff's dismissal, the Police Tribunal found against Rogerson on departmental charges including impairing the efficiency of the force, improperly associating with criminals and operating two false bank accounts. He was dismissed from the police.

Smith, meanwhile, was reorganising. In early 1986 he hooked up again with Glen Flack, who during the 1970s had been close to Smith and his longtime partner in armed robberies, drugs, corruption and other crimes, Abo Henry. Flack was a Glebe boy and knew all the local crooks, particularly the clever ones. Within weeks of his release from a long stretch in jail he was committing armed hold-ups with Smith. In one raid they stole $60,000 from South Sydney Junior Leagues Club.

Riley's value to Smith was now declining—he was not an armed robber—and their paths had diverged. But they teamed up again for occasional heroin deals and drug rip-offs, sometimes with Bill Sinclair, who had been pardoned in Thailand and returned broke to Sydney in 1982. (Fellows and Hayward were pardoned in 1988.) Having identified a potential rip-off, Riley needed Smith's muscle to carry it out and his connections with police to reduce the risks. But Smith didn't need Riley, and Riley was omitted from several of Smith's rip-offs. For drug deals Smith and Riley—and often Abo Henry and Flack—turned to Michael Hurley, a onetime partner of Danny Chubb (see Chapter 9), and to Barry McCann's partner, George Savvas. In between armed hold-ups and drug dealing with Smith, Flack also did jobs with Hurley, believing he offered better prospects in the long term.

Smith had remained friends with Savvas throughout his feud with McCann. Without McCann's knowledge Smith had bought heroin from Savvas, but it was a casual arrangement and sometimes involved a go-between. The go-between, known as 'Hollywood', had been an SP bookmaker during the 1970s and was the driver in several of Smith's armed hold-ups. Hollywood worked in a community centre in Glebe and hid heroin there for Smith and his associates.

In October 1987 Smith and Flack began what was to have been just another all-day drinking session. They began the day at the Lord Wolseley Hotel in the inner Sydney suburb of Ultimo, moved on to the Covent Garden Hotel in Haymarket for drinks with Rogerson and another former detective, Graham Frazer, then had a few more beers and several bottles of wine over a Chinese restaurant lunch. They returned to the Covent Garden for several rounds of beers and at about 4 p.m. went to the Australian Youth Hotel at Glebe for a few more drinks. Rogerson and Frazer bowed out, but Smith and Flack headed to the beachside Coogee Sports Club for a final schooner. On the way, they had a minor collision, got into a fight with the driver and passenger of the other car, and Smith stabbed the passenger, Ronald Flavell, four times in the stomach. The father of four died. The next day Smith and Flack were charged with murder.

The police were entitled to think they had got Smith at last. But in February 1988, four months after the murder, there was a break-in at Randwick Police Station and police diaries and other documents relating to the Flavell investigation were stolen.

On bail for the murder, Flack and Smith continued their crimes. On New Year's Day 1988 Flack, Hurley and others burrowed into the National Australia Bank in Sydney's Chinatown and stole money and jewellery said to have been worth millions. During 1988 Flack and Smith committed at least four robberies and one attempted robbery before being arrested on Boxing Day as they were about to rob a council chambers of its Christmas payroll.

This time Smith and Flack did not get bail. Smith remained in custody until he was sentenced in March 1989 to thirteen years' jail. Almost a year later a jury took just two hours to find him guilty of the murder of Ronald Flavell. He was sentenced to life in jail. On the same day he was fined $60,000 for contempt after he refused to give evidence at Flack's trial. Smith later claimed that in the weeks after his arrest for Flavell's killing, his solicitor, Val Bellamy, told him that Abo Henry had paid $50,000 to a former police officer, Mal Spence, 'to do something', but Spence said he needed another $50,000. Smith's conviction for the murder was more good luck than good police work.

Flack beat the murder charge and cut a deal, pleading guilty to conspiring to commit an armed robbery, motor vehicle theft and firearms offences. He was released in May 1993, having served four and a half years.

Eleven months later, as part of an NCA investigation into drug trafficking, state and federal police executed a search warrant on the Housing Commission home of Flack's mother. They seized a briefcase containing $433,000 in cash that had been hidden in the hallway cupboard. Her son had a key to the house and visited her 'about twice a week', Mrs Flack said, but he did not stay at the house. He kept 'a few clothes in a back room'. She denied any knowledge of the briefcase or the cash, and when told how much cash was in the briefcase she responded, 'Oh my God.'

No charges were laid but the NCA kept the money. There was evidence that several of the notes had been in circulation for only a few months. Mrs Flack lodged a claim for the cash on the ground that it had been found in her house. Three years later the Federal Court found in her favour, awarding her the cash and costs. An NCA appeal failed. It is not known what Mrs Flack did with the cash but those who knew her describe her as a generous woman who doubtless shared her luck with her son.

Within months of receiving his first life sentence, Smith was dreaming up ways to get out of jail or at least have his sentence reduced. There were police on the outside who Smith felt had lived off him, either corruptly or by getting good arrests on information supplied by him. There were others he hated for having tried to lock him up. Now it was time to pay them back. He would admit to corruption that had occurred and make it up where it had not. In October 1990 he wrote to the Independent Commission Against Corruption offering his services as an informant. During the ensuing series of interviews with ICAC officers, he is believed to have named more than a hundred New South Wales police as being corrupt.

Public hearings began in November 1992 and continued for almost a year. The inquiry—covering both public and private hearings—resulted in 147 witnesses being called, almost 13,000 pages of transcript and more than 600 exhibits. Its report, published in February 1994, noted that Smith and his partner Abo Henry were 'notorious, professional criminals with a proven tendency to lie when it suits them'. Both Smith and Henry had claimed that they would nominate corrupt police but would not dob in their criminal associates. The commission commented: 'In the main, *although not entirely* [emphasis added], that stance was maintained throughout.'

In his book *Abo: A Treacherous Life*, Henry insisted that he only learned Smith had become an ICAC informant after

Smith had been interviewed several times. According to Henry, it was only the impracticality of murdering Smith and a well-founded fear that Smith would roll on him that induced him 'reluctantly' to corroborate Smith's testimony. He claims that even this cooperation was limited, since much of Smith's evidence to ICAC consisted of exaggeration and outright lies. Smith's book *Neddy* tends to support Henry's claims. The book was frequently at odds with Smith's evidence to ICAC, while early drafts were even less consistent. Having failed to get his sentence reduced by going to ICAC, Smith did the rounds of law enforcement and related agencies offering 'new' information about the 1970s and '80s—information he had, for some reason, forgotten to tell ICAC.

The explanation for Smith's dubious evidence lies partly in the fine print of the indemnity he was given for cooperating with ICAC. The indemnity was limited to 'the commission of any offence, other than homicide, which any member of the New South Wales Police Service, past or present, aided, abetted, counselled or procured' and about which Smith agreed to give evidence, either before a court or before ICAC. In other words, the only crimes Smith could talk about freely were those that involved police. Consequently, his stories were always tailored to include police as major participants. Generally he followed the same principle in his book. Where he wrote about crimes not involving police, the stories were so hazy on details that no prosecution against him could be launched. There is no doubt that Smith had corrupt dealings with a number of police over the years, but they were fewer than he pretends.

In April 1994 the then New South Wales police commissioner, Tony Lauer, told the *Sydney Morning Herald*: 'The system bred the man [Rogerson]. It's a good thing the system doesn't exist [any more] . . . The culture in the late '70s, the willingness to close ranks, to not see fault in a fellow officer, to not disclose improper conduct doesn't happen anymore.'

Lauer appeared not to have learned anything from his notorious and mistaken endorsement of Rogerson thirteen years earlier. His claim that 'the system doesn't exist [any more]' was an even bigger error. A few years later, as the Wood Royal Commission was exposing widespread and systemic corruption within the police on an almost daily basis, he resigned.

In 1994 Smith had reminisced to a cellmate about the mayhem he'd been part of back when he was a big man of Sydney crime. The man was a police informant and taped Smith confessing to a number of murders. In October of that year, Task Force Snowy was set up to investigate the taped claims. However, the tapes were leaked to Sydney solicitor Chris Murphy, who was then a columnist with the *Sun-Herald*. On 22 January 1995, front-page headlines screamed: 'Sensational secret tapes recorded in jail: I KILLED SIX: NEDDY SMITH'. Details of the recordings were reported over three pages, and more reports appeared over the next couple of weeks. The Wood Royal Commission into Police Corruption questioned Murphy about the source of the leaked documents, but he claimed the material had been given to him anonymously. For Task Force Snowy, the leak was devastating: 'We lost the element of surprise and opportunities for covert surveillance were blown,' said Detective Chief Superintendent John Laycock, who headed the taskforce. 'It cost us any opportunity of getting Smith's accomplices.'

Snowy reinvestigated thirteen murders committed between 1976 and 1988 and a number of shootings. Corruption allegations threaded their way throughout the investigation and overlapped with similar allegations in previous inquiries, including that of the gang war task force, the ICAC inquiry into the relationship between police and criminals, and the ongoing Wood Royal Commission.

Smith was eventually charged with seven murders, including Huckstepp's. On the prison tapes, Smith had claimed he attacked her from behind and lifted her bodily by the throat, strangling her until she went limp. Then he dragged her, face down, into the pond and stood on her corpse to keep her head under and make sure she was dead. He was recorded as saying it was 'the most satisfying thing I ever did in my life'. DNA evidence presented at the trial also linked him to the killing, but he was acquitted. He was convicted of the shooting murder of Harvey Jones, a brothel keeper, in 1983, and sentenced to life. The magistrate declined to commit him for trial on the other murders, and following his second life sentence for killing Jones, the Crown did not pursue those charges.

In early 1994 Bill Duff, a mate of Smith and Rogerson, was arrested with 57 grams of heroin worth an estimated $40,000 and more than $17,000 in cash. His trial would not come up for another couple of years. Broke and facing several years in jail, Duff used his remand time to build up a war chest. The money would once again come from drugs. Introduced to Richard James Simpson, a well-known amphetamine 'cook for hire' to outlaw motorcycle gangs and other criminal groups, the former policeman persuaded Simpson to teach him the tricks of the trade. Using a workshop at Bankstown airport controlled by the Bandidos bike gang as their lab, Duff's group produced 5 kilograms of pure methylamphetamine, which when cut broke down to around 50 kilograms, worth about $5 million on the street.

In preparation for their next cook, Duff did the rounds of Sydney pharmacies and bought 8,000 Sudafed tablets, from which the group extracted about half a kilogram of pseudo-ephedrine. A month later Simpson was jailed over an earlier cook. Plans for the second cook were further disrupted when Duff was sentenced to three years' jail for the 1994 heroin charge. Within a couple of years he was out on parole. But in May 1999 police carried out a series of raids on a network of clandestine drug laboratories across western and south-west Sydney. One target of the raid was the Duff group's workshop at Bankstown Airport. Chemical tests showed it had been used as an amphetamine laboratory. The search also turned up a large cache of Bandidos' weapons, including semi-automatic military rifles and handguns, and ammunition. Duff was on parole for the 1994 heroin charges when, on 4 June 1999, he was charged over the lab, but the charges were eventually dropped.

Also arrested in the sweep on drug labs was another former police officer, Bill El Azzi, one of Domican's allies in the 1980s gang war. Duff had introduced El Azzi to Simpson as someone who could advise him on court tactics and ways to attack police evidence at trial. Although he didn't prevent Simpson's jail sentences, El Azzi became an apprentice cook. El Azzi had been charged with conspiring with Victor Camilleri and Kevin Theobold to murder Michael Sayers during the gang war, but the charges were dismissed. He then avoided conviction for possessing cannabis and importing heroin, possessing an unlicensed firearm and corruptly receiving a reward. In 2003, however, he was convicted of conspiring to manufacture amphetamines and sentenced to seven years' jail. El Azzi's main accuser was Simpson, the man who had introduced him to amphetamine production; El Azzi had made the mistake of stealing Simpson's wife.

The amphetamine network had used around fifty different laboratories in and around Sydney. Police estimated that this loose syndicate, which the raids of 1999 largely broke, had over the previous decade been responsible for producing and distributing more than 200 kilograms of pure methylamphetamine, which translated to 2000 kilograms of street-quality 'meth' worth around $200 million.

Neddy Smith will never be released from jail. But that is not his only prison. In the early 1980s he was diagnosed with Parkinson's disease. His condition has worsened greatly in recent years. Some would see this as a form of justice. A thug who boasted that he feared no one and who bashed and killed criminals and innocent victims alike now needs the help of others to survive. His life of luxury, violence and power is only a memory. Fellow prisoners regard him with contempt.

In just over a decade and a half from the mid 1970s, while Smith traded in heroin, corruption and violence, there were more than forty murders among his circle of 'friends'. He was a violent man in a violent trade in violent times. A former detective who was involved in Smith's 1978 arrest over the Sinclair–Fellows–Hayward conspiracy says that some of the police involved had considered taking half the heroin found on Neddy's brother, Edwin, and planting it in Neddy's home to ensure his conviction, but this plan was thwarted when Neddy's solicitor arrived at the scene much sooner than they expected. The former detective went on to say: 'In those days Neddy would have been convicted and sentenced to ten years, and it would have been for something he had done. With Neddy in jail, Roger and Bill [Duff] would probably have been still in the police, a lot of people, criminals and innocent victims, would be still alive, and the heroin trade might have looked a lot different.'

How big an impact did the early arrival of that lawyer have on crime in New South Wales over the next quarter of a century? What impact did it have on the lives of thousands of drug addicts, and on the political debates and decisions Smith and Rogerson influenced?

In Smith's words: 'I have watched them and seen how they act, for example criminals, instead of looking after their friends' wives and families when they get buckled they can't wait to get over their mates' places to fuck their best friends' wives . . . crims only give each other up, rob each other and fuck their friends' wives . . . I hate crims today. Even the weakest lowest of the criminals can make plenty of money through drugs and then they turn into monsters . . . Drugs have fucked this country completely and you can say I had a hand in doing [it], I cannot deny it.'

Chapter 8

'Stan the Man' Smith and Lawrence McLean

Mates to the end

By the mid 1970s the partnership between 'Stan the Man' Smith, Lennie McPherson and George Freeman was on the wane. Smith's new partner was Lawrence McLean, who was on the way to becoming Australia's largest cannabis importer.

Lawrie McLean and Stan Smith were close mates. They had been doing business together since the 1960s, first as professional shoplifters, then as small-time drug dealers in Sydney's eastern suburbs. McLean called Smith 'Specs', a nickname few others got away with using. By the mid 1970s they were growing cannabis through a network based in the

Byron Bay area, on the far north coast of New South Wales. They had also begun importing high-grade cannabis 'Buddha' sticks and hash. A decade later McLean was being supplied by one of the world's biggest cannabis dealers, Phillip Sparrowhawk, masterminding multi-tonne importations into Australia. He was also an associate of an even bigger international trafficker and associate of Sparrowhawk, Howard 'Mr Nice' Marks.

McLean, who used more than a dozen aliases during his criminal career, was born in Melbourne in 1941 and turned to crime while still in his teens. Within a few years he was working as an SP bookmaker. After moving his illegal business to Sydney, he befriended several of the people who would later become part of his drug network. During the 1960s McLean carried out a series of lucrative burglaries on Sydney's affluent upper North Shore. He was caught and charged, but absconded on bail. He spent some time in the infamous Kangaroo shoplifting gang, which carried out well-organised raids on exclusive stores in the UK and Europe. He also began to make his name as a drug dealer.

In 1972 he moved to Byron Bay and bought some land with Stan Smith, a fellow graduate of the Kangaroo gang who now made his money providing protection to the McPherson–Freeman network and the drug trade. McLean was joined in Byron Bay by one of his Sydney crime partners, twenty-five-year-old Neville Hugh Scouller. They quickly built a profitable business trafficking locally grown cannabis to Sydney and Brisbane.

Within a year of his arrival in Byron Bay, McLean was charged with possession of cannabis when police searched his property looking for Stan Smith, who was wanted in Melbourne on a drugs charge. McLean gave a false name and

'STAN THE MAN' SMITH AND LAWRENCE McLEAN

was released. Despite a warrant for his arrest, he continued to live openly in Byron Bay. In the same year Scouller was arrested at nearby Ballina, charged with possession of drugs and granted bail.

In 1974 Maxwell Garry Bowman, a thirty-year-old international drug trafficker, joined McLean and Scouller at Byron Bay. Bowman had been convicted of drug trafficking in France and Switzerland in the early 1970s. Between those episodes he had been arrested in Karachi, Pakistan, for drug trafficking, but beat the charges. Bowman was a longtime associate of McLean, Stan Smith and Jimmy Sweetman, with whom Smith had been convicted of drug trafficking half a decade earlier.

By the mid 1970s a loose network of more than forty drug traffickers was living the good life in the Byron Bay area. Most had connections in Sydney, Melbourne and Queensland's south-eastern coastal strip.

In October 1975 McLean fled Byron Bay when he and a woman friend wanted for cannabis trafficking escaped a drug squad raid on his property. He moved across the border to Queensland and remained involved in marijuana growing in remote areas of the state as well as importing the drug from Thailand. Two years later he was arrested with Scouller at Mona Vale, on Sydney's Northern Beaches. Both the state drug squad and the then Federal Narcotics Bureau had been tipped off about a large cannabis deal. Police missed the deal but McLean and Scouller were charged with possession of a small amount of cannabis. By then there were several warrants out for McLean's arrest, but he gave a false name and police failed to make the link. Once again he got bail— and once again he disappeared.

Returning to Queensland, McLean continued his drug business, sending shipments as far afield as Melbourne. By the late 1970s McLean was wanted by the Australian Federal Police for 'forging and uttering' false Australian passports for drug-buying trips. In May 1978 Kenneth Derley, who had spent much of the past two years trafficking drugs with Murray Riley, offered McLean and a Brisbane dealer $200,000 to find a boat that could be used to pick up a five-tonne cannabis shipment for Riley that had been dropped off at Polkington Reef, near the Solomon Islands (see Chapter 3). McLean said he couldn't get a boat, but suggested the yacht *Anoa*, which was then in Cairns. They bought it and eventually landed almost three and a half tonnes of the drug at a small inlet near Port Macquarie.

Between 1977 and 1980 New South Wales was getting too hot for some criminals, with two royal commissions into drug trafficking—Woodward's and Willams's—running concurrently. Jack 'the Fibber' Warren was one of several criminals who shifted their businesses to Queensland. The Fibber continued to spend time in the Philippines looking after the sex and gambling investments of Lennie McPherson and the drug interests of his old associate Danny Chubb, while keeping an eye out for commissions and scams of his own. One of his main contacts was an old mate from Kings Cross, Lord Tony Moynihan. A hereditary peer who had served in the Coldstream Guards, Moynihan fled England in the mid 1950s rather than face assault complaints laid by his father and then wife. During a stint playing bongo drums in Kings Cross nightclubs he got to know Warren and other members of Sydney's underworld. Moynihan left Australia in a hurry—he is thought to have owed money to several dangerous characters—and in 1963 surfaced in Karachi as the bongo-playing husband of a belly dancer known as Princess Amina. A few years later Moynihan's father died and he returned to Britain, without Amina, and took his seat in the House of Lords. After running up a string of debts and almost sixty fraud-related charges, he bolted again, this time to Manila, where he married for the fourth time. His new father-in-law was a major-general in the Filipino army with a chain of massage parlours and close ties to President Ferdinand Marcos. Socially and financially secure, Moynihan quickly became a person of corrupt influence and a useful contact for Australian criminals.

In 1979 Stan Smith spent several months in a Melbourne jail over possession of a few grams of cannabis six years earlier. On his release he returned home to Whale Beach, in northern Sydney. Not long after, his twenty-two-year-old son, Stan, died of a heroin overdose. Only a year before, Stan Sr. had told the Woodward Royal Commission, '[M]y eldest son, who is 21 years of age, is currently serving a gaol sentence for drug-related offences and has been a hopeless heroin addict for some years now.' A few weeks after young Stan's death, a North Shore heroin dealer in his twenties was found dead in a park at Narrabeen Lakes. He had been run over many times by a car, and had taken some time to die. It was clearly personal.

About this time Smith moved to Caloundra, on Queensland's Sunshine Coast, and caught up with several longtime colleagues, including the Fibber. By now Smith's interests lay primarily with McLean, though he maintained business and personal relationships with McPherson and Freeman. McLean was seeking both to expand his cannabis operations and to reduce his risk of detection. His answer to both problems was to transplant his operations to the Philippines. Through the Fibber, McLean was reintroduced to Moynihan, who claimed he could, for a fee, arrange anything in the

Philippines. Under the protective umbrella of the corrupt Marcos government, McLean was soon granted access to land outside Baguio, in the mountains 250 kilometres north of Manila, for 'agricultural purposes'. The arrangement survived the fall of Marcos in 1986. More than a decade later McLean was still paying several hundred thousand dollars a year for protection.

Having established a marijuana plantation, McLean shipped drugs to Australia in yachts, landing the drugs mostly along Australia's east and south coast and using Smith as his main distributor.

The Fibber's son Barry had moved to Pattaya in Thailand in the late 1970s and dabbled in drug trafficking. Around late 1981 Barry was visited by Phil Sparrowhawk, who had been given his name by a corrupt Bangkok lawyer known for defending drug traffickers. In his book *Grass*, Sparrowhawk relates how he'd been left with 4 tonnes of cannabis after a deal fell through. Barry took over the cargo and arranged for its importation into Australia. Sparrowhawk claims to have pocketed $2 million from the deal. Flush with success, Barry agreed to arrange another shipment of 500 kilograms of Kashmir hash. Not long after it went through, he died in Bangkok of a heroin overdose. Barely breaking stride over his son's death, the Fibber flew to Bangkok, met up with Sparrowhawk and took him to Manila, where he introduced him to Moynihan, Neddy Smith and 'Joe Smith' (as McLean was known). Neddy Smith was to play no further part in the relationship, but over the next few years Moynihan and McLean would do plenty of business with Sparrowhawk.

McLean started buying some of his cannabis consignments from Sparrowhawk, who describes in his book how the importations to Australia were done, without revealing their number or frequency. According to Sparrowhawk, by the time they met, 'Joe' McLean was a big-time cannabis dealer who 'didn't touch a deal less than five tons'.

'I was supplying Joe with the Thai grass he would be importing into Australia via Holland. Although geographically Thailand was closer to Australia than Holland, it was still cheaper and smoother for me to send it to Amsterdam and for Joe to get it shipped to Oz from there.' Sparrowhawk also credits Joe with 'organis[ing] the private yachts that brought the grass into his country and the initial onward distribution'.

Sparrowhawk introduced the Fibber to Howard Marks, the man who had brought Sparrowhawk into the cannabis trade. An Oxford graduate, Marks ran an international cannabis trafficking operation that was making multi-tonne importations into Ireland, Europe, the UK, Canada and the US. To protect his network from police, he juggled more than forty aliases, including 'Marco Polo' and 'David Nice', used more than eighty telephones and created more than twenty companies around the world.

According to his book *Mr Nice*, Marks was sceptical of Moynihan's claim to be the dependable Mr Fix-it of the Philippines but decided he would be a useful person to know. At his palatial home on the outskirts of Manila, Moynihan introduced Marks to 'Joe Smith' McLean, whom Marks described as looking like 'a cross between Crocodile Dundee and Kirk Douglas'. The pair took an immediate liking to each other. In no time they were smoking dope and swapping stories.

Marks recalls 'Joe' telling him: 'What I'm after is a good contact in Pakistan. I got my own guy [Sparrowhawk] in Bangkok that gives me great gear . . . I've been bringing dope into Australia all my life. I need someone reliable to get shit out of Pakistan.' Marks's response was, 'Call me whenever you want, Joe.' He introduced McLean to his Pakistan connections, whom McLean used to organise a series of huge cannabis shipments into Australia.

About eighteen months after Marks and McLean met, the arrests of several members of Marks's network spooked him into backing out of the cannabis trade. But he'd left it too late. In July 1988 raids in five countries netted Marks and about twenty members of his syndicate. Several, including Marks's brother-in-law and Moynihan, rolled over as they cut deals with the US Drug Enforcement Administration (DEA) in return for reduced jail sentences. Moynihan had an insurance policy: for at least a year he'd been taping every conversation he'd had with Marks.

While Australia was never one of Marks's drug markets, Australian police played a pivotal role in his downfall. As one of his US-based drug yachts visited Australia on its way to pick up a 20-tonne shipment from Pakistan, Australian and US DEA agents planted tracking devices on the yacht. Its later interception and the arrest of its crew were major blows to Marks's operations.

In 1990 Marks was sentenced to twenty-five years' jail over the importation of hundreds of tonnes of cannabis into the US.

During twenty years as a drug trafficker Marks had had contact with organisations as diverse as the British spy agency MI6, the IRA, the CIA, the DEA, the Mexican Secret Service and the Mafia. More than 140 identified members of his syndicate and wider network 'disappeared' and escaped arrest. Some were later arrested as they continued their involvement in drug importations and trafficking; some continue their activities to this day and others just faded away, never to be heard of again.

It has been estimated that at his peak Marks was smuggling 10–15 per cent of all cannabis smoked around the world, in consignments of up to 30 tonnes each. The DEA estimated his personal fortune at $200 million, though Marks disputes this, claiming his profits were eaten up in seized importations for which he had to pay, debts owed for drugs delivered, large-scale bribery (he said he paid CIA agents to keep the DEA agents away from his operations), and an extravagant lifestyle.

Released in 1995 after serving less than a third of his sentence, Marks now appears in one-man shows where he talks about his life and times. He describes himself as 'a temporarily unemployed dope smuggler' who smokes 'between twenty and thirty joints' a day.

Arrested in Bangkok around the same time as Marks, Sparrowhawk spent four years in Thai jails before being extradited to the US and sentenced to sixteen years' jail. In 1992 he was deported to the UK—broke. The DEA had seized his £30 million (about A$70 million) drug fortune, which he kept mostly in cash.

After telling police what he knew about Marks and Sparrowhawk, and testifying in court against Marks, Moynihan briefly 'disappeared', then turned up in Manila again. In 1991 he took his fifth wife and a few months later died of a heart attack, aged fifty-five. At the time, he was running a brothel in Manila and had a string of debts. His obituary, according to the *Daily Telegraph Book of Obituaries*, read, 'Lord Tony Moynihan, bongo-drummer, confidence trickster, brothel-keeper, drug-smuggler and police informant'. Some Sydney criminals who knew Moynihan are not convinced he is dead. They say the DEA and the CIA organised his 'death' and that he now works undercover for them: unlikely, yes, but a colourful story, befitting a colourful character.

During 1987, as Australian law enforcement organisations were assisting US and other authorities in the pursuit of Howard Marks, the newly established National Crime Authority was also investigating a number of New South Wales and Victorian criminals living on the Gold Coast. Among them were the Fibber, McLean (on his visits to Australia) and their networks. It has been claimed that the investigation was compromised when corrupt Queensland police tipped off its targets. Eight million dollars were said to have been swiftly withdrawn from a bank and sent out of the country. The investigation collapsed, the cash was never found and the cannabis importations continued.

Hearing that Moynihan had rolled, the Fibber fled the Philippines and returned to Australia for good. Rejoining his colleagues on the Gold Coast–Sunshine Coast strip, he continued to work at the drug trade and anything else that promised a quick profit.

Mick O'Brien had never been a fit man but his health was now failing. Years of heavy drinking and smoking were taking their toll. After Bob Trimbole fled Australia in 1982, O'Brien visited him several times, often with large amounts of cash. But O'Brien's own finances were drying up. He needed a new employer and found one in Victor Thomas Spink.

One of the crime boss Hurley's teenage hoodlum pals, Spink had been jailed and deported from the United Kingdom for shoplifting. Back in Australia in the late 1970s, he was sentenced to three years' jail for a $54,000 mailbag robbery at Port Macquarie, New South Wales. On his release he moved into drugs and became a heavy punter with good inside knowledge. Along with Michael Sayers, Spink featured prominently on the so-called jockey tapes—illegal recordings by New South Wales police that linked jockeys, course callers, bookmakers and organised crime figures, including 'Aussie Bob' Trimbole, to race fixing. When news of the recordings was leaked to the media more than a decade later, the state government was forced to hold an inquiry. According to the Premier, the jockey tapes 'rocked racing in New South Wales and undermined the confidence of punters in the administration of this important industry'.

Spink and another ex-shoplifter, Raymond Dumbrell, became the principal Sydney-based distributors for the Fibber's cannabis importations during the early to mid 1980s. Encouraged by the cash-strapped O'Brien, they started looking for ways to become importers themselves.

Unlike the Fibber, who had his cannabis brought by a mother ship to a vessel waiting about 100 kilometres off the Queensland coast, Spink, Dumbrell and O'Brien planned to bring their shipments into Sydney in a container. Since the Fibber's overseas contacts were going to supply the drug, he and some of his network would be invited to be part of the importation. Michael Hurley would be offered a fee for the use of his mates on the wharves and in Customs and law enforcement to get the drugs through.

In late 1987 or early 1988 around a tonne of cannabis—a relatively small amount by the Fibber's standards—was successfully imported through Sydney. Some months later

O'Brien began hearing rumours that federal law enforcement authorities were sniffing around. In an effort to protect himself, O'Brien approached Bruce Provost, an Australian Federal Police officer on secondment to the National Crime Authority. While speaking generally about drug dealing, O'Brien mentioned a recent cannabis importation but gave no details. He alleged that Trimbole's son Craig was involved in the cannabis trade and was also importing cocaine. In return O'Brien hoped to find out how much law enforcement authorities knew about his own role in the drug trade and whether he was a police target himself. He did not get the information he wanted—Provost was too experienced to fall into that trap—but he went away convinced that if anything were to go wrong he would be safe. (In this O'Brien was partly correct: at the time the police were watching Spinks and Dumbrell, not him.)

Over Christmas 1988 a container of foodstuffs was landed at White Bay in Sydney. A random check by Customs found that it contained more than a tonne of cannabis. Law enforcement authorities headed by the National Crime Authority now took over. The container was watched as it was loaded onto a truck to be taken to a Sydney bond store and held for inspection by Customs. However, police had been tipped off that the drug would be taken from the container at Marrickville before being delivered to the bond store. The police operation did not go as planned. It was soon obvious that the driver was aware of the surveillance. He stopped the truck at Annandale and went to a nearby hotel where he was seen making a telephone call for instructions from his criminal bosses. The container, with the drugs still on board, was delivered to the bond store. Surveillance was maintained for several nights before the National Crime

Authority seized the container and 1.6 tonnes of cannabis. No one was arrested.

Within weeks O'Brien was back talking to Provost—this time about the cannabis seizure. In March O'Brien was charged by the National Crime Authority with possession of a handgun found in his Rosehill home. He fled to Queensland on bail but was arrested on 18 April for his role in the importation and extradited to Sydney. Rolling over, he quickly gave up the others. On 12 August he was placed in the Federal Police Witness Protection Scheme. Four days later the NCA swooped, arresting and charging ten people in connection with the importation. Spink, Dumbrell, the Fibber and Hurley escaped arrest. Six months later O'Brien decided not to give evidence against his colleagues. He did, however, make a number of complaints about the National Crime Authority, claiming he had been lured into the importation by an undercover National Crime Authority informer.

In court, six of the ten charged were discharged while the other four were committed to stand trial. But the Commonwealth Public Prosecutions' Office did not proceed with the charges. In May 1991 O'Brien was discharged from the Witness Protection Scheme. Eight months later he was dead, shot once in his Granville unit with a heavy calibre handgun. The night before his assassination, O'Brien had made several phone calls. One of these was to Ann Marie Presland who, for fifteen years, had been Bob Trimbole's lover.

No one has ever been charged with O'Brien's murder, but according to the coroner there was 'an abundance of suspects'. After all, O'Brien had given up his colleagues in the East Coast Milieu, his partners in the importation and members of the Trimbole family.

*

With O'Brien's inquest behind him, the Fibber was straight back into business, but his luck didn't last. In August 1994 the National Crime Authority, assisted by state and federal police, arrested more than twenty people, including Spink, then fifty-one, and Dumbrell, forty-two, and raided over a hundred homes in Sydney, Brisbane and Melbourne after intercepting a 15-tonne cannabis shipment from Pakistan. Five tonnes was seized on board a boat that had put into Hervey Bay, 250 kilometres north of Brisbane. A further 10 tonnes was found in deep water near the Chesterfield Reef, about 600 kilometres west of New Caledonia. It had been hidden there after a French maritime surveillance aircraft spotted the mother ship. The cannabis was to have been imported to Australia in two further shipments, each of 5 tonnes. It was the fifth multi-tonne importation by the group—each importation is believed to have been at least 5 tonnes. Though the shipment had been obtained on credit, some costs had to be paid up front: the syndicate was more than $1 million out of pocket.

Forty-seven-year-old Hurley had somehow escaped arrest. Another syndicate member, fifty-eight-year-old Vincent Roy 'Roy the Boy' Radovan escaped jail, if not arrest. Radovan was a former professional shoplifter and close business associate of the murdered Michael Sayers. In the early 1980s he was a beneficiary of the prisoner early release scam that involved the then Labor Corrective Services Minister, Rex 'Buckets' Jackson, and Neddy Smith. Radovan was released after serving just sixteen days of a six-month jail sentence, having no doubt passed a few thousand dollars to the minister via Jackson's loyal emissary, Neddy. A few months after being granted bail he died of a heart attack.

When the importation case went to court it was every man for himself. Spink abandoned Dumbrell and most of the others involved in the syndicate. Described in court proceedings as 'the controlling mind of the importation', Spink was sentenced to nine years' jail. His 'very able and active lieutenant', Dumbrell, received a thirteen-year sentence. The court explained that Spink's lighter sentence was due to his early guilty plea, his 'favourable character evidence', his 'significant financial loss in terms of wasted outlay in relation to the criminal venture' (which included the confiscation of assets worth more than $20 million) and finally the fact that he 'rolled over'. The assistance Spink gave authorities was never publicly disclosed. Curiously, the 'dog' tag never appeared to worry him, despite the murder of his former colleague Mick O'Brien.

Spink was allowed weekend release during the last of the six years he spent in jail. On his release in 2002 he moved into the Vaucluse mansion where he lives today. In mid 2008 a Swiss court allowed him to keep US$500,000 he had deposited with Citibank in Zurich under a false name in 1987, plus twenty-one years' interest. Spink claimed the source of the cash was gambling, not drugs.

Victor Spink's ultimate double cross, however, did not involve any of his criminal associates but rather his long-time friend and lawyer Chris Murphy, who lost a 2002 claim against Spink of around $500,000 in unpaid legal bills. Radovan was another member of the syndicate who didn't pay Murphy—Roy the Boy's death cancelled all his debts.

Dumbrell served nine years before being released in late 2003. The Fibber was sentenced to four years' jail but served only one year. He died in 2003 at the age of seventy-nine.

At his funeral he was described as a great bloke, 'generous to a fault, though often with other people's money'. But not even death could keep the Fibber out of trouble. Dumbrell gave evidence in the New South Wales Supreme Court that more than $4 million stashed in a safety deposit box in Amsterdam belonged to the Fibber and should be given to his wife Frances. Dumbrell claimed that although he had opened the box in 1993 using a false passport, had accessed it several times and used it to store false identification documents, including passports for the Fibber and his wife, the cash was rightly the Fibber's and had been legitimately earned. (He didn't say how.) Unfortunately for Dumbrell and the Fibber's wife, the judge didn't believe him and the money was forfeited. No doubt Dumbrell's evidence would have offended the Fibber, who prided himself on never having done an honest day's work in his life.

According to Phil Sparrowhawk, at the time of his arrest in Bangkok he was discussing with McLean a planned importation to Australia of at least 5 tonnes of cannabis. McLean was also arrested after a kilogram of cannabis Sparrowhawk had given him was found in his hotel room. For McLean, it was only a hiccup: he was released after a few days in jail and promptly left Thailand.

He now took full advantage of the opportunity created by Marks's and Sparrowhawk's demise. Having gained access to Marks's Pakistan connections, McLean expanded his own network to the UK and the US. Within a few years it almost rivalled that of Marks in his heyday.

Rival traffickers, however, were outraged that McLean, an outsider, was barging in on their markets and helping himself to their profits. They started feeding information to law enforcement authorities—tip-offs that would eventually bring McLean undone.

In late 1989 two of Stan Smith's longtime Balmain associates, Michael Hurley and Malcolm Field, approached him for help. They wanted to arrange a large cannabis importation but couldn't afford to pay the whole cost up front. Smith arranged for their introduction to McLean. On 11 February 1990 Field flew to the Philippines to meet McLean, who in turn arranged an introduction to local suppliers and to one Ronald Milhench, who would be the middleman. McLean took no further part in the deal. It would prove a wise move.

A former British SAS trooper, Milhench was discharged from the Army in September 1966 and found work in the insurance industry. In February 1974 Milhench was travelling in a car with his wife, Kathleen, when it veered into a lake off a straight stretch of road in Staffordshire, England. Kathleen drowned. Milhench, who was driving, had recently doubled her life insurance, and her death netted him £40,000. Two months later Milhench's business went bust. He was subsequently jailed over a range of offences from illegal firearms possession to fraud. He had forged a letter from the then British Prime Minister, Harold Wilson, on Wilson's personal notepaper, purporting to support a property deal Milhench was trying to arrange. After his release he became involved in drug and people smuggling in various parts of Asia, Australia and New Zealand. In 1983 he made the Philippines his base, and it was there that he came to the attention of McLean.

McLean hired Milhench to find a man named Stuart Perry, who had absconded with $1 million of his money. Perry had form: the Costigan Royal Commission into the activities of the Painters and Dockers Union had identified him as a significant figure. He had been part of the thriving Noosa Heads drug trade in which Snapper Cornwell's partner Barry Bull was prominent. Perry was also a business associate of the Melbourne criminal Ian Carroll, a member of the gang that got away with $6–12 million in the so-called Great Bookie Robbery of 1976. Over the next nine years six members of the gang, including Carroll, were murdered in underworld disputes. At McLean's behest, Milhench pursued Perry all over the world before running him to ground in the Philippines. Perry's body has never been found. Both Howard Marks and Phil Sparrowhawk claim Perry was thrown out of a helicopter.

If Hurley and Field had known all this when McLean introduced them to Milhench in 1990, they might not have been quite so eager to do business with him (see Chapter 9).

In 1995, at the age of sixty-three, McLean returned to Australia and settled in Main Beach, on Queensland's Gold Coast. He immediately set about arranging yet another multi-tonne shipment of cannabis.

To orchestrate the deal he turned, as usual, to Martin Waldemar Jonsson, who lived on the mid-north coast of New South Wales. Jonsson owned the Panamanian company Springfield Corporation, which operated four commercial cargo vessels sailing between Southeast Asia and Australia. Jonsson had for some time been the linchpin of McLean's operation, picking up drug cargoes in Southeast Asia and bringing them to prearranged drop-off points, usually about 100 nautical miles off Australia's coast, where they would be transferred to smaller vessels for landing in Australia. In an intercepted telephone conversation with another member of his syndicate, McLean said of Jonsson: 'This guy is the most important person in my business because he owns the ships and can bring the gear in and take the money out. Without him I'm sunk. I can't get the stuff in and I can't get the money out. Also, it's the way I use to get in and out of the country.'

On 15 November 1995 Jonsson's *Neptune Wind* left the Philippines for a location near Thailand where it took on 11 tonnes of compressed cannabis. It then sailed to a point off Kangaroo Island, about 110 kilometres south-west of Adelaide, where the shipment was unloaded, taken ashore and driven to Melbourne. About 2 tonnes were sold. Over the next few months the remainder was transported to Sydney by campervan in batches of about a tonne. McLean shared the driving.

The final destinations were the suburbs of Balmain and Gladesville, where the van would be parked, the keys left on a rear wheel, and a phone call made to the buyer. He would drive the van to a nearby garage for unloading and return it to a prearranged spot for collection by McLean. The principal Sydney buyer and distributor was Stan the Man. Smith received the drugs on credit and paid McLean $6 million a tonne. In more than twenty years, he had never failed to settle a debt.

By mid 1996 the January importation was complete and the drugs were in the hands of distributors. McLean simply had to wait for the cash to roll in so he could pay his overseas suppliers and the $2 million owed to the Australian end of his importation syndicate, and take his share of the profits. Meanwhile he set about planning his next shipment. He placed an order for 10 tonnes with a longtime Thailand-based middleman, Marc Gustave Bogerd. The cannabis was to be delivered towards the end of the year for shipment to Australia around January 1997.

But trouble was brewing for McLean. His latest importation had attracted the attention of federal police, who placed McLean and several members of his syndicate under intensive electronic and physical surveillance. McLean, however, was confident he knew how to escape detection. As he explained to a syndicate member who later rolled on him: 'I'm going down to South Australia and work out a place for my group to stay when we're down there . . . I want my group to go down there and start to get known by the locals so that they don't look out of place . . . I think down there the coastal surveillance is much more lax than in other places . . . We've done one from there before.'

The plan was to break the final leg of the importation into two stages. In the first stage they would meet the mother ship, unload the cargo onto smaller boats, and take it to Kangaroo Island where it would be stored. The next stage would be a short trip to the mainland aboard the island's car ferry. But the plan fell apart when the cottage where they wanted to store the cargo proved impossible to rent.

Four alternative landing points were scouted. But by now several syndicate members were sure they were being watched. To test his suspicions, McLean arranged a feint. He told his collaborators: 'Go out and stay out late one night and come back and see if you get a challenge . . . 'Cause mate at this stage you've committed no fuckin', they've got no crime been committed . . . We could pull up right now and there's nothing.' Their dummy run went unchallenged, but McLean was worried. 'They [the police] are all over them [the syndicate members in South Australia],' he told other colleagues.

Some were advised to take their cars to the garage for a service and 'have a real good look underneath'. A police bug was found under one syndicate member's car in Adelaide. McLean acted immediately: 'Everything's closed down until Christmas... nothing until after Christmas... I'll just change the job.'

By March 1997 McLean was frustrated. The police attention was holding up the shipment. Not to take delivery of a consignment once ordered would be bad for his reputation. An indignant McLean told his Philippines-based money launderer, John Liuterio, commonly known as John Liu: 'That was perfect what I did last time [January 1996] ... when we go to do it again a year later they've had the money and they've... fucked the whole rort.'

To make matters worse, the January 1996 importation wasn't selling as fast as McLean had anticipated. As late as October 1996, while discussing the new importation, McLean was told by one of his Sydney distributors: 'We are having trouble selling the last lot.' The market was flooded with cannabis both imported by independent groups and produced by Australian-based growers.

Stan Smith also complained about the cannabis glut in Sydney. He urged McLean to cancel the next cannabis shipment and get cocaine instead. There was a cocaine drought and demand was very high, he said. He and Smith had agreed never to traffic in heroin—an agreement they stuck to throughout their careers. But cocaine was different. McLean was unmoved. There would be no cocaine, he said. But he told a syndicate member, 'I just cancelled another lot [the 10 tonnes of cannabis].'

Unfortunately for McLean, it wasn't that simple. The Thai connection, Marc Bogerd, had already taken delivery of the consignment. The importation had to proceed, he said; at best it could be delayed a few months. So an increasingly nervous McLean resumed planning for the shipment. By March, however, he was so concerned about police surveillance that he decided to quit Australia aboard one of Jonsson's cargo vessels and continue organising the operation from overseas. Before he could leave, the police swooped. McLean and several other members of the syndicate were arrested. At least one member escaped, however, skipping Australia with $45 million of McLean's profits.

McLean was hardly penniless, however. Police seized almost $9 million of assets, bought in an attempt to launder his black-market earnings. They included the Bunyip Inn Guesthouse in Berry, south of Sydney, which McLean claimed to have bought for a 'lazy one million', another million in cash found hidden at the inn, and twenty-five thoroughbred horses that had cost McLean around $300,000. Several of the horses were at Riverview, the property at Warwick, Queensland, which McLean had bought for around $350,000 with money laundered between the Philippines and Australia. Around $500,000 in cash and several hundred thousand dollars' worth of gold and jewellery belonging to McLean were seized from Jonsson's home, and more than $5 million in cash, hidden under frozen meat, was found on Jonsson's boat *Neptune Wind*.

Police had recorded McLean telling a syndicate member how Jonsson smuggled money out of Australia and deposited it on his behalf in a Philippines bank:

> The old man [Jonsson] is a very careful bloke. Whenever I give him the money to send out he sorts it all beautifully. He's got a vacuum packing machine that heat seals slabs of money. What he does is he keeps these in his freezer [at home] until a suitable boat comes through to take it away. He's got chains and padlocks on his freezers. His family... thinks he's mean. But they don't know, you see, what is actually happening... He's taken money out for me a couple of times. It works, mate. It's pretty easy really to get the money out and overseas.

The wholesale value of the January 1996 importation was estimated at between $66 million and $77 million. The aborted importation was worth $60 million to $70 million. During discussions with a syndicate member about his difficulties shifting the ten tonnes, McLean made it clear how much the importation was worth to him: 'It's all right, mate, I'm not gunna sweat me guts out and not make this $10 million.' McLean's personal fortune at the time was estimated to be $110 million.

In 1998 the sixty-seven-year-old McLean pleaded guilty to conspiracy to import cannabis and money laundering. He was sentenced to sixteen years' jail but appealed against the severity of the sentence and in 2002 it was revised to twelve years (from the date of his arrest). For a time he was one of the oldest inmates in the New South Wales jail system.

In maximum security McLean kept to himself and expressed horror at the violence he witnessed in jail. Released in 2005, he returned to Melbourne, where he now lives quietly in his late mother's home. He still visits Sydney from time to time and can be found drinking with his old mate Stan Smith in the hotels and clubs of Gladesville and

Balmain—the suburbs where ten years ago tonnes of cannabis were being bought and sold and millions of dollars in cash handed over.

Over more than fifteen years from the late 1970s, the McLean–Smith partnership is believed to have brought around 140 tonnes of cannabis to Australia in some fifteen shipments. In addition, McLean lent a hand to close friends who brought in perhaps another half dozen shipments of between 10 and 15 tonnes each. McLean's syndicate, like that of Howard Marks, was spread across five countries—Australia, the Philippines, Thailand, Germany and the United Kingdom—with a core membership of about fifty people. Outside Australia it remained largely intact—as did most of McLean's $110 million fortune. As with Marks, McLean's years in the drug trade have provided him with generous 'superannuation' benefits. Unlike Marks, however, McLean has chosen not to turn his exploits as a drug trafficker into a theatre piece.

Stan Smith was never charged with any offence relating to McLean's drug importations. He and his wife live on Sydney's lower North Shore, from where they run a number of night clubs and manage property investments in the city's inner suburbs. Smith also spends time working with welfare groups in the former docks area of Woolloomooloo, feeding the poor.

Over the years stories have circulated about Smith's alleged heroin use and McPherson's antagonism towards Smith on that score. Both stories are wrong. Smith never used heroin. His son's addiction and death deeply affected both Smith and his wife. Stan had a life-long hatred of heroin and never sold it. Always a pragmatist, he knew he couldn't stop the heroin trade but he could refuse to be part of it. He could also remind people that they would forfeit his support if they dealt in heroin. The same pragmatism also meant that people could rehabilitate themselves by abandoning the heroin trade to pursue acceptable alternatives—acceptable to Smith, that is.

The stories about Smith's use of heroin began in the late 1970s when police raided his Whale Beach home. Syringes and ampoules of what appeared to be drugs were found. The stories spread and have been repeated over the years. However, the ampoules contained vitamin supplements. Smith was a fitness fanatic and was using the supplements to build stamina and endurance.

Chapter 9

'Mikel' Hurley

From Balmain Boy to head honcho

Michael Hurley, who would at one point be worth $50 million, was born in 1946 in the inner-Sydney suburb of Pyrmont, where he grew up in poverty, one of eight children. He was an indifferent student, repeating third class three times. Leaving school at fourteen, he worked at various jobs before taking a job on the wharves. There he fell in with seasoned thieves whose speciality was shoplifting and the theft of goods from the docks. He began mixing with a group of like-minded men from the Balmain–Glebe area and this small gang—which included Danny Chubb as chief organiser, Malcolm Field and Michael Hurley (who would become drug-trafficking partners during the 1980s and '90s)—became known as the Balmain Boys. During their first few

'MIKEL' HURLEY

years together the Balmain Boys stole large sums in cash from licensed clubs, intercepted postal transfers of cash, and organised large-scale pilfering from Sydney's wharves and Customs bond stores. They usually had inside information and sometimes inside help.

Once they lifted a container full of Scotch whisky. Driving a truck up to the container, they presented false documents claiming ownership and with some help from wharfies who were in the know, drove off with the container. The driver—Danny Chubb—gave a friendly wave to security at the gate as he headed out. For weeks the whisky was served in most of the city's better-known pubs and nightclubs.

In 1977 Hurley was convicted of breaking and entering a Customs bond store at Mascot and stealing almost $1 million worth of Citizen watches. Sentenced to four years' jail, he was out in less than two.

While he was away, Hurley had asked his close friend George Freeman to look after his wife Lena. Freeman obliged—all too eagerly. After a short affair with Freeman, Hurley's wife went to work as a madam in an eastern suburbs massage parlour. Hurley was naturally furious, and brooded heavily on Freeman's treachery. After a day of heavy drinking, Hurley, in a state of alcohol-induced bravado, mouthed off about shooting Freeman. Unknown to Hurley, his wife's stepfather, John 'Jack' Muller was thinking of doing the same thing. On the night of Anzac Day 1979 Freeman was ambushed and shot in the driveway of his Yowie Bay home. He survived a shot in the head but lost the sight of one eye.

Hearing of the attack, Hurley panicked. Who had heard him make his threat a few weeks earlier? Freeman would surely know about it—and if he didn't, he soon would. The terrified Hurley went to ground, but kept sending messages to Freeman: 'It wasn't me, George. Honest, it wasn't.' Hurley was lucky: Freeman had seen the shooter. Asked by police for the name of the shooter, Freeman insisted he didn't know, but it was a lie. While he recuperated he always kept a companion to watch over him (and provide an alibi in case someone was to die suddenly).

Six weeks later Hurley's father-in-law was dead, shot three times in the head at close range in the driveway of his eastern suburbs home. Muller, a standover man, was generally disliked by those who had dealings with him. Interviewed by police, Freeman declined to answer any questions, just as he had declined to answer any questions years earlier over the murder of John Stewart Regan. And the result was the same: no one was ever charged with killing Muller. Police and gangsters alike noted the irony—one crook was dead and two others might have been, all because of a marital bust-up, not some gangland war. As relative calm returned to Sydney's underworld, Hurley came out of hiding and resumed his career in organised crime.

In October 1980 Hurley and others stole a 95-carat, $2 million diamond known as the Golconda d'Or from a locked glass case at Sydney Town Hall, in front of about sixty people. They used the timeworn shoplifters' tactic of having a few people stage a distraction for security, sales staff and onlookers while another in the gang committed the crime. Hurley and his young brother Jeffrey were charged with the theft, but charges were dismissed when witnesses could not tell the brothers apart well enough to identify which of them was the thief.

While Hurley was in jail during the late 1970s for the

Citizen watch and other thefts, the Balmain Boys continued their robberies, but their interests also moved with the times. Drugs became the new focus for some of them, notably Danny Chubb. After Chubb's murder Hurley scaled up his drug dealing. In his book *Neddy*, Smith describes how during 1986–87 he and Murray Riley were 'dealing with the "Friendly Gang" then, selling for them'. The gang was led by Hurley, fellow Balmain Boy Ray Johnson and Glen Flack, Smith's former partner in armed robberies and drug dealing.

The Friendly Gang's most spectacular coup was the New Year's Day 1988 robbery of the National Australia Bank in the Haymarket–Chinatown district. The thieves broke into the bank from an adjacent building and emptied dozens of safety deposit boxes for what is believed to have been a multi-million-dollar haul. The exact value depended on whether the boxes were rented by 'fabulously wealthy Dixon Street traders' or 'merely humble folk who had had bits of jewellery, passports and things of sentimental value in safe-keeping', as reporter Malcolm Brown wrote in the *Sydney Morning Herald* at the time. The Australian Taxation Office obviously took the former view, as they carried out a major investigation into the theft that left some members of the Chinese community claiming that they'd been robbed twice. Hurley later complained to colleagues that there was not as much in the bank as he had been told or as much as everyone thought. Inside information had cost him a lot; getting into the bank was also a costly exercise and physically trying. Even Hurley felt he had been robbed.

In the following two years the Hurley gang stole, in single heists, $1 million worth of cigarettes from Flemington, $400,000 worth of electrical equipment from Botany, $60,000 worth of cigarettes from Ultimo and another

$200,000 worth of cigarettes from Homebush. They were joined on some of these jobs by Malcolm Field, another Balmain Boy, who now lived in France but sometimes returned to Sydney to work with Hurley and his gang.

Field was an experienced thief by the time he was old enough to drive. While on bail for burglary, he embarked on a new career as an international thief and fraudster. Using false passports, he travelled to Thailand, Denmark, the UK, France, Yugoslavia, Canada, the US and Bahrain before he was arrested in Paris in 1974 and briefly jailed for theft. On one of his frequent passing visits to Australia, Field was charged in 1977 with possessing and using false passports. Granted bail, he fled on another false passport. He was next arrested in Stockholm and spent twenty months in a Swedish jail. Back in Australia, an arrest for a minor traffic offence revealed Field's outstanding warrant for passport offences. He was placed on a good-behaviour bond. Unsurprisingly, he obtained another false passport and left Australia.

For the next two years he moved between Singapore, the Philippines and the UK. Returning to Australia in October 1985, he and a partner named Cedric White bought a $150,000 ocean-going yacht and called it *Knot Guilty*. He continued his travels but kept in regular contact with Hurley, whose criminal star was on the rise. By now Chubb was dead and Hurley had parted ways with the McPherson– Freeman alliance. He had already had one alarming run-in with Freeman, and while he paid the old crooks due deference, he did not want another. Being independent would serve Hurley well. While his competitors went to war, he kept his head down and got on with business.

*

As Hurley and Field consolidated their criminal careers, two professional rugby league players took their first steps in organised crime. Leslie Mara, who had played mostly for Balmain, and Ricky Montgomery, a former South Sydney Rabbitoh, found their way into Hurley's gang. Montgomery quickly acquired an extensive criminal record that included convictions for possessing a prohibited weapon, stealing, assault and robbery, and supplying drugs. It was almost inevitable that he would end up in the drug trade: he was a compulsive gambler and always in debt. He had wanted to become a professional shoplifter, but was told he was ten years too late and that drugs were the way to go. Once he saw the profit margins, he needed no further encouragement.

Mara was introduced to crime and to the Hurley gang by Balmain old-timer Ray Johnson, said to have been the explosives man on the 1988 Chinatown bank job. By the mid 1980s Johnson had settled on the New South Wales central coast and was moving into drugs, particularly cocaine, while making extensive property investments in Queensland. In March 1995 he was arrested with Les Mara and Mara's mate Mark Smith, driving a van containing housebreaking implements and 100 stolen tennis racquets. Mara and Smith beat the charges; Johnson fled overseas on bail.

Back in Sydney, Johnson was arrested in February 2001. Police later raided a house where he was staying, and charged him with having a semi-automatic 9-millimetre pistol, a shotgun, a stun gun, a large variety of ammunition, a police identification badge signifying the rank of Inspector, housebreaking implements, a knife and goods stolen or otherwise unlawfully obtained, and resisting police in the execution of their duty. He was jailed until April 2006.

Despite their highly successful thefts, in the 1980s the Hurley gang started wondering if it was worth the effort. The profits from thefts are not always what they seem. The professional thief will usually receive between a third and a fifth of what stolen property is worth. Split between a gang of four, a $1 million property theft could yield as little as $50,000 for each member—a good night's work, perhaps, but for a crew like Hurley's, only enough to fund a couple of months of high living.

Hurley started seeing far greater potential in the drug trade. He dabbled in heroin dealing before 'Stan the Man' Smith told him heroin was not an acceptable commodity. Still, 'We want a slice of action in the dope trade,' Hurley told Smith. The proposed solution would keep a couple of old Balmain Boys laughing for years to come.

Smith arranged for Hurley's mate Field to meet his own partner in the Philippines, Lawrie McLean (see Chapter 8). Field told McLean that he and Hurley wanted several tonnes of cannabis to import and they wanted it in a hurry. They had some cash, but not enough. The deal was to be done mostly on credit. McLean put them in touch with suppliers in Southeast Asia and Ronald Milhench, who would be the go-between and organise the transportation.

Throughout 1990 and 1991 Field made numerous trips to Hong Kong, Singapore, the Philippines and Thailand as planning for the importation progressed. At one point he was arrested trying to board a plane in Sydney with yet another of his many false passports. He was fined $1000, a minor inconvenience. A new false passport was a simple matter and the planning resumed.

To deliver the 12 tonnes of cannabis, Milhench recruited his occasional partner Fred Van Pallandt, half of the 1960s husband-and-wife singing duo Nina and Frederick. After two decades in comfortable retirement in Spain, Van Pallandt divorced Nina and moved to an island resort about 130 kilometres south of Manila, in the Philippines. For some years he had been using his yacht, the *Taiping*, to transport tonnes of cannabis around the world for Milhench, Howard Marks and Phil Sparrowhawk.

In late 1992 Field and Hurley's shipment was loaded on the *Taiping* and taken to a spot off the south coast of New South Wales for collection. It fetched a total of around $80 million. So as not to flood the market, Hurley took charge of organising and coordinating the drugs' sale. Ricky Montgomery was one of the main Sydney sellers, making $15 to $20 million for the gang from the more than 2 tonnes he sold. Field was responsible for handling and managing the gang's profits.

Because much of the operation—including transport—had been conducted on credit, the costs were higher than if the gang had paid cash: they now owed $20 million. As is so often the case in the drug trade, the huge profits only fuelled people's greed. In December 1993 Field paid Milhench half the money: $10 million to be shared with Van Pallandt's transport team. Milhench decided to keep this payment entirely for himself, unaware that Field and Hurley had no intention of paying anyone the second $10 million. When Van Pallandt asked Milhench for his money, Milhench said Field hadn't paid. Van Pallandt flew to Sydney to confront Field; the same day, Field flew to France. Van Pallandt returned to the Philippines a very unhappy man.

Field, Hurley and Milhench knew Van Pallandt was now telling anyone who would listen that he wanted his share of the profits—or else. The 'or else' could be a problem for

Milhench, Hurley and Field. Did it mean Van Pallandt was thinking about giving them up to law enforcement agencies? Or telling underworld contacts these men did not pay their debts? Van Pallandt had made himself their biggest problem.

Six weeks after Van Pallandt returned to the Philippines, he and his partner, Susan Tapon, were dead. On 15 May 1994 the couple had dinner at their beachfront home with a local businessman. A short time after he went home, a motorised dinghy landed on the beach in the dark. The killer walked up to Van Pallandt's home, put a gun to his head and shot him twice. He fired two more shots into Susan's back as she tried to escape. The killer then calmly walked to the dinghy and motored it back to the mainland, about an hour away, where it was found abandoned the following morning.

Van Pallandt's home had not been disturbed. Nothing had been stolen. In a cupboard police found two handguns, some valuables and a sealed envelope. It contained a letter to Susan dated three months before and signed Van Pallandt. In part, the letter read:

> If something happens to me before I get payed [sic], get in touch with [XXX]. Ask his help. Whatever is my share to be sent to my children. My bank is [XXX]. The account number is [XXX]. This account is in the name of [XXX]. No more information is necessary just show this letter to [XXX] and he will contact [XXX] and do the rest. Whatever is in the safebox at [XXX] is for you. Thank you for this and for all the years together.

The hits on Van Pallandt and Tapon had been carried out with military precision. 'The shots through the head indicate it was the work of a professional,' police said. Local police suspected Milhench, who'd been in the British SAS. Milhench, however, had an alibi—or did he?

Two days before the murders, Milhench had flown to Australia to have a hair transplant. Nine days later he returned to the Philippines with new hair—but only part of his time in Australia could be accounted for. Law enforcement authorities believe that as soon as he arrived in Australia Milhench travelled to Darwin and, using a false passport, returned to the Philippines where he carried out the executions. He returned to Australia on the false passport the next day, leaving a week to have his hair transplant before using his real passport to fly home.

Three weeks after the murders, Milhench again flew to Australia. He now wanted the $10 million owed to Van Pallandt for himself. Within days he deposited $1 million in the bank—in used, small-denomination notes. Milhench later told police the money was profits from business ventures in Hong Kong and Manila. A few days later the cash was withdrawn by cheque, Milhench left Australia, and the million dollars 'disappeared' in the international financial system. Tipped off that Milhench was on his way to Europe to look for him, Field returned to Australia. The safest place for him was Sydney, where he had friends and Milhench did not.

Milhench was still looking for Field in December when he was arrested in Hong Kong in possession of a handgun, thirty-four rounds of ammunition and a forged British passport. He told a court that the gun was his daughter's and had been packed accidentally when he had to flee a Florida hurricane. Somehow the gun and ammunition had passed undetected through the airport checks. According to Milhench, when he realised he still had the gun and ammunition he found himself in a quandary. He considered throwing them away, 'but to a gun enthusiast that would be almost sacrilegious'. His reason for having the false passport, he said, was that he had been secretly recruited as a DEA agent by Lord Tony Moynihan. The passport was to enable him to create a false identity so he could infiltrate and expose a group of Filipinos involved in the smuggling of illegal immigrants.

Sentencing Milhench to a total of five years' jail, the judge described him as 'a man who fantasised about living a James Bond type lifestyle'. Milhench served only a year in Hong Kong; he spent the balance of his sentence in Britain. After his release he returned to the Philippines, where he is believed to live in relative luxury. He never did find Field, and the final $10 million instalment was never paid.

For Hurley, the two years since the 12-tonne Milhench–Van Pallandt cannabis shipment had been very profitable —to the tune of several million dollars—and the NCA had missed him entirely when they arrested Spink and Dumbrell. But not everything went his way. In 1993 he was convicted of obtaining money by deception; the following year he was in court over his possession of a fake New Zealand passport, but the charge was dismissed. The same year Hurley was diagnosed with cancer and considered changing his lifestyle. He even contemplated a move to Switzerland. Hurley was, however, a creature of habit and could not change. How could an old Balmain Boy run his crime business from Switzerland? As the saying went, 'If you're not there, you're not in it.' And Hurley wanted—needed—to be in it.

While working on the 1994 cannabis importation, Hurley

and Field also set about hiding the multi-million-dollar profits from their importation two years earlier. Hurley had long been a regular customer of De Costi Seafoods, at the Sydney Fish Markets. When George Costi's longtime partner Harry Demetriou wanted to leave the business, Hurley saw a good investment opportunity and a vehicle for money laundering.

Theo Kiriaszis was a well-known personality around the fish markets and an associate of Hurley and Field. When he heard Costi was looking for a potential partner, Kiriaszis introduced him to a potential investor named John Harte. Over a period of months, Costi and Harte met in Sydney, Singapore, Indonesia and New Zealand to discuss business possibilities. Around April 1994 the pair reached an agreement. Harte would pay $2.5 million for a half share of De Costi Seafoods and make a loan of $2.5 million more as working capital. A year passed before Costi learned that John Harte was Malcolm Field. During this time he also learned that Michael Hurley—'one of my best private customers'—was also 'in some way' involved. Later Hurley would tell Costi, 'half of Malcolm's business is mine.'

Things turned sour for Costi as Field and Hurley demanded a greater return from the business while, unknown to him, using its cash flow to launder illegal money. By now Costi was well aware of Hurley's reputation and had seen Field's violent outbursts when he didn't get his way. During 1996 Costi agreed to buy Field out, but first he had to find the funds. Until then, Hurley had demanded that cash from the business be given straight to him. At various times he would return sums to Costi with orders that the money be deposited in the business and then transferred to Green Island Trade, a Singapore-registered company belonging to Field. At other times Hurley produced large amounts of cash that had not originated from the seafood business but which Costi was asked to look after. Between February 1997 and February 1999 more than $1.2 million was transferred to Green Island Trade. Field's and Hurley's demands on Costi—Hurley even asked for $40,000 a year 'for his kids' schooling'—continued until 2001, when their arrangements were investigated by the New South Wales Crime Commission and it moved to confiscate their assets. Costi co-operated and gave evidence to the commission. Hurley cut his losses and forfeited about $600,000 to the commission, selling the family home to pay the bill. Mara, who was also involved, and Field also forfeited significant assets.

In May 1994 the Wood Royal Commission began its investigations into police corruption, in which Hurley and his gang were likely to feature prominently. This, added to the loss of the Spink–Dumbrell cannabis cargo and Hurley's cancer diagnosis, would have persuaded most men to lie low. But the drug markets demanded an endless supply and Hurley was under pressure from his distributors to come up with more dope.

For a short time the answer seemed to rest with Snapper Cornwell, who thought he had latched onto 2 tonnes of locally grown cannabis. Unfortunately for Cornwell, the deal was a police sting. Now Hurley could do little but bide his time.

The Wood Royal Commission exposed publicly for the first time Hurley's status in the Sydney underworld. Norman Beves, a longtime associate and professional shoplifter, was played intercepted telephone conversations in which he referred to Hurley as the head honcho of organised crime.

The intercepts also showed that not all the Hurley gang's crimes were well planned, and even when they were, they were not always well executed. Beves became the butt of jokes in both the criminal underworld and the media when his public examination revealed how he and a shoplifting colleague, 'Bone-Crusher' Popovic, had been chased from a newsagency in suburban Earlwood with more than $9000 in stolen cash. Bone-Crusher made his escape on foot while Beves ran to the getaway car, which was parked in a nearby car park. As he tried to drive off, pursuers jumped on the car, shouting and abusing Beves and ripping off windscreen wipers, rear-view mirrors and even door handles. In his panic, Beves put the car into reverse and lurched backwards, crashing into the car behind him before he finally managed to speed off. He soon abandoned the car and escaped in a taxi. The hapless Beves's embarrassment continued when it was revealed that the getaway car, a BMW sedan, was leased in his name. One well-known Sydney identity and tough guy who heard the story just shook his head and lamented, 'This is bad for business. How are we supposed to get respect when people hear about things like this?'

Chapter 10

The Coogee Mob

The head honcho's new gang

Hurley's crime group, which by the mid 1990s was known as the Coogee Mob, was one of several—Maroubra's notorious Bra Boys was another—that police referred to collectively as the East Coast Milieu. When the Wood Royal Commission closed its doors in 1997, it was time for the Milieu to get back into big-time drug trading. There were plenty of new opportunities and a big demand to be met. In mid 1999 Michael Hurley and Malcolm Field imported and successfully distributed an estimated 20 kilograms of ecstasy—about 60,000 tablets—from the Netherlands. Around the same time they imported 4 tonnes of cannabis in a shipping container landed at Sydney. Former footballer Ricky Montgomery was, once again, a principal distributor.

THE COOGEE MOB

In November that year Montgomery and fifty-six-year-old George Murchie, a longtime associate, were arrested and charged with supplying a large commercial quantity of cannabis after 750 kilograms of the drug, valued at around $7.5 million, were recovered from a safe house in Maroubra. It was part of the Hurley–Field importation. Murchie was sentenced to seven and a half years' jail and Montgomery to three years' jail on charges of supplying quantities of cannabis, but the major charge, relating to the 750 kilograms, was dropped. Montgomery also forfeited significant assets to the New South Wales Crime Commission. Released a few months later—his jail sentence had been backdated to the time of his arrest—he immediately set about making up for lost time and money.

Murchie was an old mate of Norm Beves and had received a mention during the Wood Royal Commission. In 1990 Beves had called on Murchie to provide a false alibi to the court when Beves was charged with driving while disqualified. But Commissioner Black was more interested in Beves's suggestion, captured on telephone intercepts, that Murchie be approached to provide a false alibi for the bungled robbery of the newsagency at Earlwood in 1996. Murchie was not called before the commission.

Bra Boy Jed Samuel Campbell was arrested with Montgomery and Murchie and, like them, was sentenced to jail. A relatively junior member of the Bra Boys and the Coogee Mob, Campbell grew in stature by keeping his mouth shut, declining an offer to roll over and save himself. Angela Kamper and Charles Miranda, in their book *My Brother's Keeper*, recount how Campbell read the Bible in jail and found Ezekiel 25:17: 'Blessed is he who, in the name of charity and good will, shepherds the weak through the Valley of Darkness, for he is truly his brother's keeper, and the finder of lost children. And, I will strike down upon thee with great vengeance and furious anger those who attempt to poison and destroy my brothers!'

It was this, the authors say, that gave birth to the tattoo 'My Brother's Keeper', worn by Koby Abberton and a core group of the Bra Boys.

The 1999 importation wasn't as profitable as Hurley had hoped—the cannabis was of poor quality—and while it provided the Coogee Mob with some spending money, it badly dented their reputation. The following year Hurley and Field turned their attention to ecstasy. In mid December 2000 Field travelled to Malaysia on a false passport and arranged a shipment of 34 kilograms of the drug, about 100,000 tablets, to be sent to Sydney hidden in computer equipment. The wholesale value of the importation, which was sourced from Southeast Asia, was between $1.5 million and $2.5 million; the street value was estimated at around $7 million.

Field returned to Sydney just before Christmas on a fake British passport. There he met up with Cedric White, his longtime colleague and co-owner of the yacht *Knot Guilty*. Field travelled around Sydney and Queensland under various false identities, attempting to retrieve the computer equipment and the ecstasy. But the drugs had been detected and the consignment was under surveillance. A few weeks later, Field was arrested and charged with importing the ecstasy and possessing and using a false British passport.

A garage in the inner Sydney suburb of Annandale, leased in a false name by Field, was searched. It was found to contain 150 kilograms of cannabis—the last of the 1999 importation—as well as scales for weighing drugs and other property that could be used in packaging drugs. Despite Field's links to the garage, he was not charged.

THE COOGEE MOB

Meanwhile, Snapper Cornwell was planning his next cocaine importation. He was having a lean time by his standards, having spent much of the 1990s in jail. But in 2001, with his latest shipment en route to Australia, Cornwell was heard complaining to one of his partners that 'the Coogee fucking mob' wouldn't sign up to take their share of the importation.

What Cornwell didn't know—and the Coogee Mob were not about to tell him—was that they had several of their own shipments at various stages of importation and were busy distributing other drugs that had already been imported. Meanwhile Hurley, Field and Mara were under pressure from law enforcement authorities. The Crime Commission was pursuing them over their assets and their money laundering through De Costi Seafoods, Field was still trying to get out of jail, and the Mob now had grounds for suspecting they had an informer in their midst.

In mid 2001, while Field was doing a stint in jail (bail having been refused) Hurley and Mara travelled to Ireland on business. Hurley went to the Bank of Ireland and attempted to draw funds from a Jersey account opened by Field six years earlier. The account was in Hurley's name and held US$270,000 dating back to 1993–94, but the bank refused the withdrawal. Police were watching, too.

Travelling by train to Zurich, Switzerland, Hurley and Mara made several unsuccessful attempts to access a safe deposit box held at the UBS Bank, Zurich, in the name of Ronald William Bender. Like the Irish bank account, it had been opened by Field years earlier. Swiss police detained Hurley, searched and interrogated him, and then let him go. The safe deposit box was found to contain only travel documents and an unused British passport with Hurley's photograph, but a false name.

Now sixty-one, Field pleaded guilty in 2002 to possessing and using a false passport and was sentenced to a year in jail. One month later he was found guilty of importing ecstasy and sentenced to thirteen years' jail. Explaining what many considered to be a light sentence, Judge Armitage said he had taken into consideration Field's diagnosed 'acute and severe asthma', which worsened after he was jailed. At the time of sentencing, Field was suffering 'chronic airflow limitation . . . [and] . . . severe adult onset asthma,' the judge said, adding that he also took into account 'that the serving of his sentence will be more arduous than it would have been if he did not suffer from the condition diagnosed by Professor McKenzie, particularly having regard to the very real difficulties he will encounter in avoiding tobacco smoke [in jail]'.

In the two decades before his arrest the previous year, Field had travelled the world using at least fifteen false passports. He had taken more than 200 international flights. He lived in France, even though the French government had barred him in 1975 because of his criminal record. Throughout the 1990s, when not organising drug importations into Australia, he lived in his luxurious multi-million-dollar Villa Carisan in Cannes. During this period Field and Hurley conducted their business through a network of companies and bank accounts in the UK, Ireland, the British Virgin Isles, the Cook Islands, France, the Philippines, Switzerland, Singapore, Malaysia, New Zealand and Australia.

As Field's jail sentence began, Hurley and Mara were convicted of attempting to pervert the course of justice. Hurley had been caught on tape telling his seafood partner George Costi how to answer questions and how to avoid answering when called before the Crime Commission. His message to Costi was clear: don't implicate me. Instead Costi

THE COOGEE MOB

went straight to the police. In July 2002 Hurley was sentenced to two years' jail. He was released in early 2003. In sentencing him the judge took into account Hurley's alcoholism and noted that jail would be 'onerous' for him. Mara followed Hurley to jail but was out after just a few months. Field, who refused to cooperate with the court, was given an indefinite jail sentence for contempt of court—a sentence he is serving concurrently with his thirteen years for importing ecstasy.

Another member of the Coogee Mob was Bondi local Shayne Hatfield, a professional surfer who was also a standover man and drug trafficker. Hatfield met Hurley in the early 1990s when both were attending Alcoholics Anonymous. Their first meetings extended to coffee to discuss their problems with alcohol, but quickly turned to the illegal drug trade. Hatfield was an independent trafficker, though from this time he and Hurley cooperated. Hatfield obtained drugs from Hurley and at other times supplied cocaine to him.

By the late 1990s Hatfield was a distributor for one of Sydney's biggest drug trafficking rings. The ring was controlled by a Colombian woman in her fifties who still lives in Sydney's eastern suburbs. Everyone knows her as Aunty.

Aunty came to Australia in the 1970s and is the face of an Australian-based syndicate that imports and distributes around a tonne of cocaine every eighteen months. Her husband stays in the background, but has the necessary power and influence with Colombian cocaine barons. Aunty and her husband have been operating for around seventeen years. During that time it is estimated that they have carried out at least ten and possibly as many as fourteen importations (totalling between 10 and 14 tonnes of the drug) landing it through various ports around Australia and by using offshore drop-offs to smaller boats that bring the drug ashore. The cocaine is sold in bulk, primarily to networks in Sydney, but it also makes its way to other state capitals.

The retirement of some distributors, the arrest and jailing of others, and the expansion of Hatfield's own network meant that by the early 2000s he was dealing directly with Aunty. In mid 2004 Aunty's syndicate made another successful importation of around one tonne. Hatfield took the opportunity to buy in bulk and soon had 200 kilograms for sale.

One of Hatfield's distributors was a young criminal in his mid twenties who has been given the pseudonym 'Tom' by law-enforcement authorities. Tom has never held a job or had a legitimate income, except for a couple of weeks soon after he left school. He was a cannabis smoker at school and on leaving at seventeen he quickly moved into the drug trade as a supplier. His progression from small-time dealer to large-scale trafficker was swift. He became part of a network run by an outlaw motorcycle gang whose drug operations were centred in Adelaide but spread to most states and territories of Australia.

As well as cannabis, Tom trafficked in ecstasy and cocaine. He carried a gun. Once he kidnapped another dealer who had ripped off his South Australian bikie drug suppliers and put him in a car for delivery to the Adelaide gang. Tom told a court that he never saw the drug dealer again but that he didn't consider it a kidnapping because 'He never asked to get out [of the boot].' Tom was also involved in a shooting where an accomplice fired around thirty shots from an Uzi submachine gun fitted with a silencer into a competitor's premises. Arrested several times, Tom bribed police in the 'tens of thousands of dollars' to reduce or beat the charges and at other times bribed them for information they might have had about his activities or the activities of his associates.

By 2000 Tom was selling 1-kilogram lots of cocaine supplied by Hatfield. Tom regularly travelled overseas on holidays and operated a Swiss bank account. Around mid 2004 he put in $100,000 cash with Hatfield for a share in a 10-kilogram purchase of cocaine from Aunty. They were now partners, but it was Hatfield who gave the orders. Over the next six months Hatfield moved 200 kilograms of Aunty's cocaine, although Tom was confused about the quantity they sold. In an intercepted telephone conversation with Hatfield, Tom suggested it was 300 kilograms.

About a quarter of the cocaine found its way onto the streets of Kings Cross. Large amounts also reached Sydney's west and southwest and the parties and social groups of Sydney's eastern suburbs.

Hatfield and Tom's main distributors included Steven 'Mags' Sevastopoulos and Rodney 'Hooksey' Monk.

According to Tom, Sevastopoulos was a heavy cocaine user and a compulsive gambler, particularly on poker machines. During the second half of 2004 alone, Tom sold him around 75 kilograms of cocaine, which he sold on through his networks to the streets of Kings Cross.

Monk, president of the Sydney chapter of the Bandidos biker gang, was a longtime drug trafficker and go-between. In the last six months of 2004 he brokered the sale by Tom of 25 kilograms of cocaine at $5000 a kilogram. Monk would introduce the buyer to Tom and supervise the exchange of cocaine and cash; his reputation was a guarantee to both buyer and seller. The sales took place in affluent Paddington and Woollahra, not far from Monk's apartment.

Monk's ten to twelve buyers were part of a drug network he had developed on behalf of the Bandidos.

The second half of 2004 was a busy and profitable time for Hatfield and Tom. In a few transactions Tom sold more than 100,000 ecstasy tablets for Hatfield, while six months of daily cocaine sales netted around $30 million cash. Tom paid Aunty a total of $24 million. He estimated that Hatfield made about $4.5 million, while he made 'not too far short of a million dollars'. One day in November, a gleeful Tom spread just over $10 million in cash across a table at Hatfield's mother and stepfather's home and had Hatfield and himself, wearing balaclavas, separately photographed standing behind it. But they wanted more. While selling Aunty's cocaine, the two men plotted with Hurley and Mara to import their own cocaine behind her back. That would make them an extra $100,000 a kilo.

Opportunities for importing and trafficking in drugs, particularly cocaine and ecstasy, were a constant topic of conversation among the East Coast Milieu. Hatfield introduced Hurley and Mara to Sean Michael Coulson, or Sean Peter North as he called himself, and Ian Robert 'Rocky' Chalmers, and soon a new cocaine importation crew had been formed.

Newcastle-born Coulson was an excellent skier and had spent a lot of time in the snowfields. He had enjoyed a bit of dope since his teens and had graduated to 'party drugs', particularly ecstasy and cocaine. He soon realised that dealing was an easy way to support his lifestyle—it certainly beat working.

While still at school Coulson had teamed up with another risk taker, Rocky Chalmers, who was a year younger. He introduced Chalmers to cannabis and later to the party drug set. Chalmers, unlike Coulson, went on (briefly) to a successful banking career and an addiction to cocaine and alcohol. In his late twenties, Coulson left Chalmers and flew off to the European snowfields. A likable character, Coulson made friends easily and was never without a girlfriend. Over the next few years he drifted around the ski resorts, smuggling ecstasy between countries and peddling party drugs wherever he went. It was a good living, but his focus was on having fun and he was taking risks.

In 1996 Coulson was arrested carrying ecstasy into Greece. His fellow courier rolled over and gave him up. He spent the next few years in a Greek jail. Released at the end of 2000, he returned to Sydney and registered for the dole, which was immediately paid to him. He changed his name to Sean Peter North, obtained a new passport in that name and—still collecting unemployment benefits—left Australia in February 2001 to resume his world wanderings.

Coulson remained overseas for the next seven months, visiting Hong Kong and various countries in Europe and South America, making friends and catching up with old jail contacts who could introduce him to cocaine suppliers. A few years later he was picked up on telephone intercepts bragging that he 'went in [to the Greek jail] with a degree in ecstasy and came out with a PhD in cocaine'.

Back in Sydney, Coulson continued to receive the dole for several months before it was cut off. In March 2002 he left Australia for Ecuador and continued his career as a global drifter, skiing at famous resorts and leaving behind a string of disappointed lovers. Drug dealing gave him money but his itinerant lifestyle meant that Coulson never tapped into the higher levels of the trade. His networks were always opportunistic and unstable.

In 2004 Coulson returned to Sydney, broke and no longer with the dole to fall back on. Rejecting the idea of honest work, he set about re-establishing himself in the drug scene.

One of the first people he called was his old mate Rocky Chalmers, by now a director of the Macquarie Bank. After a successful career in Sydney he'd moved to England in the mid 1990s and worked for Bain & Company, Barclays and Bankers Trust. But Chalmers's cocaine habit, hard drinking and gambling were liabilities that far outweighed his benefits to his employers. Returning under a cloud to Sydney, he started losing large amounts of money at the Star City Casino. His alcoholism and cocaine addiction were out of control.

Rehab curtailed the drinking but little else. In 2004, with his marriage over and his life in freefall, Chalmers and Macquarie Bank parted ways. He received a payout believed to be in the vicinity of $1.3 million and a substantial share package. Some of his debts were paid; many were not. His lifestyle ensured that no amount of cash would last long.

Chalmers's split with the bank was still a few months away when Coulson knocked on his door, but he knew it was inevitable. Despite his own problems Chalmers gave his friend a short-term loan of around $70,000. He had a chance to make a quick dollar and would repay the loan within weeks, Coulson told Chalmers. In March, with cash in his pockets, Coulson left Sydney for Argentina. A month later he was back. His South American investment turned a handsome profit: he repaid Chalmers and let it be known he still had cash in his pockets.

Chalmers was impressed. His own debts were mounting and he saw only one way out. Chalmers and Coulson discussed their first cocaine importation. It was to be a modest venture but would get them started on what, for Chalmers at least, was potentially a new career and a solution to all his financial problems. Chalmers knew some dealers because of his own habit. The pair chose one of these dealers—Shayne Hatfield—to distribute their cocaine.

Coulson, laden with cash, left for Argentina, bought a few kilograms of cocaine and had a courier carry the drug back to Sydney. The drug was sold by Hatfield. Each man got his share of the profits.

Chalmers left Macquarie Bank as the importation was under way. At the same time Hatfield took delivery of 200 kilograms of Aunty's cocaine. Over the next few months he and Tom had their work cut out distributing their share of Aunty's importation. Meanwhile Chalmers blew all his money, gambling away up to $100,000 a day. Coulson still had most of his cash from the importation and within a few weeks Chalmers was putting the bite on his mate for a loan.

In early June Coulson lent Chalmers $80,000—about the same amount he had borrowed from him a few months earlier. Unlike Coulson, Chalmers did not repay the loan. Both he and Coulson were now looking at further importations. Bigger profits required larger operations; larger operations meant more detailed planning, more cash to finance them, more people and a higher risk of detection.

Hatfield had a solution. He introduced Coulson and Chalmers to Hurley and Mara. Since his days stealing from wharves and bond stores in the 1970s, Hurley had stayed in touch with people who could get access to secure areas where high-value goods were stored and were willing to sell that access for a price. The network of corruption was loose and informal, with potential new players being regularly introduced as others left. It extended to baggage handlers and security officers at Sydney Airport, where Hurley's associate Murray Riley had been well connected since at least the 1970s. Over the years, Hurley introduced Mara to the network and he became the go-between.

Now it was time for the baggage handlers to make some extra money. There would be a series of cocaine importations, starting with 10 kilograms in October 2004. Coulson would organise the cocaine in South America; Hatfield would finance the operation; Chalmers would make the travel arrangements, organise the transfer of cash overseas and the couriers; and Hurley and Mara would be responsible for bypassing Customs to land the cocaine.

On 2 September Coulson flew to Argentina to wait for the cash and the courier, then made the buy. The courier flew into Sydney with 10 kilograms of cocaine in a briefcase. It was left at the airport and baggage handlers, bypassing Customs, removed it and gave the briefcase to Mara, who passed it to Tom. A decision was made to hold the cocaine for a short time until the last few kilograms of Aunty's cocaine could be sold. Tom buried it in bushland in northern Sydney, where he had successfully hidden drugs and cash for years. The profits from the sale of Aunty's cocaine were buried nearby.

But there was a hitch. Hatfield, Hurley and their team were prepared to wait for their money, but the baggage handlers wouldn't. They had done their job and wanted to be paid. On Hatfield's orders Tom gave $300,000 to Mara. Two days later Coulson returned to Sydney. Mara and Hurley were paid $540,000 for their part. The baggage handlers, happy now, were eager for another run.

A fortnight later a cashed-up Coulson left Sydney. During the next two months he visited Ecuador, Chile, Madrid,

Amsterdam and London before returning to Sydney in late December. In South America Coulson met his contacts and discussed importations for 2005. He also caught up with some old friends in Europe who were in a position to steer him towards ecstasy suppliers—there was a surging demand for ecstasy and several of the East Coast Milieu's recent importations had failed.

Buoyed by their initial success, Hatfield, Tom, Hurley, Mara, Coulson and Chalmers planned to import around 200 kilograms over the next twelve months. As they gloated, however, a number of fellow traffickers were arrested. For a while they worried that some might roll over or that the cocaine seized might lead back to them. But within weeks things returned to normal. Over the next few months Aunty was paid in full—around $24 million in cash—and Tom sold 3 kilograms of their own cocaine.

By mid December Tom decided he'd had enough. He would roll and cut a deal for himself. He telephoned Mark Standen, the Assistant Director of Investigations at the New South Wales Crime Commission. Within days he was working for the commission. He later told a court why he rolled: he was 'tortured emotionally' and had had 'a gutful of my involvement with one particular person [Mara]', he said.

Others associated with Tom claim he rolled because a major cocaine dealer he'd been supplying had been arrested and Tom feared he might roll over. The dealer, Thomas 'Tony' Vincent, had been arrested during a police raid on Vincent's Lady Jane restaurant and nightclub in the city. The sixty-four-year-old's involvement in organised crime went back to Kings Cross during the 1970s and '80s. It was claimed in court that his business, variously described as a restaurant, gentlemen's club, strip joint and sex club, was a front for his crime activities.

Vincent was charged with supplying cocaine, offering to supply cocaine in large commercial quantities and related charges. Two employees of Lady Jane were also charged with supplying cocaine. A fourth person was charged with supplying and possessing cocaine and possessing stolen goods.

At the time of Vincent's arrest, Superintendent Ken McKay of the State Crime Command described him as the leader of a major drug syndicate trafficking large amounts of cocaine in the city centre. McKay called him the patriarch of one of Sydney's biggest crime families.

Hooksey Monk, to whom Tom had sold 25 kilograms of cocaine, was a Bandido 'employee' of the club and over the years Tom himself had sold up to 100 kilograms of cocaine to Vincent—a couple of points Tom left out of his explanation for his rollover. Tom also forgot to mention that on the day Vincent was arrested he had been on his way to the Lady Jane club to deliver a kilogram of cocaine. As he turned the corner into Market Street he saw the police raid in progress. Tom politely asked if he could make his way through the police lines and continued on down the street—carrying a bagful of cocaine.

Twelve months later Vincent and ten others were charged with a $150 million superannuation fraud. The money had been transferred to Greece, Hong Kong and Switzerland. Unfortunately for Vincent and the gang, the fraud was quickly spotted and all but $3 million was recovered.

In February 2007 Vincent was sentenced to ten years' jail for drug supply. A year later he pleaded guilty to a lesser charge relating to the superannuation fraud and was sentenced to three years' jail. He will be at least seventy before he is eligible for parole.

Another reason Tom rolled over could have been that he had sold 3 kilograms of the October importation behind the backs of Hatfield and the others and kept $230,000 for himself. If his partners had found out, Tom would have been a dead man.

In later court proceedings, Tom agreed that the 'principal carrot' he had dangled in front of the Crime Commission was Hurley, Mara and Hatfield. 'Dead right,' he said when asked if he was offering up heads on a plate. This was not the first time Tom had done a deal to get himself out of trouble: he had previously bribed police and traded information about other criminals to beat charges or have evidence against him weakened.

As Tom began working for the Crime Commission—sort of—he kept his day job of drug trafficker. He didn't bother telling the commission that he was still selling cocaine and pocketing the proceeds; that there had been an importation of 10 kilograms about two months earlier and that most of that drug was buried, waiting to be dug up; that Aunty even existed, let alone that she had imported at least 200 kilograms of cocaine in the previous twelve months (in fact it was closer to a tonne); or that he had a couple of million dollars in cash lying around from drug sales.

He did, however, tell the commission about the plans for more importations. The aim was now to arrest Hurley, Mara, Hatfield and the team as they brought up to 30 kilograms of cocaine through the Qantas baggage handling area in February 2005.

Within a fortnight of meeting Standen, Tom left Australia for a month-long skiing holiday in Europe. While overseas he kept in touch with his drug partners and made sure arrangements for the deal were on track. He also kept the commission informed.

Just before the cocaine was due to come in, Tom returned to Sydney and met up with Hatfield. It was time to sell the rest of the October 2004 importation. Tom now told the Crime Commission about the buried 7 kilograms and the plan to sell it. A decision was made to allow the cocaine to run. Tom took police to the bushland hiding place and the cocaine was retrieved. He still neglected to mention the $750,000 buried nearby.

The next day Tom took his own drug presses and glucose powder to the Crime Commission and packaged the cocaine for sale, cutting it with the glucose to increase the amount. He then rang his buyers and the sales began. But this would be their last purchase from Tom. The next time they saw him would be in court, with an indemnified Tom in the witness box giving evidence against them.

Over the next month the cut cocaine went to various buyers in lots ranging from 250 grams to 2 kilograms. Six kilograms were allowed to run to the streets. (In September 2008 the High Court of Australia ruled the authority for Tom to sell the cocaine was invalid. The matter is now back before the courts for legal argument.) One kilogram was recovered and the buyers arrested in Melbourne. Now the second importation was imminent. But even the potential for millions of dollars in profits was not enough to ensure honour among the drug traffickers. Tom had already stolen from Hatfield and was in the process of setting up Hatfield, Hurley, Mara and other colleagues. Now Hatfield was proposing to rip off Hurley and Mara, and Tom was to be his partner.

The plan was simple. Hatfield proposed they fit 'as much cocaine into the case as possible, up to 30 kilograms' although Hurley and Mara would be told there was only 20 kilograms and the baggage handlers would be paid only for that amount. The million dollars they were to make from the extra 10 kilograms would be shared by Hatfield and Tom. Most of the team had been involved in the first importation four months earlier, and the responsibilities of the principals were largely the same. Hurley and Mara would arrange the baggage handlers. Hatfield would manage the finances and, with Chalmers, the couriers. Chalmers would also book the travel and organise for cash to be transferred to Coulson in South America. Coulson would fly there to buy the cocaine. A university student and pro surfing colleague of Hatfield, Ryan Chandler, carried some of the money to Coulson. In a bad error of judgement, Phillip Tyler, a thirty-three-year-old addict, was hired as a courier.

Almost nothing went as planned. The importation had to be delayed because the cash had not arrived. On 22 February, a few days before the deal was to take place in Argentina, an agitated and very angry Coulson was picked up on intercepted telephone calls leaving a message for Chalmers: 'I want my fucking money and I don't give a flying fuck . . . the people I'm talking to, they are angry . . . there's a lot more to lose than just fucking money, isn't there.' Chalmers did not return the call. He spoke to Coulson only after Coulson had left several more messages threatening to have him killed if he did not answer the phone.

Eventually a new date, 15 April, was set, chosen to coincide with the roster of particular baggage handlers at the airport. A frustrated Coulson returned to Australia to finalise arrangements with Hatfield. Late in March, Chandler and Coulson left Sydney to buy the cocaine and put it on the plane. All up, Hatfield arranged for Coulson to be given around $200,000 cash for the cocaine and expenses.

Coulson expected to pay between $5800 and $6400 a kilogram. In Sydney it was expected to fetch around $160,000 a kilogram.

On arriving in South America, Coulson found there would be a further delay. As he told his Sydney connections, because of the previous delays the South American suppliers had sold the cocaine to other buyers. But it was a relatively small transaction for the South American cocaine trade so either Coulson was lying to his connections or he was dealing with small-time suppliers. Chandler emailed Tom that there would be a delay, 'but don't worry it needs a couple more weeks to be OK'. Details were to follow.

A further complication arose when Tyler, the courier, went on a cocaine binge in Argentina and ended up in hospital. On his release the agitated gang immediately ordered him back to Australia.

Hatfield was nervous, but he eventually agreed to Coulson's request for a delay of ten to twenty days. However, this created another problem: the main contact among the baggage handlers was going on holidays, so the importation would have to be pushed back even further, perhaps until mid May.

Now Hurley was nervous. He worried that the baggage handlers were a weak link in the chain and feared that one of them might roll over.

In another twist, a bragging Hatfield showed Hurley and Mara the photograph Tom had taken a few months earlier of him standing behind the $10 million in cocaine money. They joked about sending the photograph to the Crime Commission. Little did they know that Tom was recording their conversations and that the Crime Commission already had a copy.

The importation was finally set for 4 May. Then disaster

struck. Two of the conspirators, Hatfield and Christopher Duck, a Coogee Mob associate who was to be paid $40,000 for storing the cocaine after its arrival in Australia, separately found listening devices hidden in their homes. Hurley and Mara immediately postponed the importation yet again.

Paranoia was now rife. Checks were made with police contacts. Hurley was told there was a rollover to the Crime Commission and given the dog's first name. Hurley, Mara and Hatfield confronted Tom. He denied being the rollover, but Hurley and Mara didn't believe him. The next time Hatfield met Tom, hardly a word was spoken as Hatfield drove to the North Sydney swimming pool. There he told Tom to strip down to his underwear. Hatfield also stripped and they held their meeting in the pool.

Hatfield told Tom that Hurley and Mara had told him that he, Tom, was the informer. Hatfield was suspicious, but not convinced. Still, things were getting a bit too hot. Hatfield and his partner were planning to go overseas but he promised Tom that he would continue to arrange the importation.

Five days later the Crime Commission and state and federal police pounced, raiding homes across Sydney. Over the next few days around twenty members of the Coogee Mob and East Coast Milieu were arrested and charged with cocaine importation and trafficking and money laundering. Hurley and Mara had already left town.

Police dug up $1 million in cash buried in the backyard of Hatfield's parents' house. Home units, houses, a business, cars, bank accounts and cash totalling around $15 million were seized. Around half of Hatfield's $4 million drug profits from 2004 was also taken.

Just eight weeks after his arrest, in a remand cell at Long Bay jail, Hatfield wrote a suicide note and cut his throat. Rushed to hospital, he was held for a week before being returned to jail. His suicide attempt and the evidence of two forensic psychiatrists was enough to convince the judge that Hatfield was mentally unfit to stand trial. He was to be held indefinitely in the prison hospital, subject to periodic assessment by the Mental Health Review Tribunal.

On the run, Hurley had more than just the police to worry about. In the weeks before the police raids two attempts had been made on his life, reportedly by a former colleague of Hurley and Neddy Smith. Worse, despite the removal of a tumour Hurley's cancer was spreading aggressively and required radiotherapy. Rumours spread that he and Mara had been smuggled aboard a cargo ship by some of their wharfie mates and had fled the country. The Philippines and Colombia were the two most likely destinations, associates claimed.

Hurley had in fact driven to north Queensland, where he stayed for eight months, leading a relatively open, if low-key lifestyle, before returning to Sydney in January 2006. A couple of weeks later he was arrested while attempting to negotiate with police over his surrender. He was charged with both importing and supplying cocaine. For a time after his arrest, Hurley and Neddy Smith lay in adjoining beds in the Long Bay jail hospital.

Hurley immediately sought bail on the grounds that he was unable to obtain vital medical treatment in jail. When this was rejected, he tried to have his trial stopped by arguing that his advanced cancer made it impossible for him to sit through the evidence. Estimates of his life expectancy ranged from one year to five, depending on whether the doctor speaking was giving evidence on behalf of Hurley or the prosecution.

During one of Hurley's bail applications, Justice Hoeben observed that while police said Hurley had been a leading crime figure for several decades, 'An unusual feature of the applicant's criminal record is that although he has been charged with many offences between 1962 and the present time (2006), most did not proceed or were withdrawn.' Justice Hoeben was wrong: it wasn't an 'unusual feature'. It was part of a pattern common to many leading crime figures, including Danny Chubb, George Freeman, Lennie McPherson, Stan Smith and Lawrie McLean. Like them, Hurley had a criminal record that didn't nearly do justice to the crimes he'd committed, which were organised, large-scale, netted him and his associates many millions of dollars, and made him one of the true Mr Bigs of the Australian underworld. During these decades Hurley was the subject of around twenty state and federal police operations. Before 2006 he had escaped the net almost every time.

It was not the police who got Hooksey Monk. On 20 April 2006 he was shot in a laneway in little Italy, in East Sydney. Moments before, Monk and a number of other Bandidos had been at the popular Bar Reggio having a farewell drink for Russell Oldham, the former sergeant-at-arms for the Bandidos. Monk had told Oldham he was to be expelled for breaking several club rules and that he could no longer wear the club's colours or ride with the gang. An argument followed and Monk, Oldham and other bikies left the bar for the outside lane. Oldham pulled a gun and fired three shots, hitting Monk twice in the head.

Oldham had a history of violence and was on parole after serving six years of a nine-year sentence for the manslaughter of two men shot dead in a house at Bankstown. He was involved in drug trafficking and was using crystal methamphetamine, or ice. None of this was a problem for the Bandidos, but Oldham had breached one rule that put him beyond the pale: he was having an affair with his female parole officer.

Monk's funeral procession had a guard of more than 150 Bandidos and other outlaw gang members in full colours. At the church, Bandido Arthur Loveday (who had been convicted of murder but who was later pardoned, and who had a long history of violence and drug trafficking) described himself as Monk's protégé and Monk as 'a sensitive New-Age biker'. He called for an end to violence. Loveday had been involved in the September 1984 Milperra massacre that saw seven people, including a fifteen-year-old girl, killed.

In shooting Monk, Oldham had signed his own death warrant. A Bandido told the *Sunday Telegraph*, 'I reckon [Oldham] will probably shoot himself before the police do.' Three weeks later, Oldham walked into the water at Balmoral Beach, on Sydney's north shore, and shot himself in the head.

In November 2006, after eighteen months on the run, Les Mara was arrested at Callala Bay, 200 kilometres south of Sydney and not far from where Lawrie McLean had landed one of his multi-tonne cannabis importations a decade earlier. Mara had been staying at a friend's holiday home in the small township. After fleeing Australia he had spent time in South America and Ireland before returning to settle in Callala. Mara pleaded guilty to the charges against him and was sentenced to twenty years' jail. He will be sixty-seven before he next tastes freedom.

Phillip Tyler pleaded guilty to being a drug mule; his nine-year sentence was reduced on appeal to seven and a half.

Ryan Chandler, the student who had couriered money to South America to pay for cocaine, also pleaded guilty and was sentenced to a non-parole period of six years. Friends described Chandler as 'a non-smoking, non-drinking surfer who didn't stay out late'. In his pro surfing profile Chandler described himself as 'definitely not someone who works 9 to 5' but rather a man who liked 'socialising with great people and prayer/meditation'. His stated 'dislikes' included drugs and alcohol.

Another of those picked up in the swoop on the Hurley mob was Ian Charles Finch, a fifty-year-old former New South Wales detective. In January 2006 he pleaded guilty to trafficking in cocaine and was sentenced to a minimum of three and a half years' jail. Finch was the brother of one of the officers investigating the Hurley crew—a bitter pill for an otherwise jubilant police team.

Rocky Chalmers was found guilty of organising the drug flights and was sentenced to five and half years' jail. This was more than doubled on appeal, to twelve years.

Christopher Duck, who was to warehouse the imported cocaine, was sentenced to eight and a half years' jail.

Despite repeated applications for bail and a permanent stay in proceedings due to his cancer, Hurley was ordered to stand trial in February 2007. He never appeared in court, but not for the reasons he wanted. On 23 January the head honcho died in hospital, aged sixty-one. It was not cancer that killed him but injuries sustained two weeks earlier when he slipped and fell in the shower. He lingered for three days after his family decided to turn off his life support.

An estimated 600 mourners attended Hurley's funeral at St James Catholic Church in Glebe. It was a gathering of the East Coast Milieu, some of the surviving Balmain Boys, old drinking mates, journalists and the odd undercover cop. 'Stan the Man' Smith was there—he even had a tear for his old mate—and so was Ricky Montgomery. But the funeral wasn't all serious. Hurley's partner in crime, Les Mara, who was in jail on the cocaine charges, sent an email that read, 'I'm sorry I can't be there today . . .' Montgomery was only a bit luckier than Mara; the wake would be his last drink for a long time. The next day he joined Mara in jail.

After his release in mid 2001, Montgomery got straight back into the drug trade. This time he was not distributing for Hurley but for other members of the loose-knit Coogee Mob. In 2003 he and his crew were arrested trying to import 30 kilograms of cocaine. Montgomery's first trial resulted in a hung jury, but in 2007 a second jury took just a couple of hours to find him and his crew guilty. Montgomery was sentenced to eighteen years' jail.

After almost a year and a half of claiming to be unfit to stand his trial, Hatfield entered a plea of guilty to his charges and at the time of writing was awaiting sentence.

Of the more than $2 million he handed to the Crime Commission, Tom claimed $760,000 had been earned legitimately from gambling and other sources. He had not had a job other than drug trafficking for more than ten years and he admitted to making almost a million dollars from cocaine sales in the last six months of 2004. But he explained that the profits from drug sales had been used to maintain his lifestyle while his legitimately earned income had been saved. The Crime Commission accepted his story and let him keep the money. It also agreed to pay him $50,000 a year for four

THE COOGEE MOB

years. Tom was also indemnified for his past ten years of crime. He still hasn't done a day's jail.

The Coogee Mob carried on the tradition of ill-health set by other captured underworld figures. Neddy Smith was an alcoholic with Parkinson's disease; Frank Hakim, Louis Bayeh and Lennie McPherson claimed poor memory, mental illness and a variety of other medical conditions. Hurley was an alcoholic with terminal cancer; Les Mara was an alcoholic who claimed only to have become involved in crime out of loyalty to Hurley; Shayne Hatfield was an alcoholic who attempted suicide and self-harm several times, lost his mind and was certified mentally unfit to stand trial. Malcolm Field suffered 'chronic airflow limitation' and severe adult-onset asthma, which a court felt would be worsened by encounters with tobacco smoke in jail. The rollover Tom had attempted suicide and been certified by his doctor as 'suffering from stress-related illness/psychological depression'. Among the Montgomery crew, Montgomery tried unsuccessfully to have himself declared mentally unfit to stand trial, while one of his co-conspirators was a cocaine addict and alcoholic and another, Stephen James, received treatment for depression and other psychiatric problems.

Despite the disruption to the East Coast Milieu caused by the jailing or death of its better-known bosses, the cocaine markets continued to flourish. Temporary interruptions to supply did not affect prices. Aunty remains one of the country's biggest cocaine importers. Ecstasy also remains freely available and stable in price while the relatively new drug ice has exploded on Australian markets.

The use of baggage handlers and airline staff caused public and political outrage at the time of the 2005 arrests, but it should not have. The problem had been identified as far back as the 1970s Woodward Royal Commission and the Nugan Hand–Murray Riley inquiry of the 1980s. The Mr Asia and McCann–Savvas syndicates also used corruption at the point of entry to facilitate their importations. An international flight attendant, Steven James, was arrested and jailed in 1992 in possession of 2 kilograms of cocaine; before that he had used his job with Qantas to make at least two successful importations. A decade and a half later the potential for corruption remained undiminished.

As vulnerabilities in airport security were being publicised through the Coogee Mob trials, another set of embarrassing weaknesses was leaked to the media. Writing in the *Australian* newspaper, journalists Martin Chulov and Jonathan Porter described two Customs investigations that identified shortcomings in security at Sydney Airport, including theft, drug smuggling, criminals screening baggage and serious terrorist risks. Two years later, none of the findings had been acted on.

A three-month review of security at major Australian airports by the former chief of Britain's National Criminal Intelligence Service, Sir John Wheeler, supported the earlier findings, and Prime Minister John Howard immediately pledged $200 million to ensure that security shortcomings were rectified.

Within two years ongoing security failures at Sydney Airport were again exposed. In the lead-up to the APEC meeting in Sydney in 2007, *Daily Telegraph* reporter Justin Vellejo and photographer Toby Zerna demonstrated the vulnerability of the airport to a terrorist attack. Security forces, police and the federal government were embarrassed. The journalists were charged and convicted of trespassing. As the *Telegraph* wrote, this was another case of 'shooting the messenger instead of solving the problem'. The government offered no explanation for its years of inaction.

Chapter 11

Cabramatta

Rise and fall of a heroin capital

In the 1980s three developments dramatically changed the south-western Sydney suburb of Cabramatta. One was a wave of corrupt activity by a few police. The others were the first large-scale movement of heroin into Cabramatta and, tied to it, the emergence of Vietnamese street gangs. A decade later Cabramatta became the centre of a media and political frenzy. Drugs and violence, coupled with criticism of the police in the wake of the Wood Royal Commission, made almost daily headlines. In response, the New South Wales Legislative Council established a Parliamentary Committee into Policing Resources in Cabramatta, controlled by the opposition Liberal–National parties and Independents, to identify what had gone wrong.

For all its deliberations, and despite the often hysterical claims of a few Cabramatta activists, the committee never got to the bottom of the Cabramatta story. Among other things, it concluded: 'The committee does not believe corruption has played any role in the situation which had unfolded. It is a credit to the past and current management of Cabramatta LAC [Local Area Command] that this can be said.'

This view was echoed by the chief Cabramatta whistleblower, former police sergeant Tim Priest, in his book *To Protect and to Serve*, co-written with the academic Richard Basham. 'Clearly, it [Cabramatta] had all the ingredients for corruption,' Priest and Basham wrote. 'But if corruption existed among the rank and file Cabramatta cops, it was certainly well hidden from the likes of Tim Priest. Even the exhaustive investigations of the royal commission had been unable to uncover any corruption in the command.'

But they and the parliamentary committee were both wrong. Even as the royal commission continued to expose corruption elsewhere, a secret police investigation codenamed Medlar—whose existence and results were known to the royal commission—was focusing on police corruption in Cabramatta and neighbouring Fairfield. The investigation was led by Clive Small, then a chief superintendent in the New South Wales Police, one of the authors of this book.

Cabramatta was policed from Fairfield until the late 1980s, when the suburbs were divided. For a time they were policed by separate commands, although criminal investigations continued to operate out of Fairfield. This arrangement continued for a few years, until Cabramatta got its own detective force.

From the early 1980s crime in the Cabramatta–Fairfield area was controlled by a small group of local detectives known as the Rat Pack. Just as former Detective Sergeant Trevor Haken, the Wood Royal Commission's number one rollover, oversaw a system of corruption that included officers more senior than himself, the relatively junior head Rat was the linchpin of a corrupt organisation that embraced experienced police and major organised crime figures.

One police officer who had several run-ins with the Rat describes the latter's hold over other police. As a junior and, for a time, undesignated officer, he 'ran the show, so to speak, and gave directions to myself and other senior police'. Though rumours of the Rat Pack and its activities were widespread and several police had felt its power, the Pack remained untouched and untroubled for years.

The secret police investigation into its activities found that the Rat Pack was involved in drugs and money rip-offs, the theft of money from illegal card games, perverting the course of justice and fabricating evidence. Its members received free meals, alcohol and money from at least one licensed club. The double-cross and triple-cross of police colleagues and criminals was all in a day's work. Between 1988 and 1992 police corruption provided the foundation for Cabramatta's emergence as the heroin capital of Australia.

The Rat joined the police in the mid 1980s. A self-confessed corrupt ex-detective and Wood Royal Commission rollover code-named WS14 testified that corruption was rife at the North West Region Major Crime Squad and elsewhere. He told the secret police investigation of plans by the Rat to rip off Salvatore 'Sammy' Lapa, a well-known local drug dealer and brothel owner with a conviction for bribing

CABRAMATTA

police, on 15 November 1988. Corrupt police had been spying on other corrupt police, trying to work out who was ripping off whom. At the last minute the National Crime Authority unexpectedly arrived on the scene. According to WS14's evidence: '[A] delivery of heroin . . . was supposed to take place in a park in the Cabramatta area and the money was supposed to be exchanged at a house . . . they basically wanted us [the Drug Unit] to go to the park and intercept this load of heroin that was coming. They [the Rat and some other local detectives] were going to go to the other address [where the money was to be handed over].'

WS14 didn't trust the Rat, and 'during the evening we followed [him] . . . to a meeting he had . . . where he met with a fellow named Brown who was Sam Lapa's bodyguard.' (John Anthony Brown, then aged twenty-eight, was a criminal with convictions for drugs, violence, fraud and property offences.) Later that evening WS14 confronted the Rat and his team at the Fairfield Police Station. The Rat admitted that he was going to rip off Lapa, 'but Lapa couldn't . . . get the money and the job ended up being a controlled delivery by the National Crime Authority. The authority arrested Lapa and he was eventually convicted [in 1993] of heroin supply charges and sentenced to fifteen years' jail.'

A few months later, in July 1988, one of the Rat's informants was arrested and charged with being an accessory before the fact to murder. Given bail, the informant was arrested several weeks later for drug offences. The Rat told the Sydney District Court how valuable his informant had been but failed to mention to the presiding judge that the man was already on bail for the accessory to murder charge and for other offences. Oblivious to these facts, the judge granted bail. Not satisfied with deceiving the court, the Rat then proceeded to change the man's bail conditions without telling the court. In effect, the Rat had the informant reporting to him personally and under his control without reference to the courts.

The informant later told police that he had set up around sixty drug users and dealers for the Rat to rip off. In many of these cases the Rat Pack stole both the money—up to $20,000 at a time—and the drugs. Some of the stolen money and drugs were used to pay the informant and other drug dealers who provided information to the Rat Pack. One former drug dealer ripped off by the Rat Pack explained why he had never complained: 'At the time I was mixed up in the heroin business and I was arrested a number of times. I became used to being treated that way by police. I have been loaded, I have had money and drugs stolen from me, and I have been assaulted.' It was easier to be compliant and get on with life than it was to resist, he said. It was just part of the 'costs' of being in the Cabramatta–Fairfield drug trade.

Illegal card games were a favourite target for the Rat Pack. WS14 described how the Pack was involved in 'extorting money from different [illegal] gaming premises . . . [and] . . . loading up people that hadn't paid them'. On one rip-off they stole about $40,000 and on another more than $30,000. A Fairfield criminal who has an extensive criminal record for drug dealing, theft and violence, including one charge of murder, admitted to a corrupt relationship with the Rat, who once told him: 'The best thing about being a cop is you can walk into any gambling den, flash your badge, they run for their lives, 'cause they'll just leaving [sic] the money and we just collect all the money and no one knows anything, they're not ... gonna report it missing because they're doing illegal gambling and we rake in thousands and thousands of dollars.'

At times the rip-offs involved violence. WS14 and another informant central to the investigation described how the Rat's team broke up Victor Reljic's illegal card games a few times, even though he had an 'arrangement' with the Pack over a range of criminal activities. Reljic was a drug dealer and illegal gambling operator. A few years earlier the Rat Pack had arrested him and charged him with supplying heroin and related offences.

In January 1990 the Rat Pack, wearing balaclavas and brandishing pistols, raided Reljic's gambling club at Canley Vale and bashed Reljic and two others. A few months later Reljic went to the Fairfield Detective Office for a 'private meeting' with the Rat, who later claimed Reljic was demanding money to not be investigated. The day after the meeting, WS14 and other members of the now discredited North West Region Major Crime Squad arrested Reljic. Reljic, said WS14, claimed 'that he'd been loaded [with the heroin] and quite frankly I believed he'd been loaded myself from Sipka who'd organised it no doubt'.

Nikola 'Nick' Sipka was a drug trafficker, brothel keeper and gambling den owner. He and Reljic had been partners in a club until they fell out in late 1989. From that moment the pair had an intense and open hatred of one another. They were competitors in both the illegal gambling business and the heroin trade.

Two weeks after his arrest, Reljic was stabbed to death while leaving one of his gambling clubs in the early hours of the morning. David Radlovic, a local drug dealer and close associate of Sipka and the Rat, was charged with Reljic's murder, but the charges were dismissed. A few days after Reljic's murder, WS14 claims to have met Sipka in a Cabramatta café and told him that the detectives who had arrested Reljic over the heroin-related charges weren't happy and felt they had been used. Sipka gave WS14 $2000 'to make them happy'.

The Rat's corruption involved dealings with former Kings Cross Detective Sergeant Trevor Haken, according to one criminal source involved with him. These dealings, the source claimed, involved 'drugs, money, extortion . . . Haken was blackmailing [the Rat], who was complaining to the criminal, 'I'm sick of paying [Haken], I'm fucking sick of paying him.' According to the source, the Rat would meet Haken at a brothel in Kings Cross. He once went with the Rat in a police car to one of these meetings. The Rat left the car and met Haken, who was standing in the doorway of the brothel. The source said that earlier he had seen the Rat count out $3000 in cash; he saw him hand this money to Haken as the two entered the brothel. A short time later the Rat emerged from the brothel and they drove to Fairfield.

Sammy Lapa also used to visit the brothel and is said to have had an arrangement with Haken. The criminal explained the Rat–Haken–Lapa connection: 'He [Lapa] was a good mate of [the Rat]. He came with us one time. He was talking about seeing a bloke called "Harker" or "Harks". That was Haken. See, Lapa was doing all the gear at Cabramatta. I reckon that Haken was supplying drugs to the Rat who was unloading it around Cabramatta.'

Haken denies these claims.

At his peak, the Rat felt so secure that he even threatened

more senior police who got in his way. Two police who arrested the sister of a Rat informant heard that they were going to be set up by having drugs put in their lockers. One of the police was so concerned that he kept checking his 'locker, drawers and briefs after hearing the rumour'. He also let it be known that he had written down his concerns and put the document in a sealed envelope in the hands of his solicitor. Other police were harassed, and one was violently assaulted. The Rat's confidence seems to have been justified. No action was taken against him, and the allegations were not investigated until years later.

The hard-core graft was limited to a relatively small number of local detectives. But a broader culture of corruption had been developing since the 1970s, when the Marconi Club at Bosley Park started providing free meals and alcohol through the club's restaurant as well as paying $50 a week to each detective on the late shift through the club disco for 'security work'. In a more ad-hoc arrangement, uniformed police got free meals and alcohol. One longtime club employee described the arrangement: 'Police could order anything, the waiter would write down the order and give it to the cashier who would bill the club . . . I cannot remember any occasion where they offered to pay.' The employee went on to complain, 'Also, they never left any tips.'

Another employee said, 'This was a payment of $50 each to these detectives and was given to them in an envelope. It was one envelope each and I saw the detectives receive envelopes on a number of occasions. These envelopes were sealed but I often saw them open it and get the cash out . . . I can say that the two detectives who attended the club were on duty and they would be the ones who had the meal and got the payment.'

Club records—to the extent that they were available—supported the cash-gift claims.

About sixty detectives were attached to Fairfield over the period covered by the investigation. Some fifty serving and former detectives were interviewed. Several admitted to receiving free meals and alcohol from the club. A few admitted to accepting $50 when they attended the club disco. Various explanations were offered for the free meals. One officer said: 'As police we are always encouraged to appreciate and understand the differing cultures and ethnic groups with whom we deal... this is how I viewed the meals provided by the Marconi Club, especially after the insult I had allegedly caused by offering to pay.'

The club viewed the arrangements as 'hospitality' that ensured detectives would come in and provide security and, perhaps, that police generally would give the club favoured treatment. The club's 'hospitality' continued for at least three years after the Independent Commission Against Corruption released its report *Investigation into Sutherland Licensing Police* in February 1991. The report stressed 'the importance of police officers not accepting favours from those whose activities they must regulate. More generally, no police officer should receive any benefit which might give rise to the impression that favours might be done in return.'

Neither the ICAC inquiry nor the later Wood Royal Commission had any impact on police activities in Fairfield–Cabramatta. Operation Medlar conservatively estimated that the 'hospitality' extended to detectives and other police by the Marconi Club had been worth more than $50,000 in cash payments and around $100,000 in meals and alcohol.

In 1991 the Police Internal Security Unit, set up a few

years before to target the most serious forms of police corruption, began an inquiry into the Rat Pack and Fairfield detectives. Over the next few years several detectives were forced to resign, but there were serious shortcomings in the internal affairs investigation. They included not interviewing potential witnesses to serious crimes—or the police who were suspected of committing them. Among these crimes were the theft of money from illegal gambling clubs, the payment of bribes to police by criminals, and an attempt by some Fairfield detectives on behalf of a local criminal to set up a brothel in Perth. The detectives claimed to have contacts in Western Australia who could ensure that the brothel was not bothered by local police.

Until about 1990 the Fairfield–Cabramatta drug trade was dominated by criminals of Yugoslav, Romanian and Italian backgrounds. Of these, Sipka and Lapa were among the biggest heroin traffickers. They survived and, for a time, flourished through their unholy alliances with the Rat Pack and some other detectives. Describing the Rat Pack and the Fairfield detective office during those days, royal commission rollover WS14 said, 'Oh, if you're supervising a crime wave, it was run pretty good.'

Although the crime and corruption of the Rat Pack and its associates began to wane, corruption remained a feature of policing in Cabramatta. Lisa Maher, David Dixon, Wendy Swift and Tran Nguyen comment in their 1996 Cabramatta study, *Anh Hai: Young Asian Background People's Perceptions and Experiences of Policing,* that while the Wood Royal Commission said its investigation and exposure of corruption 'was exemplary rather than comprehensive, the results of this study indicate that significant problems escaped the commission's gaze'.

Over three months Maher and her colleagues interviewed 123 Indochinese heroin users. Sixty five per cent claimed that police had stolen money from them, and 55 per cent claimed that police had taken heroin from them during searches at least once, though they had neither been charged nor arrested. Another 18 per cent claimed police had taken their heroin and 'destroyed or disposed' of it on the spot. Describing her experiences in the Cabramatta drug market, an eighteen-year-old Vietnamese–Australian said: 'We're out here trying to support our habit and then they [the police] come and tax us for drugs or take the money. It's just fucking wrong. It's bad enough without them 'cause 5T [gang members] and them stand over us and take stuff off us. Now the police are worser than the 5T.'

Another eighteen-year-old Vietnamese–Australian reported: 'They [the police] took $4000 from my flat—me and my friend. They took it and they share with each other. They don't put on the paper. I go to court—no money, no anything. I ask them in the [police] station, they say, "You bullshitting—no money, mate."'

Another girl described her experience of street justice: 'We were smoking outside the toilets off John Street and they [the police] followed us and then they came from either side—two of them. We threw the gear on the ground and they stood on it and crushed it in the dirt and let us go.'

It would be easy to dismiss these claims as 'just druggie talk', but there is a consistency to them that is hard to ignore.

Vietnamese began moving into Cabramatta in the early 1970s and their numbers swelled with the influx of immigrants and refugees after the end of the Vietnam war. By the 1990s that flood had slowed to a trickle, but the children of some of the 1970s migrants, now teenagers, emerged as street thugs and drug dealers.

The emergence of the street gangs was almost inevitable, and the state and federal governments should have anticipated the problem. Poverty, social isolation and the marginalisation of Vietnamese youth provided ideal conditions for the development of gangs and their culture of criminality. Once established, they steadily became bolder and more violent.

In late 1987 the Melbourne *Age*, under the headline 'Call to probe Vietnamese crime gangs', reported that 'Criminal gangs in the Vietnamese community are increasingly heavily armed, are moving into drugs and gambling, establishing links with Australian crime figures, and becoming involved in standover rackets in their own community.' A later story, 'Police report predicts rise in Asian crime', quoted the then head of the Victoria Police's Asia Division, Detective Sergeant Stephen Pierce, saying: 'Whilst the Vietnamese gangs lack organisation, they pose greater dangers due to their ease of mobility and transient nature, their random selection of targets, their lack of ties and ability to enact extreme violence upon their victims.'

In South Australia Vietnamese gangs were increasingly becoming involved in heroin dealing and extortion, according to that state's then police commissioner, David Hunt. At the same time, police in Western Australia were reporting: 'There is good intelligence and anecdotal evidence that the Vietnamese [criminals] are now emerging as major importers of heroin.' In Queensland a special Asian Task Force was established.

In the mid 1980s, as Barry McCann's heroin syndicate expanded, 'Johnsonny' Bi Dinh became one of its chief distributors (see Chapter 6). From a base in Marrickville he dealt drugs and forged links to the sex trade, gambling and protection networks in the Fairfield–Cabramatta area. Johnsonny was aligned with Nick Sipka and Sammy Lapa and operated on the edges of the Rat Pack's corrupt territory. Johnsonny fed heroin to Cabramatta's Vietnamese youth through pool halls and other hangouts. He kept doing so when George Savvas took over the operation after McCann's murder, and when Savvas was arrested Johnsonny simply found himself a new importer.

One of Johnsonny's key associates was Sarin Long, who became known as 'Mummy'. It was under her umbrella that Vietnamese street gangs began to emerge. Chief among them were the Cowboys, Cats, Chin Choi, Quoc Tien and Nine Bananas. When Johnsonny withdrew from the local heroin trade in the early 1990s, Mummy set up her own importation network using couriers.

Though the subject of several state and federal police investigations, Mummy operated for another decade—until November 2001—when she and her son were arrested in possession of around 300 grams of heroin. She was sentenced to four years' jail. Released two years later, she was soon charged with supplying crystal meth, or ice, and again sentenced to four years. She was released in 2005 and still lives in Cabramatta with her family, several of whom have also served time in jail for heroin offences. Unlike Mummy, Johnsonny avoided arrest at the time by maintaining a low profile—his police record listed only relatively minor convictions. However, he continued his life of organised crime and moved into money laundering for drug and other crime syndicates. On 24 October 2008 Johnsonny was sentenced to three years and eleven months jail in the Sydney District Court on a charge of 'recklessly deal with the proceeds of crime' involving more than a million dollars. Johnsonny was one of eight money launderers described by Nick McKenzie of *The Age* the day after the trial as being 'tiny cogs' in an 'Asian-controlled global criminal network' responsible for the largest recorded drug importations into Australia, and correspondingly huge flows of dirty money out.

It wasn't long before the street gangs began to fight. Several gang members and leaders were murdered. Out of this violence the 5T was born. The gang's name is represented by one large T and four smaller Ts, typically tattooed on the forearm. The name derived from the first letter of the Vietnamese words: Tình (love/sex), Tiền (money), Tội (crime), Tù (jail/prison), and Tự Tử (die/death). The tattoo is said to have first appeared among Vietnamese youth gangs in the Californian juvenile justice system.

The 5T gang's most prominent members were Van Ro Le (a man, but known as Madonna) and Dung Hing Le, who joined in their late teens, and Tri Minh Tran who was four years younger. All three were charged in August 1989 with the fatal stabbing of twenty-seven-year-old Phu Tuan Nguyen in Cabramatta. The motive is not known. Madonna and Le were sentenced to jail for manslaughter. Tran was acquitted. A few years earlier he had been arrested with a sawn-off shotgun. He gained hero status in the 5T and the respect of other gangs. Tran now became the gang's undisputed leader until Madonna rejoined the 5T on his release from jail.

The gang grew from around eleven core members and fourteen associates in 1992 to around forty core members and 100 associates at its peak in early 1995. Members lived a communal lifestyle, with up to fifteen members sharing a house. The proceeds of crime were shared and used to live on. Feared and well organised, the 5T under Tran operated with impunity, dealing drugs, robbing illegal casinos and extorting money from local Asian businesspeople. In 1994 a number of these business victims banded together and reported the extortions to police. Several 5T gang members were arrested and charged. A few were convicted, but many of the charges were dropped when witnesses failed to attend court and others declined to give evidence.

More than any other gang or individual, the 5T was responsible for expanding the drug trade in Cabramatta and establishing a flourishing drug market on the streets. Supplied by local importers, they sold high-quality and cheap heroin to street dealers, cutting out middlemen to reduce costs and improving the efficiency of the loose-knit distribution networks. They attracted both users and dealers from far and wide.

The train to Cabramatta was known as the 'smack express' by drug users, dealers and police alike. By 1997 a police intelligence assessment estimated that at least 1000 people arrived at Cabramatta station before lunchtime each day to buy heroin. 'Drug transactions can be realistically measured in the thousands each day. At any time there can be in excess of 100 individual dealers on the street, operating in groups of five to ten and ranging in age from fourteen to fifty (although the usual range is fourteen to twenty-five), both male and female.'

By the late 1980s Phuong Canh Ngo was making his name as a power broker in Cabramatta. Ngo arrived in Australia in 1981 as a refugee in his mid twenties and settled in Queensland before moving south a couple of years later. Once in Cabramatta, Ngo went into various businesses and became active in local politics. In 1987 he became the first Vietnamese-born Australian to enter local government when he won a seat as an Independent on Fairfield City Council. He became deputy mayor in 1989, a position he held for a year. In 1990 the then Liberal Premier Nick Greiner appointed Ngo as an Ethnic Affairs Commissioner.

But political opponents were already raising questions about the source of Ngo's wealth. During the late 1980s Ngo had begun to form connections with the Liberal government. It was alleged in the New South Wales Parliament in 1998 that senior members of the government had helped Ngo make contact with business leaders who in turn became involved in the development of the Mekong Club. Under Ngo the club became more than a place where the local Vietnamese community could socialise. It became a personal power base which he used for illegal gambling and to launder money.

In 1991 Ngo became involved in a bitter struggle for the state seat of Cabramatta, standing with three other independents against the incumbent, John Newman. Again, it was alleged that senior members of the government played a significant role in Ngo's campaign. 'I have a good photo of Mr Greiner and Mr Ngo walking side by side,' Andrew Refshauge told the Parliament, adding that Liberal MP John Hannaford 'did the scrutineering for Mr Ngo'. Ngo's preferences in the election were directed to the officially endorsed Liberal candidate.

While John Newman won the seat, the Labor Party realised the potential threat posed by Ngo and saw his potential value as a way to attract the still largely untapped Vietnamese vote. After the 1991 election it set about actively courting Ngo. He soon counted the former ALP federal minister Graham Richardson and state head office heavy John Della Bosca among his network of connections. They were well aware of Ngo's political ambitions. Ngo formally joined the Labor Party in 1993 and revived an ALP branch at Canley Vale. His fortunes continued to rise when the Labor government appointed him to the South West Area Health Service Board. Refshauge's warnings about Ngo no longer seemed to be a concern to the party, and Refshauge himself appeared to have lost interest in attacking Ngo or his activities.

The ALP clearly signalled the value it attached to Ngo and the Vietnamese votes he could attract in 1993, when the Mekong Club was officially opened by the then Governor-General Bill Hayden, a former Opposition Leader and senior minister in two Labor governments. The state party hierarchy soon began considering a political career for Ngo as an opponent to the Liberals' Helen Sham-Ho. Ironically, it was Sham-Ho who, six years later, led the Upper House Parliamentary Inquiry into Policing in Cabramatta, which was to cause major embarrassment to both the government and police.

On 5 September 1994 Ngo and Della Bosca discussed political and union matters over lunch. At about 9.30 that evening John Newman was assassinated in the driveway of his Cabramatta home. He was returning from an ALP branch meeting. As his fiancée looked on, the gunman stepped out of the shadows and shot Newman twice in the chest. There is no suggestion that anything Della Bosca said triggered the shooting.

CABRAMATTA

Newman had been a vocal activist against local street gangs and drug dealers and had strongly opposed what he saw as Ngo's Vietnamisation of the suburb. He had especially criticised the opening of the Mekong Club. His murder carried echoes of the state's first political assassination, the 1977 murder of Donald Mackay in Griffith, and it put Cabramatta under intense police and political scrutiny.

The murders had several aspects in common. Both occurred in recognised drug centres: Cabramatta was by now recognised as the country's heroin capital and Griffith at the time of the Mackay murder had been its cannabis growing capital. Both murders involved the Labor Party. Ngo was power hungry and had political ambitions, and saw the party as the vehicle for achieving them, while Mackay was a Liberal Party member actively campaigning against the drug industry and its connections with Labor.

The assassination made Newman a symbol of the fight against crime gangs and the drug trade. The Labor Party's Reba Meagher won the ensuing by-election in a landslide. A year later, Ngo headed the ALP ticket for Fairfield Council and was elected.

Yet Newman was a flawed character whose violent temper had made him many enemies. After his murder, Cabramatta Police Inspector Alan Leek said of Newman, 'Anyone who didn't do John's bidding became his enemy. I likened him to one of those American mayors. He was trying to run the whole town.' At the coronial inquest, Fairfield councillor Nick Lalich told police that Newman 'had hundreds of enemies' (the police thought he had thousands). ICAC investigated Newman and found him to have been 'imprudent' but not corrupt. The investigation into his murder found irregularities in Newman's finances and significant unexplained income. His assets declaration as a politician was, to say the least, misleading.

In 1991 Newman had been associated with a woman with significant underworld connections. On at least one occasion Newman took her to a Parliamentary function as his companion. Among her underworld friends was Nick Sipka and his crew. Another was Redento Grissillo, named by the Queensland Criminal Justice Commission as being involved in illegal gambling. He was a business partner of Les Jones, whose network included Sammy Lapa and who, in 1991, was convicted of conspiring with Frank Hakim to bribe a police officer. Newman had also been a close associate of Benito Esposito, who in 1980 had been charged with possessing $350,000 in forged American bank notes; Newman wrote Esposito a glowing reference that helped him get a bond. A year earlier Newman had been the guest of honour at Esposito's wedding and delivered the toast: 'I can't think of a more significant event in my lifetime than coming along tonight to celebrate Benny's wedding.' In 1986 Esposito was sentenced to ten years' jail for conspiring to cultivate 6000 marijuana plants valued at $6 million. Newman also had at least one meeting with heroin trafficker and Sydney gangster Tony Eustace before Eustace was murdered in 1985.

Another of Newman's underworld associates was Zare 'David' Kirikian. A trafficker and middleman based in Cabramatta–Fairfield, Kirikian supplied cannabis, cocaine and heroin and was connected to local Vietnamese traffickers. At one point his network extended to the Gold Coast and Perth. In November 1990 Kirikian and others were arrested by the National Crime Authority and charged over the supply of cannabis and cocaine. At trial he was found guilty of supplying cannabis and sentenced to four years' jail. In late 2000, in a joint operation involving the National Crime Authority, the Queensland Police and the Queensland Crime Commission, Kirikian and others were arrested and charged with supplying heroin. Kirikian pleaded guilty and was sentenced to six years' jail.

In March 1998 the inquest into the Newman assassination was terminated when Phuong Ngo and two former Mekong Club employees, Quang Dao and another, identified by the courts only as TVT, were arrested and charged with his murder. Two years later, in June 1999, their trial was aborted when the trial judge ruled that the tactics of the prosecutor amounted to misconduct.

Some months after their aborted trial Ngo and Dao were charged with demanding money with menaces and stabbing a local businessman in March 1994. The charge arose from a dispute between the businessman and Ngo. It was alleged that Ngo asked the businessman to come to his office at the Mekong Club, where he demanded $30,000. When he refused to pay, Dao allegedly held him down while Ngo stabbed him through the hand. The businessman did not report the matter to the police but did report it to his doctor and to his solicitor.

In late 1999 TVT rolled over in a deal with the New South Wales Crime Commission. He nominated David Dinh, a former 5T gang member, as the man who had shot Newman. In May 2000 Ngo and Dao faced their second trial but it ended with a hung jury. The third trial began in mid 2001. This time the alleged shooter, Dinh, stood beside them in the dock. After a three-month trial Ngo, the mastermind of the assassination, was convicted of murder by a 'joint enterprise'. Dinh and Dao were acquitted. It was a controversial result. A month later Ngo was sentenced to life imprisonment, never to be released. Ngo and Dao were subsequently acquitted at trial of extortion and wounding charges over the stabbing of the businessman. By now Ngo was broke.

At a Supreme Court bail application before the first murder trial a group of almost 300 local Vietnamese community leaders delivered a petition demanding that Ngo not be granted bail. They knew the community would be safer with Ngo in jail. So far as it is known, this is the only occasion such a petition has been presented to a court in New South Wales.

The murder of Newman on 5 September was not Ngo's first attempt on his life. During the trials of Ngo and others the prosecution alleged that in the six months before the killing, Ngo made or planned five other attempts on Newman's life. In March Ngo had asked an associate to obtain a weapon and hire a hitman. A man identified by the courts as CC was approached but declined the contract: Newman was too big a target. Around the same time Ngo asked others associated with the club to obtain weapons. He amassed three handguns and a sawn-off rifle. Hitmen were hired. Over the next few months two hitmen, whose names have been suppressed by the courts, made three attempts to kill Newman. One was at the Thien Hong Restaurant at Cabramatta, another was at the Greyhound Club at Yagoona, and the third was outside Newman's house. On this last occasion the hitmen accidentally fired the gun while playing with it in the car, putting a bullet hole in the floor. In a panic and almost deafened, they fled the scene. New hitmen were hired and plans were made for the killing, but they were never carried out. While most of the names were suppressed

CABRAMATTA

by the court, those hired ranged from a heroin addict and low-level dealer to Mekong Club employees, gamblers, security guards and a local gang member, Tri Minh Tran.

Tran was the leader of the 5T and had been working as a strong-arm man for Ngo, who had offered him $10,000 to murder 'someone', without naming the victim. On learning it was John Newman, Tran rejected the contract as being too risky. He feared reprisals from the police and rival crime figures. A year after turning the contract down, Tran was killed in a gang feud. Ngo delivered the eulogy at his funeral.

Even in jail Ngo stirred controversy. In 2002 it was alleged that he was influencing Fairfield Council decisions from his jail cell. ICAC found this to be untrue. The next year jail officials identified Ngo as the leader of a Lithgow jail gang called W2K, or Willing to Kill, when they intercepted a coded message. The head of Corrective Services, Commissioner Ron Woodham, declared Ngo to be 'one of the most dangerous prisoners we have'. Ngo was alleged to have arranged for visitors to pay between $300 and $400 into the credit accounts of four prisoners to provide protection and buy favours. 'That's a lot of money to a prisoner,' Woodham said. Fearing an escape from the jail, authorities transferred Ngo and the four other prisoners to five different maximum-security prisons. Ngo was sent to Goulburn Super Max jail, where he is serving his sentence under twenty-four-hour surveillance and isolated from other prisoners.

Many extravagant claims have been made about Ngo, focused on the 5T gang, which some believe he controlled, and on more shadowy networks of organised crime that have never been identified. Several years after Ngo was jailed for the murder of Newman, Richard Basham wrote: 'Ngo will continue to exert a chilling presence over his fellow

Asian Australians.' Basham never explained the basis for his assertion, what the 'chilling presence' was, or how it was being exerted.

In fact there is no evidence of Ngo's 'chilling presence'. Deputy Commissioner Nick Kaldas, who as a detective superintendent led the investigation into Newman's murder, debunks the myth of Ngo's continuing power and influence with local street gangs and the underworld. He says that before his arrest Ngo certainly flaunted his connections with politicians and business people and used the 5T on a 'contract basis' as 'muscle' to coerce people into making him loans and then deferring repayment. But it was a loose form of control, and there was no evidence that Ngo was involved in either importing or trafficking in drugs.

When sentencing Ngo, Justice Dunford pointed to the contradictions in his character: 'There was a large amount of evidence . . . concerning the prisoner's work for the community and I am satisfied that he worked very hard . . . building bridges between Asian and other groups . . . and assisting constituents with their problems . . . he fostered an Asian language and culture school at weekends . . . He was also instrumental . . . in having the Fairfield Drug Intervention Centre established.' He went on to observe that Ngo's downfall had been brought about by his 'naked political ambition'. However, it is perhaps Ngo who best explained the contradictions. Speaking in 1994 he said, 'I see myself just like a prostitute. I don't care who I sleep with as long as I achieve things for the community that I represent.' Ngo did not specify which community he was referring to.

At the time of going to press, a judicial inquiry was reviewing the evidence that led to Ngo's conviction.

*

CABRAMATTA

The former 5T gang leader Madonna was released from jail in 1995. Rejoining the gang, he unsuccessfully challenged Tri Minh Tran, who was not about to surrender the leadership. Rebuffed, Madonna broke away from the 5T, taking several of its members with him. At first the new gang was known as Members of the Brotherhood (MOB) and later as Madonna's MOB. It had a core group of about twenty members and a larger number of associates. A major difference between the gangs was that Madonna's MOB allowed anyone with the right 'qualifications' to join, whereas the 5T restricted membership to those of Vietnamese origin. Madonna's MOB moved out of Cabramatta and based itself in Campbelltown. Its activities centred on the Sydney CBD and Bankstown. The gang was particularly violent and was involved in a series of shootings in Sydney as it attempted to control new territory. Madonna told several gang members that his plan was to increase gang activities and violence in the Sydney area in an attempt to draw police away from Cabramatta, leaving that suburb exposed to a quick and violent takeover by his gang.

The departure of Madonna and the ongoing fights with Madonna's MOB significantly weakened the 5T's influence on Cabramatta's heroin trade. New gangs emerged to challenge the 5T. There were several shootings and murders. In August 1995 the 5T lost its leader when Tran, then twenty, and nineteen-year-old Hao Thanh Nguyen were shot dead by rivals in a 5T-controlled flat in Cabramatta. Another member of the 5T, twenty-year-old Hieu Dinh Trin, was wounded. Each was shot at close range with two .32-calibre pistols. No one was charged, but the shootings occurred shortly after the 5T had bashed Madonna. A 1995 Cabramatta police assessment concluded that Madonna 'has now placed himself in a position that [sic] he is forced to dominate the gang membership or be killed by rival members bent on revenge for the double murders of Tran and Nguyen'.

Tran's murder, the shooting of several other 5T members, internal conflicts, inter-gang violence, and police arrests saw the 5T splinter and start to decline. A seventeen-year-old Cabramatta heroin user, Duc (not his real name), was quoted describing the drug market and the post-Tran change in the 5T in Lisa Maher and David Dixon's study, *Running the Risks: Heroin, Health and Harm in South West Sydney*. According to Duc, '5T is always coming around [taxing] because since the leader got shot they are starting to use and they need the money too so they take it from us. There is also more dealers now—too many dealers—and they all competing [with] each other, so that makes it harder to sell too.'

An outbreak of gang violence in late 1995 caused the police executive to shift at least some of its attention from the Wood Royal Commission to the streets of Cabramatta. The result was the formation of a local gang squad. Initially its operational priority was the 5T but as the gang splintered, the squad's attention extended to the new gangs. The next year, closed-circuit television cameras were installed around Cabramatta. Despite these innovations, the then District Commander, Paul McKinnon (who went on to run security during the Sydney Olympics), told the Cabramatta command: 'We have limited fallback options, mainly for staffing reasons... our detective strength is depleted by serious internal issues and the Police Royal Commission fallout.'

Once again the Cabramatta heroin markets adapted to ensure their survival. Dealers moved their business away from the railway station and stopped open street dealing; instead they began using mobile phones to arrange deals. A new system of drive-by deals evolved. Dealers became moving targets, reducing the risk of street rip-offs by rival traders as well as arrest by police.

In late 1997 the 5T once again splintered when twenty-one-year-old 'David' Van Dung Nguyen and twenty-two-year-old Khanh Hoang Nguyen (not related) broke away and formed their own gangs, known simply as Khanh's gang and David's gang. Khanh's gang had around twenty-five Vietnamese youths as members. It was involved in local drug dealing, though its networks extended to South Australia and Victoria. Violence was limited to defence of its territories and disputed drug and gambling transactions. David's gang, with about ten members, was smaller but more violent. They were the aggressors in a series of savage encounters with Khanh's gang during 1999 and 2000.

After a restructure of police management in 1997 as a result of the Wood Royal Commission, the gang squad at Cabramatta was closed down and a new squad, the Patrol Intelligence Team (or PIT team), was formed. At the same time a separate operation, Puccini, began with police from surrounding areas brought in to provide a high-visibility presence in the central business district and nearby railway station. In late 1997 the PIT team was closed down, largely because of staffing shortages. Nevertheless, Puccini was having some impact. An eighteen-year-old Vietnamese–Australian described the effects to the authors of the *Anh Hai* study: 'Now the customers are less. They are scared to come to Cabramatta because now there are too many police and they are stopping them at the station before they even get out and searching them.' On a less positive note, she continued, 'There are more dealers now but less customer it seems.' In other words, the operation was targeting the users, but the dealers were having a free run. Within months of the PIT team being disbanded, political pressure forced police to reinstate it.

On New Year's Eve 1998 Madonna shot and wounded twenty-four-year-old Tien Nguyen, a member of the 5T, in a gang dispute. Later, armed with a gun, he went to the Mekong Club where he had an argument with Phuong Ngo. Several patrons of the club saw Madonna slap Ngo across the face. It was an egregious insult to an important man. At the time Ngo was the principal suspect for John Newman's murder. A week later Madonna was bashed by members of the 5T in a Fairfield café. Within a few months he was dead, shot outside a hotel at Bankstown. Quoc Toan Nguyen, a twenty-five-year-old member of the 5T, was charged with the murder but acquitted. Around the same time, Ngo himself was arrested and charged with murdering Newman.

Continuing violence in the local drug trade saw a review of Puccini in 2000. Significant shortcomings were found in the areas of covert operations and drug investigations. Drug transactions were now occurring in home units while police patrolled the streets of the shopping area. The morale of Puccini officers was low, and though it was 'officially' under the command of Cabramatta there was little consultation and coordination with local police. A more locally managed and directed Puccini was proposed with a new focus: 'street dealers, fortified locations, and suppliers who supply the street dealers'. But police commitments to the Olympic Games meant that, once again, Cabramatta was a low priority. Instead of making the necessary changes, the operation was wound down and effectively closed during 2000.

CABRAMATTA

Tit-for-tat violence continued between the four gangs led by Khanh Nguyen, David Nguyen, Hoan Ha La and Khanh Quang Do. Hoan Ha La's gang, known as La's gang, was a recent arrival on the Cabramatta heroin scene. Its emergence in the late 1990s prompted the final break-up of the already severely weakened 5T. David's gang and Khanh's gang also lost members to La's gang, giving it a core membership of about fifteen members.

Khanh Quang Do was leader of a Vietnamese street gang known as the Bankstown Boys. They were viewed as intruders in Cabramatta and were in a state of constant conflict with the local gangs. Rival gang members were kidnapped or shot; home units were sprayed with gunfire. From mid 1999 to mid 2001 there were roughly seventy gang-related incidents of violence across south-west Sydney, peaking with around twenty shootings in Cabramatta in the first months of 2000.

If Sarin Long, or Mummy, had released the heroin scourge on Cabramatta, she found a tenacious rival in Duong Van Ia, known as Van Duong. His family arrived from Vietnam with nothing in the mid 1970s and opened a business barbecuing pork for the restaurant trade. A compulsive gambler, Van Duong used his contacts to befriend Duncan Lam Sak-cheung (commonly known as Duncan Lam and nicknamed 'Big Nose Cheung'), a longtime heroin trafficker and trusted distributor for Chinese triads operating out of Sydney's Chinatown. Van Duong approached the heroin business the same way he approached his gambling— taking calculated risks aimed at huge wins.

In 1993 Van Duong was arrested and charged with supplying and possessing almost 250 grams of heroin, but it didn't slow him. While under committal for trial as a heroin trafficker, he was among Sydney Harbour Casino's top six high rollers. In just six months during 1996 his turnover at the casino was $94 million; in his peak month it was $24 million. Van Duong had a cheque account at the casino that enabled him to withdraw up to $750,000 on any night.

In July 1997 criminals kidnapped Van Duong's pregnant mistress, Miss Kim, a nightclub dancer who lived in a palatial home he'd bought for her. The kidnappers demanded $200,000 ransom. Van Duong turned to the police for help. He collected the ransom in cash and met the kidnappers. As the exchange was about to take place, police arrested the kidnappers. Three months later New South Wales Police Commissioner Peter Ryan banned Van Duong and more than twenty other criminals from the casino. It was a minor inconvenience to Van Duong, who simply flew to the Crown Casino in Melbourne or to Jupiters Casino on the Gold Coast, where he was welcomed with open arms to the high-rollers' facilities.

By the mid 1990s Van Duong was the sole supplier of heroin to the 5T and the major supplier for several other gangs. His buyers called him Brother Number Six. By now Sarin Long had become a distant second to Van Duong in terms of importance, and other suppliers didn't count. The streets of Cabramatta were awash with heroin and the violence increased as the 5T sought to take control.

Van Duong employed some of his seven brothers to distribute heroin. In February 1997 one brother, Duong Quoc Dung, was sentenced to eight and a half years' jail after pleading guilty to possessing almost 4 kilograms of pure heroin. In March the same year another brother, Van Duong Thoai, was charged with supplying heroin and later sentenced to jail. In 1998 Van Duong was arrested and charged after a police sting in which Van Duong was caught supplying $75,000 worth of heroin. Van Duong pleaded guilty and was sentenced to eight years' jail. In the same year, the 1993 possession charge against Van Duong was dropped and he was found not guilty at trial on the heroin supply charge. Millions of dollars from Van Duong's heroin deals are believed to have been laundered through accounts in Hong Kong and Vietnam, with substantial amounts invested in real estate in Vietnam.

Van Duong's heroin supplier, Duncan Lam, came to Australia from Hong Kong on a visitor's visa in 1976 and became a citizen five years later. Lam held various jobs including caterer, waiter, director and restaurateur, but first and foremost he was a heroin trafficker, and he soon established contacts with the 14K and Wo Sing Wo triads in Sydney and Hong Kong, receiving his share of heroin importations for distribution once they were landed in Sydney. Over a fifteen-year period as the middleman between the triads and Australian traffickers, Lam is believed to have moved about 500 kilograms of heroin, worth about $500 million on the streets.

Lam narrowly escaped arrest several times over the years, but in 1987 he was arrested and charged with importing over 10 kilograms of heroin in 1985. Eighteen months later he was acquitted. In May 1997 Lam was believed by federal enforcement agencies to have been involved in what was at the time Australia's largest heroin seizure: 78 kilograms of heroin with a street value of $78 million hidden in cans of pineapple imported from southern China. A colleague of Lam's in the heroin business, Leung Yiu Man, was arrested and agreed to set up Lam for the police. A few weeks later, wired up, Leung arranged to meet Lam at the Dragon Chamber restaurant in Ashfield. Leung entered the front of the restaurant; Lam was already inside. Both men fled out the back door and left the country.

Some time later, Lam returned to Sydney and in February 1999 he and four others were arrested over a deal involving 1.4 kilograms of heroin. Another 15 kilograms and more than $300,000 in cash and gold bullion were found in safe houses. Lam was also charged with the 1997 pineapple-cans importation. In March 2001 Lam was jailed for sixteen years. Leung was arrested in Thailand over passport offences. Back in Sydney he followed Lam to jail over the 1997 importation.

With Lam's departure and eventual jailing, and the jailing of Van Duong and two of his brothers, Van Duong's heroin operation began to struggle because the trusted connections at the highest levels of the chain had been broken and there were no readily available replacements. This internal upheaval coincided with a new police crackdown against heroin-related violence.

New South Wales Police Strike Force Portville and its successor, Strike Force Scottsville, drastically cut the violence and caused the collapse of the major Cabramatta gangs. Over two and a half years, these two strike forces resulted in around 100 arrests and more than 160 high-level charges, including six of murder, eight of conspiracy to murder, ten of attempted murder, six of kidnapping and thirty-one of firearms possession, together with numerous drug supply and possession charges. Thirty firearms, mostly handguns, were recovered. Nineteen search warrants were executed on drug houses and twenty-four heroin dealers were evicted.

The leaders of the three major street gangs were arrested,

charged and convicted. David Nguyen, then twenty-three, was arrested and charged with attempted murder, firearms possession and drug supply. He beat several charges, but was eventually convicted of kidnapping and malicious wounding and sentenced to jail. Khanh Nguyen, twenty-four, was arrested for a number of offences including armed robbery, supply of drugs, firearms possession and perverting the course of justice. He beat all charges. South Australian drug supply charges against him were eventually dropped.

However, in 2004 Khanh Nguyen, Duong Ngyen, Minh Thy Huynh and a seventeen-year-old given the code name ATCN by the court were charged with the shooting murder of eighteen-year-old Linda Huynh and the wounding of her friend in a Cabramatta pool hall just after the New Year as she attended a friend's birthday party. Security cameras caught the shooting on film. Nguyen and the three other men walked into the hall in single file and made no attempt to hide their identity. They were armed with a gun and a samurai sword. As Nguyen was heard to yell, 'Shoot them, shoot them!' in Vietnamese, Hunyh was shot at close range in the chest. But it was a bungled hit: the target was actually a member of another gang. Hunyh had simply been in the wrong place at the wrong time. All were convicted and given lengthy jail terms. In sentencing the four, Justice Hulme observed that none had shown any remorse over the 'cold-blooded' killing. 'Indeed,' he said, 'the murder was the most brazen offence that I have come across in my time on the bench. The offenders desired, or were at least content for, their ... actions to be known.' All appealed their convictions and sentences. Nguyen's conviction was upheld and he was sentenced to 27 years and four months' jail. The other three were granted retrials. In August 2008 they pleaded guilty to manslaughter and other related charges. At the time of going to press they were awaiting sentencing.

Hoang Ha La, then twenty-one, was also picked up in the Portville and Scottsville swoops. He was arrested and charged with conspiracy to commit murder and a number of violent assaults, including the attempted assassination of Khanh Quang Do. In February 2001 Do and another member of his gang were shot and wounded as they stood on the verandah of a house in Cabramatta. A third gang member escaped unharmed. Around thirty shots from up to six guns were fired at them. It was the second attempt on Do's life in three weeks. Several charges against La were dismissed, mostly because victims and witnesses refused to give evidence, but he and three other members of his gang were convicted of shooting Do. La was also convicted of drug offences. All were given lengthy jail sentences.

David's, Khanh's and La's gangs broke up with the arrest and conviction of their leaders. Khanh Quang Do recovered from his wounds and retreated to a relatively quiet life. The 5T is no longer active though from time to time there are reports of people still claiming membership of the gang. A police assessment carried out across south-western Sydney in December 2001 revealed that the decline in youth gang activity that had begun in 2000 was still continuing. At the end of 2001 Cabramatta reported no evidence of street gang activities. It was the first such report in more than fifteen years. The assessment concluded: 'While youth gangs can re-emerge, at this time they are not a significant problem in the Region [south-western Sydney].'

The primary weaknesses of the street gangs operating in Cabramatta—and for that matter across the south-western suburbs—included their failure to make financial investments to secure their own future. There was no active participation in legitimate businesses. Profits were usually spent on drug use, gambling, typical teenage purchases and day-to-day living. The gangs had no legitimacy within the broader law-abiding community. Their survival was almost totally reliant on the strength of their leaders.

Gangs had been appearing and quickly disappearing ever since the mid 1980s. Some members were absorbed into other gangs, others operated for a time as individuals in the drug trade, while others returned to law-abiding lives. All contributed in some way to the street violence and drug activity that marked Cabramatta, but no single gang ever monopolised the local drug trade. Entry into street-level drug dealing was always relatively easy and alliances at this level were largely ad hoc and ephemeral.

In just over a decade, street gang violence in and around Cabramatta was responsible for more than sixty murders and 200 shootings. The local member of parliament, the Hon. Reba Meagher, highlighted the scale of the drug problem in Cabramatta during the 1990s. On 17 November 2000 she told parliament that Puccini had 'resulted in 10,361 people being arrested for drug offences, more than 15,000 charges being laid, with 593 charges being laid for supply'.

With the decline of the gangs, a heroin shortage and the changes in policing, crime in Cabramatta fell dramatically. Relative to other parts of the state, the change was even more striking. The number of needles and syringes given out to drug users in the Cabramatta–Fairfield area also fell sharply, as did drug-related deaths and ambulance call-outs to suspected overdose incidents (down 96 per cent).

But organised crime in Cabramatta did not end with

heroin importations and distribution through local street gangs. Operation Trendelberg, conducted by Cabramatta police, investigated several hundred house-breaking and other property offences, a number of sexual assaults, the remittance of around $12 million to China under almost 600 different names, and a range of immigration offences. Three people were arrested and charged with a total of 120 counts of conspiracy to commit property break-ins, nineteen counts of break, enter and steal, two counts of sexual assault and six other property offences.

In March 2001, almost a decade late and under pressure from an opposition-controlled Parliamentary Inquiry into Policing Resources in Cabramatta, then New South Wales Labor Premier Bob Carr announced a four-year, $18.8 million package of initiatives targeting drugs and drug-related crime in Cabramatta. Later, another $9.3 million was promised. It remains to be seen whether this commitment by the government to Cabramatta endures or whether it fades now that Cabramatta is no longer in the headlines.

The dismantling of Cabramatta's gang culture has left a vacuum. Lacking adult mentors, the youth gangs had to find their own way to adult crime. While some members have graduated to adult and organised crime, the gangs as a whole do not appear to have evolved. Several leading figures seem to have turned their backs on crime. Others, however, have simply moved out of drugs towards more traditional criminal activities such as protection and extortion—the very areas from which Lennie McPherson, George Freeman and 'Stan the Man' Smith emerged as powerful organised crime bosses in the 1960s. While keeping a low profile, these former gang members and other organised crime figures are quietly building new networks and forming alliances—

notably with Lebanese gangs—for the purpose of trafficking drugs and firearms.

History suggests that the present quiet may be just the lull before another storm, but the next storm will be different: more organised and more strategic. The new storm may already be breaking. As Australia's heroin shortage took hold, Vietnamese crime gangs were forced to diversify and have now begun to emerge as major players in the burgeoning hydroponic cannabis industry. They have learned the lesson that McPherson and his cronies learned in the 1980s: 'You just can't go shooting people left, right and centre.'

Afterword

Four decades ago organised crime in Australia was transformed by the availability of illegal drugs, above all heroin. It underwent another dramatic change around 2000, this time in response to a shortage of the same drug. The open street dealing, with its associated violence and overdoses, largely disappeared from view. With the problem out of sight, governments became complacent. But if heroin is scarce, other drugs are not. Cocaine, ecstasy, amphetamines and cannabis continue to provide huge profits to organised crime.

Organised crime is like a virus, constantly mutating to exploit new opportunities and defeat new enemies. Some gangs have been dismantled but others have sprung up to replace them. Organised crime has continued to grow at a pace that far exceeds the capacity of the authorities to contain it.

In *Organised Crime in Australia: NCA Commentary 2001*, Gary Crooke QC, then Chairman of the National Crime Authority, wrote: 'Today there are no less greedy or unscrupulous people in our community. However, the opportunities available to them to profit from criminal activity have increased enormously.' Organised crime, said Crooke, did not receive 'detailed attention at the highest levels of government on a par with the national security issues of defence, foreign intelligence and security intelligence'. Crooke left readers in no doubt that organised crime constituted a serious and ongoing threat to Australia's national security.

In August 2004 *The Age* newspaper reported on a confidential major crime conference held in Melbourne. The conference identified almost a hundred organised crime groups operating nationally, thirty-two of which were assessed as being a 'high threat'. These high-risk groups had been investigated for decades but, in the words of one expert, 'Frankly, we haven't laid a glove on them.'

Three years later the Australian Crime Commission (the successor to the disbanded National Crime Authority) told a Federal Parliamentary Joint Committee: 'The most likely future scenario is that Australia will continue to be threatened by an increasing variety of serious and organised criminal groups (SOCGs)... Furthermore, the criminal capabilities of SOCGs are likely to strengthen.' The cost to the nation, in monetary terms alone, is already enormous. In 2008, in a report entitled *Organised Crime in Australia*, the commission estimated that 'organised crime costs Australia in excess of $10 billion every year'.

As this book went to press Nick McKenzie of *The Age* reported Alistair Milroy, chief executive of the Australian Crime Commission, saying that between $4 billion and $12 billion in drug money was being sent offshore annually. McKenzie pointed out that this figure was '10 to 30 times [greater than] the public estimate provided by AUSTRAC, Australia's anti-money-laundering agency'. McKenzie also noted that recent drug busts, including the 2007 seizure in Melbourne of more than 14 million ecstasy tablets, had made little or no difference to the availability or price of

AFTERWORD

drugs. Others have made the same point. It throws into serious question the strategies now employed by government and law enforcement agencies for combating organised crime.

On 11 October 2008 a statue of Donald Mackay was unveiled in Griffith as a permanent tribute to his contribution to the community and the fight against organised drug crime in Griffith. Speaking at the unveiling, Paul Mackay observed that his father had been murdered 'only four hundred metres from where we're now standing' and that although the body had never been found there were people 'alive today in this community' who undoubtedly knew its whereabouts. He noted that recent events showed it was 'business as usual in the Griffith underworld ... and that Griffith's reputation as a drugs capital will unfortunately continue'. The town, he concluded, 'would benefit from fewer visits by the national media and more visits from investigative police and forensic accountants from the Australian Taxation Office'.

This book doesn't claim to be exhaustive. It is one history, but not the only history. Another account of organised crime in Australia is possible, beginning in the same place, with many of the same people, but branching out in dramatically different directions. That is the subject for another book.

What Happened to . . . ?

Aunty lives in Sydney's eastern suburbs and continues to import and distribute cocaine.

Barry Richard Bull died in 2004 at his home on Queensland's Sunshine Coast.

Leo 'The Fibber' Callaghan (aka Jack Warren and Patrick William Warren) was jailed over a 1994 multi-tonne cannabis importation. Released after serving only one year, he lived on the Gold Coast until 2003 when he died at the age of seventy-nine.

Daniel Michael Chubb was murdered at the start of the 1984–85 gang war.

Richard Bruce 'Snapper' Cornwell is in jail.

Kenneth Robert Derley is currently in jail, serving twelve years for drug and fraud offences.

WHAT HAPPENED TO . . . ?

'Johnsonny' Bi Dinh was jailed in October 1997 for money laundering on behalf of an Asian-controlled international drug syndicate.

Khanh Quang Do survived two assassination attempts and now lives a relatively quiet life.

Thomas Christopher 'Tom' Domican is still well connected to major crime figures in New South Wales, Victoria and Western Australia. He now spends much of his time in Western Australia.

William 'Bill' El Azzi continues to protest his innocence of any wrongdoing and lives in Sydney's western suburbs.

Anthony 'Pommy Tony' Eustace was shot dead on 23 April 1985 as he waited near Sydney's Airport Hilton Hotel. A victim of Sydney's gangland war, Eustace had been on bail for conspiring to import cannabis valued at more than $8 million.

Malcolm Gordon Field is in jail serving thirteen years for importing ecstasy.

Christopher Dale Flannery was murdered on the orders of Lennie McPherson and George Freeman to bring an end to the 1984–85 Sydney gang war.

George David Freeman died in 1990 of an asthma attack.

Albert Jaime 'Flash Al' Grassby died on 23 April 2005, aged seventy-nine. In 2007 the Australian Capital Territory Labor government erected a statute in Grassby's honour.

Shayne Desmond Frederick Hatfield attempted suicide in jail. Almost two years later he pleaded guilty to importing and supplying cocaine. He is currently serving a jail sentence.

Graham John 'Abo' Henry was released from jail in 1997 and lives in the Newcastle area. He opened a restaurant but the venture failed. Henry has been taken under the wing of another Smith, 'Stan the Man'.

Michael Nicholas 'Mikel' Hurley died in jail in January 2007, having slipped and fallen in the shower.

Duong Van Ia was sentenced to eight years' jail in 1998 for supplying heroin. He now lives in Sydney's south-west.

Hoang Ha La was convicted of the 2001 shooting of Khanh Quang Do and drug offences. He was released from jail in 2004 and lives in Sydney's south-west.

Warren Charles Lanfranchi was shot dead by Detective Sergeant Roger Rogerson in Dangar Place, Chippendale, on 27 June 1981. At the inquest into Lanfranchi's death the jury declined to find that Rogerson had shot Lanfranchi in the course of duty or in self-defence.

Van Ro Le (known as Madonna) was shot dead by members of the 5T in 1998.

Barry Raymond McCann was murdered in December 1987. His partner, George Savvas, was acquitted of the murder but was later convicted of importing heroin. Savvas hanged himself in jail following a failed escape attempt.

WHAT HAPPENED TO . . .?

Bruce Michael 'the Godfather' McCauley was released on parole in 2002 after serving ten years of a seventeen-year sentence for heroin trafficking. He lives in Sydney's eastern suburbs. In September 2006 McCauley attended the funeral of his longtime friend, organised crime boss Abe Saffron.

Lawrence Edward McLean was released from jail in 2005 and lives in Melbourne.

Leonard Arthur McPherson died in jail in 1996.

Leslie Robert Mara is serving a twenty-year jail sentence for importing drugs.

Phuong Canh Ngo is serving a life sentence (never to be released) for the murder of John Newman. At the time of going to press, a judicial inquiry was reviewing the evidence that led to Ngo's conviction.

Khanh Hoang Nguyen was sentenced in 2007 to twenty-seven years and four months' jail for murder and related offences.

'David' Van Dung Nguyen was convicted of kidnapping and malicious wounding. He was released from jail in March 2008 and lives in the Cabramatta–Fairfield area.

The Rat was never convicted of corruption and now lives in Sydney.

Murray Stewart Riley lives in Queensland.

Roger Caleb Rogerson lives in Sydney's south-west and is writing his autobiography.

George Savvas escaped from the Goulburn Correctional Centre in July 1996 and was recaptured eight months later. After another escape attempt failed he hanged himself in his jail cell in May 1997.

Michael John 'Mick' Sayers was one of the first casualties of Sydney's gangland war. In February 1985 he was assassinated outside his Bronte home in Sydney's eastern suburbs.

Antonio 'Tony' Sergi has never been charged with any crime. He now runs the family-owned Warburn Wines, one of New South Wales's largest wine producers.

Pasquale 'Pat' Sergi is a wealthy property developer with strong ties to the Labor Party. During the mid 1990s he helped his close friend Joseph 'Joe' Tripodi win the safe Labor seat of Fairfield.

Arthur Stanley 'Neddy' Smith is in jail serving three life sentences for murder.

Stanley 'Stan the Man' Smith runs several legitimate businesses and does volunteer work with welfare groups feeding the poor of Sydney.

Victor Thomas Spink was released from jail in 2002 and since then has lived in the Vaucluse mansion he bought during his career as a drug trafficker.

WHAT HAPPENED TO . . . ?

Gianfranco Tizzone served a jail sentence for his role in the murders of Donald Mackay and Douglas and Isabel Wilson and other crimes. He died in Italy in 1988.

Tom's whereabouts are not known although he is sometimes seen in hotels around Sydney. In return for rolling on his colleagues, Tom is to be paid $200,000 over four years. He was also indemnified for past crimes and allowed to keep $760,000 in cash (which he claimed to have won gambling).

Tri Minh Tran and another 5T member were shot dead and a third gang member was wounded in a Cabramatta flat in August 1995. The shootings occurred after Madonna had been bashed by the 5T.

Bruno 'Aussie Bob' Trimbole fled Australia in 1981 and died in Spain in 1987.

Bibliography

Much of the information used in writing this book was obtained first-hand in the course of police investigations, from court records and from personal interviews conducted by the authors. Some sources have been cited in the text; others, for obvious reasons, must remain anonymous. The authors are grateful to all the people, named and unnamed, without whose courageous cooperation this book could not have been written.

Books and monographs

Bob Bottom, *Shadow of Shame: How the Mafia Got Away with the Murder of Donald Mackay*, Sun Books, Melbourne, 1988

——, *Without Fear or Favour*, Sun Books, Melbourne, 1984

——, *The Godfather in Australia*, A H & A W Reed, Sydney, 1979

Roderick Campbell, Brian Toohey and William Pinwill, *The Winchester Scandal*, Random House, Sydney, 1992

John Dale, *Huckstepp: A Dangerous Life*, Allen & Unwin, Sydney, 2001

Warren Fellows, *The Damage Done*, Pan Macmillan, Sydney, 2003

George Freeman, *George Freeman: An Autobiography*, George Freeman, Miranda, 1988

BIBLIOGRAPHY

Darren Goodsir, *Line of Fire*, Allen & Unwin, Sydney, 1991

Angela Kamper and Charles Miranda, *My Brother's Keeper*, Allen & Unwin, Sydney 2006

Lisa Maher, David Dixon, Wendy Swift and Tram Nguyen, *Anh Hai: Young Asian People's Perceptions and Experiences of Policing*, University of NSW Faculty of Law Research Monograph Series, 1997

Howard Marks, *Señor Nice: Straight Life from Wales to South America*, Harvill Secker, London, 2006

——, *Mr Nice: An Autobiography*, Vintage, London, 1998

Damian Marrett, *Undercover*, Harper Collins, Pymble, 2005

Alfred McCoy, *Drug Traffic: Narcotics and Organised Crime in Australia*, Harper & Row, Sydney, 1980

Athol Moffitt, *A Quarter to Midnight: The Australian Crisis—Organised Crime and the Decline of the Institutions of State*, Angus & Robertson, North Ryde, 1985

Hugh Montgomery-Massingberd (ed.), *The Daily Telegraph Book of Obituaries*, Pan, London, 1996

Keith Moor, *Crims in Grass Castles: The Trimbole Affair*, Pascoe, Apollo Bay, 1989

Keith Moor and Geoff Wilkinson, *Mugshots 2*, News Customs, Southbank, Victoria, 2006

Antonio Nicaso and Lee Lamothe, *Angels, Mobsters and Narco-Terrorists: The Rising Menace of Global Criminal Empires*, John Wiley & Sons, Mississauga, Ont., 2005

Letizia Paoli, *Mafia Brotherhoods: Organised Crime, Italian Style*, Oxford University Press, New York, 2003

Jay Pring, *Abo: A Treacherous Life—The Graham Henry Story*, ABC Books, Sydney, 2005

Tony Reeves, *Mr Big: The True Story of Lennie McPherson and His Life of Crime*, Allen & Unwin, Sydney, 2005

Arthur Stanley Smith and Tom Noble, *Neddy: The Life and Crimes of Arthur Stanley Smith*, Kerr, Balmain, 1993

Phil Sparrowhawk, Martin King and Martin Knight, *Grass*, Mainstream Publishing, Edinburgh, 2004

Government publications and official reports

Australian Crime Commission, 'Organised Crime in Australia', 2008

——, Annual Report 2003–2004, December 1994

——, Submission to the Parliamentary Joint Committee on the Australian Crime Commission, 'The future impact of serious and organised crime on Australian society', 2007

Lisa Cahill and Peter Marshall, Australian Institute of Criminology, 'The worldwide fight against transnational organised crime: Australia', Technical and background paper series, no. 9, 2004

Commonwealth–New South Wales Joint Drug Task Force on Drug Trafficking, 'Investigation of Harry Wainwright, Nugan Hand Limited and its associated companies and the affairs of Murray Stewart Riley and his associates as recommended by the Further Report of the Royal Commission into Drug Trafficking, May 1980', Report, vol. 1, January 1982; vol. 2, June 1982; vol. 3, October 1982; and vol. 4, March 1983

Frank Costigan QC, Royal Commisioner, 'Royal Commission on the Activities of the Federated Ship Painters and Dockers Union: Drug Trade', Final Report, vol. 5, Australian Government Publishing Service, Canberra, 1984

John Cusak, American Consulate General, 'Report to the Honourable John V. Dillon, Under Secretary, State of Victoria, Treasury Building', Melbourne, 11 August 1964

BIBLIOGRAPHY

General Purpose Standing Committee no. 3, New South Wales Legislative Council, 'Review of Inquiry into Cabramatta Policing', Report 12, September 2002
——, 'Cabramatta Policing', Report 8, July 2001
Gregory Charles Glass, New South Wales Coroner, 'Inquest Findings into the Disappearance and Suspected Death of Christopher Dale Flannery', 5 June 1997
Independent Commission Against Corruption, 'Report on Investigation Relating to the Raid on Frank Hakim's Office', December 1989
——, 'Report on investigation into Sutherland Licensing Police', February 1991
——, 'Investigation into the relationship between police and criminals: First report', February 1994
——, 'Investigation into the relationship between police and criminals: Second report', April 1994
——, 'Investigation into the Department of Corrective Services: first report: the conduct of Prison Officer Toso Lila (Josh) Sua and matters related thereto', February 1998
——, 'Report on the investigation into allegations made by Louis Bayeh about the Member for Londonderry, Paul Gibson MP', December 1998
The Hon. Mr Justice Athol Moffitt, Royal Commissioner, 'Allegations of Organized Crime in Clubs', NSW Government Printer, 1974
J.F. Nagle, 'Report of the Special Commission of Inquiry into the Police Investigation of the Death of Donald Bruce Mackay', D West, Government Printer NSW, 1986
National Crime Authority, 'Organised Crime in Australia: NCA Commentary 2001', 2001

——, 'Operation Cerberus: Italo-Australian Organised Crime', Bulletin, November 1995

Parliamentary Joint Committee on the National Crime Authority, 'Asian Organised Crime in Australia', Discussion Paper, February 1995

Christopher Sneddon and John Visser, "Financial and Organised Crime in Italy', AUSTRAC Papers 2, Australian Government, 1994

The Hon. Mr Justice Donald Gerard Stewart, 'Report of Commission of Inquiry into Alleged Telephone Interceptions', Australian Government Publishing Service, Canberra, 1986

——, 'Royal Commission of Inquiry into the Activities of the Nugan Hand Group', Report, Australian Government Publishing Service, Canberra, 1985

——, 'Royal Commission of Inquiry into Drug Trafficking', Report, Australian Government Publishing Service, Canberra, February 1983

The Hon. Justice J.R.T. Wood, 'Royal Commission into the New South Wales Police Service', Reports, vols. I–III, 1 May 1997

The Hon. Mr Justice Phillip Morgan Woodward, Royal Commissioner, 'Report of the Royal Commission into Drug Trafficking', Report, vols 1–3, October 1979

Newspapers and periodicals

The Adelaide Advertiser
The Age
The Australian
The Canberra Times
The Daily Telegraph

BIBLIOGRAPHY

The Eye
The Herald Sun
Insight Bookmagazine
The National Times
The Sun-Herald
The Sunday Telegraph
The Sydney Morning Herald
The Weekly Times

Index

5T (Vietnamese gang), 217–18, 226–32, 236
33 Club (Kings Cross), 42–4

amphetamine production, 133–5
Anderson, Frederick 'Paddles', 38, 39
Anoa (yacht), 51, 55, 140
'Aunty', xv, 181–4, 187–9, 191, 201, 244
Australian Labor Party
   branch stacking, 14, 95
   honours Al Grassby, 31–2
   Calabrian mafia and, 8–14

baggage handlers, 187–8, 191, 193–4, 202
Baldwin, Peter, 95
Ball, Terrence, 125–6
Balmain Boys gang, 162–5
Bandidos biker gang, 133–4, 183–4, 197–8
Bankstown Boys, 231
Barbaro, Domenic, 9–10
Barbaro, Tony, 7
Basham, Richard, 205, 225–6
Basham, Terrence, 56, 74
Bayeh, Louis, 72, 85–6, 90, 92–3, 201
Bazley, James Frederick, 6, 17, 19–20
Bennett, Raymond 'Chuck', 68–9
Beves, Norman, 174, 177
Bogerd, Marc, 158
Bonnette, Karl, 38
Boundy, Deborah, 69–70
Bowen, Geoffrey Leigh, 27
Bowman, Maxwell Garry, 139
Bra Boys, 176–7
Brokenshire, Dominic, 61, 63
Brown, John Anthony, 207
Bull, Barry Richard, xv, 55–9, 244
Byron Bay, 138–9

Cabramatta
   heroin trafficking at, 206–10, 213, 214–16, 218, 221–4, 227–9, 231–4, 237–9
   influence of Phung Ngo, 218–21, 225–6
   murder of John Newman, 220–5
   non-drug crimes, 238
   police corruption, 204–14
   police crackdown on gangs, 228–30, 234–6, 237
   Vietnamese street gangs, 214–18, 227–38
Calabrian mafia *see* 'ndrangheta (Calabrian version of mafia)
Calipari, Pietro, 8
Callaghan, Leo 'the Fibber', xv, 38, 244
   see also Warren, Jack 'the Fibber'
Camilleri, Victor, 86, 89, 103
Campbell, Jed Samuel, 177–8
Cann, Graham Lyall, 50–1
cannabis
   Calabrian mafia's involvement, 4–5, 29
   Chubb's operations, 80–3
   Cornwell and Bull's importations, 55–8
   glut on market, 157
   Hurley/Field/Milhench/Van Pallandt shipment, 168–72
   McLean and Scouller's trafficking, 138
   McLean's multi-tonne importing network, 137, 142–4, 152–60
   Moylans' importing syndicate, 44–5
   Riley's importation debacle, 50–2, 55
   Spink/Dumbrell/Hurley operations, 147–9
   Warren's importations, 142, 147, 150–2
Carbone, Rocco, 10
casino and gambling interests, 36–7
Chalmers, Ian Robert 'Rocky', 184–9, 193, 199
Chandler, Ryan, 193, 199
Chew Suang Heng, 84

256

INDEX

Chinatown bank robbery, 128, 165, 167
Chubb, Daniel Michael, xv, 80–4, 102, 244
Clark, Terrence, 15–19
Clarkson, Mark Alfred, 70–1
cocaine
   Aunty's syndicate, 181–3, 201
   Cornwell's venture with Diez-Orozco, 61–4, 179
   Coulson/Chalmers importations, 184–9, 192–5
   distribution by Hatfield and 'Tom', 181–4, 187–9, 192–5
   Flannery and Cross importation, 75
   Hurley/Mara syndicate, 184, 187–9, 192–5
   Vincent as dealer, 189–90
Cole, Leslie 'Johnny', 74, 88
Coogee Mob
   and Aunty's cocaine ring, 181–4
   claimed illnesses, 201
   Cornwell's relations with, 60–2
   Coulson/Chalmers and, 184–9, 192–5
   Crime Commission operation and raid, 179, 191–5, 199
   double-crossing within, 192–3
   Hatfield's drug network, 181–4, 187–9, 192–5
   Hurley/Field trafficking, 176–81
   Hurley/Mara trafficking, 184, 187–9, 192–4
   as Hurley's crime group, 176
   and Sydney Airport baggage handlers, 187–8, 191, 193–4, 202
   Tom's rollover, 189–92
Cornwell, Carmen, 57
Cornwell, Richard Bruce 'Snapper', xvi, 244
   arrested in cannabis sting, 59–60
   cocaine importation, 61–4, 179
   distributor for Moylan's syndicate, 44, 54
   forms drug syndicate with Bull, 55–8
   heroin importing with Riley's group, 46, 50
   relations with Coogee Mob, 60–1
Costa, Michael 25
Costi, George, 173–4, 179, 180–1
Coulson, Sean Michael, 184–9, 193–4
Countis, George Pierce 'Duke', 46, 48
Croft, Barry, 99
Czajkowski, Hans 'Bumbles', 20–1

Dao, Quang, 223–4
De Costi Seafoods, 173, 174, 179, 180
Della Bosca, John, 220
Derley, Kenneth Robert, xvi, 140, 244
Diez-Orozco, Juan Guillermo, 61–3
Dinh, Bi 'Johnsonny', xvi, 97–9, 216–17, 245
Dinh, David, 223
Do, Khanh Quang, xvi, 231, 236, 245
Domican, Thomas Christopher 'Tom', xvii, 245
   involvement in local politics, 95–6
   McPherson's war with, 85–6, 88–90, 92–5
   murder charges, 103–4
Drury, Michael, 75–6, 121
Duck, Christopher, 195, 199
Dufek, Nancy, 100
Duff, Bill, 70, 72, 83, 121–4, 125–6, 133–4
Dumbrell, Raymond, 21–2, 147–51
Dung, Duong Quoc, 232

'East Coast Milieu', 60, 176, 195, 200
ecstasy trafficking, 20, 30, 178, 180, 201
El Azzi, William 'Bill', xvii, 86, 92, 103, 134–5, 245
Ellis, John, 8
Eustace, Anthony 'Pommy Tony', xvii, 79, 85, 91, 245
Evans, Gareth, 12
Evans, Neil, 48

Fellows, Warren, 47, 50, 112–13, 127
Field, Malcolm Gordon, xvii–xviii, 201, 245
   and De Costi Seafoods, 173–4
   drug trafficking with Hurley, 153, 168–72, 176–81
   lifestyle, 180
   sentenced for ecstasy importing, 180
Finch, Ian Charles, 199
Flack, Glen, 127–30, 165
Flannery, Christopher Dale, xviii, 245
   accused of Wilson's murder, 71
   armed robberies, 66–7
   conflict with McCann, 73–4, 83
   and Locksley murder trial, 68–9, 72, 74, 77
   mate of Sayers, 79, 87
   and Melbourne gang warfare, 68–71, 87
   murder of, 93–5, 103, 245

257

New Year's Eve assault, 68–9, 74
relations with Freeman, 72–3, 83, 93–4
relations with McPherson, 72–3, 76, 85 245, 92–3
relations with Rogerson, 72, 74, 76
as 'Rent-a-Kill' hit man, 68–71, 74, 75–6, 91, 93
reputation for violence, 67
and shooting of Drury, 75–6, 120–1
and Sydney gang warfare, 72–3, 83, 86–7, 89–95
Flannery, Kath, 66, 69–70, 76–7, 89–90, 93–4, 103
Flavell, Ronald, 128–9
Fratianno, James 'Jimmy the Weasel', 46
Fred (police informant), 59–60
Freeman, George David, xviii, 245
attempts on his life, 93–4, 163
death, 106
early career, 34–5
Flannery's connection with, 72–3, 83, 93–4
Hurley's falling out with, 163–4
partnership with McPherson, 35–40, 72–3, 85, 106
questioned on Muller's murder, 164
and Regan's murder, 38–9
wants Sayers dead, 79, 88
'Friendly Gang', 165–6, 168
Fry, Ken, 12

gang warfare *see* Melbourne gang warfare; Sydney gang warfare
George, Johnny, 46, 48
Grassby, Albert Jaime 'Flash Al', xviii, 245
assistance to Calabrian mafia, 9–11, 13–14
character evidence for Calipari, 8
defames Barbara and Paul Mackay, 13–14
statue of, 32
Grassby, Ellnor, 14
Green Island Trade, 173–4
Griffith *see* Mackay, Donald; 'ndrangheta (Calabrian version of mafia)

Haken, Trevor, 210
Hakim, Fayez 'Frank', 80, 86, 201
Hand, Michael, 48

Hao, Thanh Nguyen, 227
Hardin, Bruce, 72
Harlum, John, 104
Hatfield, Shayne Desmond Frederick, xviii–xix, 181–4, 187–9, 191–6, 200–1, 246
Hayward, Paul, 112, 127
Henry, Graham John 'Abo', xix, 84, 85, 127, 129–31, 246
heroin
Chinese triads and, 233–4
Chubb-McCauley operations, 80–4
effect of market shortage, 237, 239, 241
Pel Air scheme, 121–4
Riley's importation syndicate, 45–52
Savvas-McCann operation, 95–102
Smith-Riley networks, 120–4
Smith-Sinclair-Fellowes syndicate, 47, 50, 52, 112–14, 127
Thelander importation syndicate, 50–2
trafficking at Cabramatta, 206–10, 213, 214–16, 218, 221–4, 227–8, 231–4, 237–9
Trimbole and Mr Asia syndicate, 14–18, 20, 73
Hill, Stephen, 48
Ho, Vincent Chin Hoon, 81–2, 84
Hoffman, Neil, 59
'Hollywood' (Smith's go-between), 127–8
House of Sergi Winery (later Warburn Wines), 4, 23
Huckstepp, Sallie-Anne, 115, 118–20
Hughes, Michael 'Popeye', 21
Hurley, Michael Nicholas 'Mikel', xix, 201, 246
attempts on his life, 196
Balmain Boys robberies, 162–5
cannabis importing with Field, 153, 166–72, 176–81
Chinatown bank robbery, 128 , 165
and Coogee Mob's drug trafficking, 181–4, 187–9, 192–5
criminal record, 149, 150, 163, 164, 196–7
death, 199–200, 246
Freeman's treachery towards, 163–4
and heists by the 'Friendly Gang', 165–6, 168
as leading crime figure, xix, 174, 176, 197

258

INDEX

links with Spink/Dumbrell shipments, 147, 149–50
money-laundering through De Costi Seafoods, 173–4
see also Coogee Mob
Huynh, Linda, 235

Ia, Duong Van, xix, 231–3, 246
Italian Anti-Mafia Commission, 28–30
Italo-Australian organised crime, 25–30
see also 'ndrangheta (Calabrian version of mafia)

Jackson, Rex 'Buckets', 150
James, Steven, 201–2
jockey tapes, 147
Johnson, Ray, 165, 167
Johnstone, Christopher Martin 'Marty', 15–17
Johnstone, Peter, 122
Jones, Harvey, 133
Jones, Kathleen (later Flannery), 66
Jones, Lesle 'Les', 97
Jonsson, Martin Waldemar, 154–5
Joseph, George, 6, 19

Kane, Brian, 68, 74
Kane, Les, 69
Karp, Ross, 81, 102–3
Kelleher, David, 119
Kelly, Ray 'Shotgun', 41
Kidd, Robert Douglas 'Bertie', 104
Kings Cross, cocaine sales, 183
Kiriaszis, Theo, 173

La, Hoang Ha, xix, 231, 236, 246
Labor Party *see* Australian Labor Party
Lady Jane nightclub, 189–90
Lam, Duncan, 231, 233–4
Lanfranchi, Warren Charles, xx, 115–19, 201, 246
Lansky, Meyer, 37
Lapa, Salvatore 'Sammy', 206–7, 210, 213, 216, 222
Lauer, Tony, 117–18, 131–2
Lawrence, John, 61–2
Le, Dung Hing, 217
Le, Van Ro *see* Madonna
Lee, Ronnie, 36
Leith, Kevin, 122
Leung Yiu Man, 233–4
Lewis, Desmond Anthony, 104

Lewis, Harry 'Pommy', 16–17
licensed clubs
money-skimming from, 42
organised crime in, 35, 37–8
Liuterio 'Liu', John, 157
Locksley, Raymond Francis 'the Lizard', 68–9, 72, 74, 77
Long, Sarin ('Mummy'), 216, 231
Lux, Sylvia, 57–9

Mackay, Barbara, 13–14, 21
Mackay, Donald
convictions for his murder, 19–20
disappearance and murder, 1, 6–8
Nagle Inquiry, 7
statue of, 243
Mackay, Paul, 13–14
Madonna (Van Ro Le), xx, 217, 227–8, 230, 246
Madonna's MOB, 227
Mafia *see* Italian Anti-Mafia Commission; 'ndrangheta (Calabrian version of mafia)
Magros, Joseph, 98
Mara, Leslie Robert, xxi, 167, 174, 179–81, 184, 187–9, 191–6, 198, 200–1, 247
Marconi Club, 211–12
Marks, Howard 'Mr Nice', 138, 143–5
McCann, Barry Raymond, xx, 246
feud with Flannery, 73, 83
feud with Neddy Smith, 85, 99–100, 126
heroin importation with Savvas, 95–102
murder of, 100–1
McCauley, Bruce Michael 'the Godfather', xx, 82, 84–5, 124, 247
McLean, Ian Victor, 71
McLean, Lawrence 'Lawrie' Edward, xx–xxi, 197, 247
Anoa (yacht), 140
arrest and sentencing, 158–9
Byron Bay cannabis business, 137–9
hires Milhench, 154
as multi-tonne cannabis importer, 137, 142–4, 152–60, 168
partnership with Stan Smith, 137–8, 155, 160
McNamara, John, 122–4
McPherson, Leonard Arthur 'Lennie', xxi, 33–42, 201, 247

259

gang war with Domican, 85–6, 88–90, 92–5
investments in the Philippines and New Guinea, 36, 140
murder of Flannery, 72, 92–3, 245
partnership with Freeman, 34–40, 42, 76, 85–6, 106–8
Savvas fraud case, 98
Medlar (police investigation), 205, 212
Meissner, Joe, 86, 95–6, 98–9
Mekong Club, 219–21
Melbourne gang warfare, 68–71, 74
Members of the Brotherhood (MOB), 227
Mengler, Carl, 7
Milat, Ivan, 105–6
Milhench, Ronald, 153–4, 168–72
Miller, Milan 'Iron Bar', 38
Moffitt Royal Commission into Allegations of Organised Crime in Clubs, 38, 42
money laundering, 26, 48–9, 217, 219, 233, 242, 245
Monk, Rodney, 'Hooksey', 183–4, 197–8
Montgomery, Ricky, 167, 169, 176–7, 200–1
Moran, Lewis, 74
Moran, Mark Anthony, 74
Moylan, Michael, 43–5, 54
Moynihan, Lord Tony, 140–2, 145–6, 172
Mr Asia syndicate, 15–18, 20, 73, 95
Muller, John 'Jack', 163–4
Murchie, George, 177
Murphy, Chris, 132, 150
Murray, Eric Leonard, 104

Nagle Report, 7
National Crime Authority (NCA)
  arrest of Cornwell and Diez-Orozco, 63
  arrest of O'Brien, 148–9
  bombing of Adelaide office, 27–8
  Cerberus project, 25–7, 28
  investigation of McLean networks, 146
'ndrangheta (Calabrian version of Mafia)
  cannabis trade, 4–5, 26
  Commonwealth Police's list of members, 20

Italian and US links, 26, 28–30
links with Labor MPs, 8–14
NCA investigation, 25–8
origins in Australia, 2–3
New South Wales Crime Commission, 174
Newman, John
  critic of Vietnamisation of Cabramatta, 221
  murder of, 219–20
  murder trials, 223–5
  underworld associates, 222–3
Ngo, Phuong Canh, xxi, 247
  convicted of Newman's murder, 223–5
  courted by Labor Party, 219–20
  Liberal Party connections, 218–19
  role in Vietnamese community, 218–20, 225–6
Nguyen, 'David' Van Dung, xxii, 229, 247
Nguyen, Khanh Hoang, xxi, 229, 235
Nguyen, Phu Tuan, 217
Nguyen, Quoc Toan, 230
Nguyen, Tien, 230
Nugan Hand Merchant Bank, 48–9
Nye, Garry, 104

O'Brien, Reginald 'Mick', 21, 146–9
O'Connor, Cornelius 'Con the Cobra', 97
Oldham, Russell, 197–8
Ong Jong Tai ('Chinese David'), 96

Painters and Dockers Union, 66, 74
Palmer, Graham 'Croc', 81
Paltos, Dr Nicholas, 18, 81, 102–3
Papapetros, Dr Peter, 98
Papua New Guinea 121–4
Passaris, Jack, 98
Pel Air, 121–4
Perry, Stuart, 154
Petricevic, Milan 'Iron Bar Miller', 38
Pochi, Luigi, 10–13
police corruption
  Cabramatta, 204–14
  see also Rogerson, Roger Caleb; Wood Royal Commission into Police Corruption
Popovic, 'Bone Crusher', 175
Prendergast, Laurence, 66, 68, 76, 90, 94–5
Presland, Ann Marie, 149

INDEX

Priest, Tim, 205
Provost, Bruce, 148
Puccini (police operation), 229–30, 237

race fixing, 36, 147
Radlovic, David, 209
Radovan, Vincent 'Roy the Boy', 150
The Rat, xxii, 206–11, 247
Rat Pack, xxii, 206–11, 213
Read, Mark 'Chopper', 69
Regan, John Stewart, 38–9
Reljic, Victor, 209–10
Riley, Murray Stewart, xxii, 83, 247
    cannabis importation debacle, 50–2, 55, 140
    failed Las Vegas casino bid, 48–9
    forms heroine importing syndicate, 45–50, 52
    joins Moylan syndicate, 44–5
    on McPherson's payroll, 42
    name change, 52
    partnership with Neddy Smith, 48, 49–50, 113–14, 121–4
    as police officer, 41–2
    travellers cheque fraud, 49, 52
Rogerson, Roger Caleb, xxii, 248
    dealings with Neddy Smith, 72, 88, 110–11, 114–18, 120, 121, 125–6, 128
    defends Chapman, 110–11
    dismissed from police force, 126–7
    Lanfranchi's shooting and inquest, 117–19
    Lauer's endorsement of, 117–18, 131–2
    links with Flannery, 67, 72, 74, 76

Savvas, George, xxii–xxiii, 86, 95–101, 105–6, 127, 248
Sayers, Michael John 'Mick', xxiii, 74, 79–80, 85, 87–8, 103
Sayers, Robert, 88
Scouller, Neville Hugh, 138
Sergi, Antonio 'Tony', xxiii, 248
    connections with Tripodi, 24
    family-owned winery, 4, 23
    knowledge of 'ndrangheta, 23
    and Mackay's murder, 7–8, 23
    relations with Trimbole, 4–5, 11
Sergi, Pasquale 'Pat', xxiii, 248
    cannabis distribution, 23–4
    Labor Party ambitions, 24

Sevastopoulos, Steven 'Mags', 183
Shepherd, James 'Diamond Jim', 20–1
Simpson, Richard James, 133, 135
Sinclair, William, 47, 50, 52, 112–13, 127
Sipka, Nikola 'Nick', 209–10, 213, 216, 222
Sloss, Albert Ross, 38
Small, Clive, 205
Smith, Arthur Stanley 'Neddy', xxiii, 248
    armed hold-ups, 125, 127–8
    association with McPherson, 35, 85
    attempts on his life, 125–6
    betrayal of Chapman, 109–12
    charged with McCann's murder, 101
    confesses to six murders, 132
    dealings with Rogerson, 110–11, 114–18, 120, 126
    feud with McCann, 99, 101–2, 126
    Flannery's association with, 72, 87
    as heroin distributor for Chubb, 83–4, 115, 120–1
    as heroin importer, 83, 112–13, 121–4
    as ICAC informant, 130–1
    murder of Ronald Flavell, 128–9
    partnership with Riley, 48, 49–50, 52, 113–14, 121–4
    as police informant, 110, 125, 131
    receives life sentences for murder, 133, 248
    relationship with Lanfranchi, 115–16
    and Rex Jackson, 150
Smith, Edwin, 113, 116
Smith, Peter, 119
Smith, Ray, 41–2
Smith, Stanley 'Stan the Man', xxiv, 248
    involvement in shootings and murders, 35–6, 160–1
    links with McPherson, 35, 39–40
    partnership with McLean, 137–8, 141, 155, 160
    son's overdose death, 141
Smith, Susan, 56, 74
Somare, Michael, 122–3
Sorby, Darryl Leigh, 20
SP bookmaking, 24, 36
Sparrowhawk, Phil, 142, 145, 152
Sparrowhawk, Phillip, 138
Spink, Victor Thomas, xxix, 21–2, 146–51, 248
Stapley, Alan, 103

Stein, Danny (also known as Steinberg), 37
Stewart, Murray Lee, 52
Stout, John Lawrence, 102
Sweetman, Jimmy, 139
Sydney Airport, 188, 193, 202–3
Sydney gang warfare
　Chubb's murder, 80–4, 102–3
　Flannery's involvement, 79, 83, 85–7, 89–92
　Flannery's murder, 92–5, 103
　McCann's murder, 100–1
　McPherson/Freeman versus Domican/McCann, 85–95, 99–100, 103–4
　Neddy Smith versus McCann, 99–100, 101–2
　Savvas fraud case, 98–9
　Savvas versus McCann, 100–1
　Sayers's murder, 79–80, 87–8, 103
　Thurgar's murder, 104
Sydney Town Hall diamond theft, 164
Szeto Yin Wah, 122

Tabone, Albert, 79
Tapon, Susan, 170
Task Force Snowy, 132
Testa, Joseph Dan, 36–8
Tham, Rudy, 46
Thelander, Wayne, 50–2
Theobold, Kevin, 86, 89, 103
Thurgar, Roy, 86, 101, 103–4
Tizzone, Gianfranco, xxiv, 6–7, 17, 19, 249
Toe Cutter Gang, 35
'Tom' (drug trafficker), xxiv, 182–4, 188–92, 194–5, 200–1, 249
Tran, Tri Minh, xxiv–xxv, 217–18, 225, 227, 249
Trimbole, Bruno 'Aussie Bob', xxv, 249
　arrest in Ireland, 18
　cannabis trade, 2–5, 14–15
　death, 18–19
　early life, 3
　and Mr Asia syndicate, 15–17
　and murder of Donald Mackay, 6–7, 13
　and O'Brien, 27
　'practical leader' of Calabrian mafia, 2–3

　relations with Antonio Sergi, 4, 11
　and the Wilsons death, 17–18
Trimbole, Craig, 21–2, 148
Trimbole, Domenic, 22
Trimbole, Rosaria 'Ross', 22, 27
Tripodi, Joseph 'Joe', 24–5
Twaddell, Graham, 45
Tyler, Phillip, 193–4, 199

US underworld, 36–8

Van Bommell, Wouter, 62
Van Duong, xix, 231–2, 234, 246
Van Pallandt, Fred, 168–71
Verduci, Giuseppe, 11–12
Vesey, Graham Gerald 'Barney', 44–7
Vietnamese gang violence, 214–18, 227–38
Vincent, Thomas 'Tony', 189–90

Wainwright, Harry, 46
Walker, Ray, 115
Walker, Robert 'Pretty Boy', 35
Warburn Wines see House of Sergi Winery
Warren, Jack 'the Fibber', 140, 142, 146, 150–2
　see also Callaghan, Leo 'the Fibber'
Warren, Patrick William see Warren, Jack 'the Fibber'
White, Cedric, 166, 178
Williams, Alan, 68, 74–5, 120
Williams, Kevin 'Weary', 70–1
Wilson, Douglas and Isabel, 16–19
Wilson, Roger, 69–71
Wings Travel, 47
Wood, Merv, 41
Wood Royal Commission into Police Corruption, 107, 132–3, 174, 204, 212, 213, 229
Wooden, Jim, 99
Woodham, Ron, 103, 225
Woodward Royal Commission into Drug Trafficking, 2, 5, 10–11, 20, 23, 31
Wran, Neville, 8, 9–10, 13

Young, Mick, 12

Zapata, Adolpho, 61–3